TYRANTS

Joseph Brodie

ISBN 978-1-63784-406-9 (paperback)
ISBN 978-1-63784-407-6 (digital)

Hawes & Jenkins Publishing
16427 N Scottsdale Road Suite 410
Scottsdale, AZ 85254
www.hawesjenkins.com

Printed in the United States of America

Dedicated to my beloved, loyal service dog Geno…
for years of continuous & faithful service
and for the years I was taken away from you.
You remained loyal & loving, and I can never
repay your service. May this book allow you
to live on in memory FOREVER as a
tribute to you & my eternal love for you.

—"Dati"

PREFACE

In September of 2017, I was arrested and charged with threatening a U.S. Official. I maintained my innocence and opted to exercise my constitutional right to have a trial before a jury of my peers because I knew I was innocent. The United States Attorney's Office alleged that I made a telephone threat and email threat against the chief of staff and other staff members of a U.S. Representative for New Jersey's 2nd District.

I was aware of the high conviction rate and publicly proclaimed skill set of the lawyers employed by the United States government. I was also aware that going to trial incurred a greater penalty than someone who accepts a plea bargain and avoids trial, thereby saving the government time and money. If an individual should choose to exercise his constitutional right to go to trial, then one will pay a greater penalty if found guilty when sentenced. It is what is known as a "trial tax." On the surface, it seems stupid and un-American to punish an American citizen for exercising their constitutional rights, but over the course of this book you will discover many similar facts. For example, our system is repugnant in that we use what is referred to as a "snitch-system" in which the government prosecutors can get co-defendants to testify against one another for lesser sentences and recommend lesser, more lenient sentences (known as 5K1) after they have provided testimony to catch "bigger fish". It also permits defendants to avoid any line of questioning by defense counsel as to providing testimony for a reduced sentence. Even banana republics reject and abhor the snitch system. It suborns perjury and perpetuates injustice.

I knew the government had a conviction rate that exceeded 95%. Still, I felt confident because I knew I was innocent. I knew what had transpired because I was present during the call and the government was not. I was on the phone with one person -and ONLY one person- when the call was made. The email was a follow up to an email from June 2017 after Congressman Scalise was shot at the Republican party's softball practice. I had warned my congressman of a man using social media to stalk elected officials in New Jersey. The congressman's office sent me an email thanking me. It was certainly not perceived as a threat then and I did not regurgitate it as a threat later. I did not have social media and abhor it altogether. I just forwarded a link to a news story I found locally and expression my reasoning for hoping to speak privately -face to face- with my elected representative, in the comfort, safety & security of his Washington, D.C. office.

I was further confident because in college I majored in political science, but I pursued the legal option to prepare myself for law school with an emphasis in constitutional law. I genuinely believed I had a better-than-basic knowledge of my rights and the system. I thought it was impossible to lose; especially since I knew that I was innocent. The truth will always set you free and the truth will always come out.

I quickly found myself repeating a mantra that my attorney and friend had told me 15 years earlier when I was going through my divorce. He was the best attorney and smartest guy I ever met. He reminded me of Robert Deniro. His name was Vince Rovito, and he ran a small practice out of a small town in Coal Region Pennsyltucky. I could never understand why he worked there when he possessed such incredible talent as a trial lawyer. It was his father's firm and he worked with his dad there before his passing and I think he just stayed. The whole aura around him and his small firm was something out of a John Grisham novel. Anytime I got myself jammed up or needed help with something, he was there, and he never lost. A "pitbull" in the courtroom and an amazing trial lawyer. Not that I was always getting into trouble, but I did have trouble readjusting after returning home from Iraq, but I will get to that in later chapters. Vince taught me many things over the years but what kept hitting my mind like a brick wall as I sat in shackles in the holding cell at the Camden New Jersey Mitchell Cohen Federal Courthouse was that it's not what you **know**… but it's what you can **prove** in court. And I was quickly about to learn that the government and its proxies were going to do everything in their power to limit my access to any evidence that existed; even destroy, tamper, and alter impeachment and exculpatory evidence to win their case against me.

It was done by the same government that I had fought for and served in Operations Enduring & Iraqi Freedom as an infantryman. I reenlisted in the Army after 9/11 after already serving in the Marine Corps pre 9/11. I was 0311 (infantry) in the Marine Corps but was discharged honorably (early) due to kidney failure. I was stationed at Camp LeJeune and told I am not entitled to any of the settlement money from the poisoned water scandal. Interestingly, my medical records were "lost or stolen" by my nephrologist at the naval hospital the day of my discharge per the NCIS report at Camp LeJeune. The Army didn't treat me much better, and the VA treated me horribly when I came home from Iraq so I shouldn't have been that surprised this same government took a giant shit all over me when I was on the verge of exposing an enormous scandal involving the VA Choice Program and at a time while veterans were lighting themselves on fire outside a VA Community Based Outpatient Clinic (CBOC) in a certain NJ congressional district to protest the poor treatment.

Have I piqued your curiosity yet? Or, do you think I am a crazy conspiracy theorist? I am assuming that if you're reading this book then it is the former and not the latter. The mere fact that you purchased this book confirms that for me and I am grateful. Writing this book for me has been therapeutic. It hasn't been easy; I was sentenced to 87 months in federal prison. I was in covid lockdown for nearly 2 years of that time and contracted the virus 3 times. I was psychologically, physically, and sexually abused by correctional officers in multiple facilities. I had to fight to defend myself; being Jewish in prison isn't always easy. You either learn to fight or be a bitch and I was no one's bitch. Ever. Plus, I was good with legal work, and numbers. I was a good earner. I fit right in with the Italians but flew solo for the most part. I learned a lot in prison, but I learned most **from** being put in prison.

Our system is broken. It's not a system the discriminates by race; it's a system that discriminates by class. The wealthy dominate the poor. Poor whites, Asians, Hispanics, and Blacks all fill prisons while the wealthy (mostly) do not. The elites, the "politically connected", or our modern aristocracy do not experience the same system of justice as the majority of us. There are exceptions to the rule e.g., when one elite offends/violates another elite and that elite weaponizes the justice department against the offending elite. But there are certainly two systems of justice. My goal is to tell you my story but also to expose the tyranny and tyrants in each and every level of the system.

The government bureaucrats who are unelected but are appointed and hired via cronyism or nepotism are a class of tyrants. They receive salaries and benefits that most people could only dream of. They possess the IQ of a rock, and their work quality is characterized as "quiet quitting" i.e., doing the bare minimum and "spinning" you to another person, department or agency so as not to do any work even if it is their responsibility. On the scumbag ladder, these are low-level tyrants, but they are like genital warts and hard to remove. When you remove them, new ones come back in their place. Think government agencies on local, state and federal levels.

Law enforcement officials are a special kind of tyrant. Typically, they spent their entire junior/senior high school years getting shoved into lockers. They graduated from high school went to an online college or local community college while living in their mom & dad's basement and began cycling steroids they purchased from Moldova online. Soon, these juiced up tyrants are tasering speeders and shooting 10-year-old trick or treaters in the park because he thought the reflective Three Musketeers candy bar was a gun. Even worse is the self-aggrandizing scumbag who possesses a veneer of respectability and floods your mailbox every election season asking for your vote for him as sheriff or district attorney. As if the tv and radio commercials ear and eye fucking you aren't enough.

If I may, I would like to quote the late Supreme Court Justice Ruth Bader-Ginsburg: "even judges can be tyrants." Yes, judges can be tyrants. Judges are supposed to be fair and impartial. They are supposed to remain fair and impartial and not allow their personal opinions to sway their judgments. Judges are supposed to base their findings on the credibility of the evidence and testimony presented. I was ridiculed at sentencing and told I was a "crazy conspiracy theorist" who made "wild, crazy, baseless, certainly lacking in evidence accusations against the New Jersey State Police, the government and anyone involved with this case" and that the court had not seen "even a scintilla of evidence that any of these wild crazy things are true." Imagine being told that at sentencing when you are telling the truth and the evidence does exist, but your judge just didn't take the time to look at it? And your court appointed lawyer told you he wasn't getting paid enough to go to trial, so he didn't have the time to go through it with you and the judge. Yes, that really happened, and I was enhanced and given additional time to my sentence for "perjury" even though there was never any concrete evidence that I ever committed perjury. My sentencing court said these things to me, and they exist in the court record and are viewable by the public. Everything I am going to tell you in this book is viewable by the public, so you don't have to worry about me telling you a bunch of lies to exaggerate my plight or make myself appear as something I am not. As you read, you will see that it wasn't me who committed perjury, but rather 8 New Jersey State Police troopers at the behest of two assistant united states attorneys. It will only get worse; I will not just tell you about what happened, but I am going to show you -or direct you to New Jersey 1:20-12713-NLH- the actual evidentiary exhibits that were tampered with by the federal government and its proxies as well as the deliberate falsification of reports and records used to imprison me.

Why? In an era of divided politics and a nation split more so than the Civil War, the focus is on the oval office but presidents come and go. The oval office has term limits whereas congress and federal agencies do not. Real power is in those agencies and institutions. It is in those where the true threat of tyranny lies. Lifetime appointments and term-limitless positions are a threat to democracy. I was put in prison because what I stumbled upon while interacting with New Jersey's 2nd Congressional District and the VA bureaucrats would have caused an uproar for reform. After implicit threats to my life from various entities in the aforementioned tyranny, I took my story and the evidence to my publisher. My publisher, my good friend attorney Vince Rovito, and my family all confirmed that this is a story that needs to be told and only I can tell it. It was a wild ride. Hang on, this one is a doozy.

CHAPTER 1

HUMBLE ORIGINS

I think it's important for any person who's about to present a viewpoint in an intelligent debate to be open and honest about any biases that they might hold. With that said, full disclosure, I want to be upfront with my readers and express my utter contempt and disdain for the Department of Veteran's Affairs. This includes the healthcare and benefits entities which are separate yet equally incompetent. In order for you to understand how I got to my current situation; I must take you back in time a bit. I will, however, spare you a lot of insignificant details.

Most people's earliest childhood memories consist of details and vague flashes of moments which they can't distinguish as being real or recall from dreams. Mine, however, are quite different. They are vivid, quite clear and I never forgot, nor will I ever forget them. My earliest experience entails that I was about 3 years old sitting on the living room floor which was covered in a horrifically ugly shag carpet appropriate for the era. The smell of popcorn cooking in the frying pan fills the air from the kitchen where my father was cooking while I sat watching the television set. My father kept telling me not to spin the knobs on the set because he was afraid I would break the new television set. We were an upper middle-class family, and my father worked as an executive in downtown Pittsburgh, Pennsylvania for a computer company. My father hated his job but had 4 sons and a wife to provide for and struggled with demons from the not-so-distant past. He possessed a genius IQ with a photographic memory which allowed him to rattle off programming code from memory in the middle of the night if systems crashed and subordinates called for help.

My father returned from the kitchen with a bowl of popcorn in one hand and a can of beer in the other. He was wearing a pair of sport shorts typical of the era. If you are old enough to know what I am referring to, good, if not then simply perform an internet search. This is the time that I had all to myself with my father. My dad. While he never admitted it, I was always his favorite. The bond lasted for life, and I was with him until his last breath. But for now, we were about to enjoy watching a game of Pittsburgh Penguins hockey on our television set. I tried to learn the game from an early age and overwhelmed my father with questions. Always showing infinite patience, he answered all of my questions and spent the intermissions playing hockey with me on the living room floor with Lincoln Logs, a common and popular toy of the era. While my father answered all questions about hockey, he couldn't seem to answer one question. What are those marks on your legs?

My father was a Marine and a Vietnam Veteran. He was exposed to Agent Orange and had periodic flareups of rashes and blisters on his lower legs for the rest of his life. My father never complained about it but as I got older, I could tell he was bitter and filled with resentment. Eventually, he would tell me as I grew older that it was "from Vietnam." When I would ask him, what Vietnam was, he would reply "it was a war." When I asked why we had the war, he would reply, "politics." That was my father; a man of very few words. Always. He tried to teach me to speak little and listen more. It didn't stick with me as well as he would've liked. I am sure of that. My overwhelming sense of integrity and justice always kept me from keeping my mouth shut. My father was smart enough to know that the world wasn't always fair & just. He tried to teach me that, but I had to learn that the hard way.

For example, when I turned 18 and enlisted in the United States Marine Corps. My father was not happy because I was repeating his mistake. My grandfather had moved mountains and worked his ass off to get my father's college tuition paid only to see my father enlist in the Marine Corps. A World War II veteran himself, he could see the signs of the time and didn't want his son to see what he saw. And here I was, about to follow in my father's footsteps. A chip off the old block; the apple wasn't falling too far from the tree. Something like that.

My father was right in the end. I loved the Marine Corps. Basic training is exactly how it is depicted in Stanley Kubrick's famous movie that we all love. I love watching that and it brings back the best memories. I enlisted to be a rifleman in the infantry, 0311, and graduated high school early. I skipped my high school graduation to challenge myself to go through Recruit Training at Parris Island South Carolina in the hottest months. My father had mixed emotions; he was proud but was also not happy. He didn't have the money to pay for my college. My parents were long divorced and his job at the computer company was a distant memory. But at least he was happy now because he was driving truck. My father liked it because he enjoyed the periods of solitude and Hank Williams Jr. The Marine Corps and the GI Bill could pay for my college tuition even though he wasn't sure that college was all that society was making it out to be. My father saw a lot of radicalization taking place on campuses during his era and I didn't know until years later that he was spit on upon after his return from Vietnam.

After Basic Training, I went home on 10 days leave. It was a blur and then redeployed to Camp Geiger for 6 weeks of Infantry School which is better known as SOI. I loved it and it was right next to Camp LeJeune. Camp LeJeune is the home of the 2nd Marine Division. This meant that I could likely get stationed there and it was what I had always hoped for. I wanted to be deployed on a 6 month "med float" (Mediterranean Sea Deployment) with a rotating Marine Expeditionary Unit (MEU). Unfortunately, Ole Uncle Sam was about to sodomize me without any lubricant and not for the last time.

The Marine Corps ordered me to Camp LeJeune but sent me to the headquarters of The Chemical Biological Incident Response Force (CBIRF). This unit was a Charlie-Foxtrot (Cluster-Fuck) and only two years old. It was mostly a dog and pony show consisting of Nuclear, Biological and Chemical decontamination Marines and Infantry Marines assigned to do "Security AND Search and Rescue" (SSRE). It was supposed to be the Marine Corps answer to any impending doom posed by a terrorist attack by weapons of mass destruction. Trainers were brought in from NYFD and members of congress visited frequently to see demonstrations ("dog and pony shows") deliberately orchestrated to inflate the Marine Corps budget for this "cutting edge" program.

For we Marines, this was Uncle Sam's way of fucking you out of your enlistment contract. It was what my father feared would happen. On paper, I was still an 0311, but in actuality I was being trained now as a fireman. My company's first sergeant was a crash/fire/rescue Marine they pulled in from the Marine Air wing stationed at New River Air Station next door to Camp LeJeune. The company gunnery sergeant was an infantry Marine but approaching his retirement. The first sergeant was "cross training" infantry Marines into fireman to the extent we never went to the field for infantry training. When we complained to our squad leaders and platoon sergeants, we received more crash/fire/rescue training. Marines went AWOL and morale was the worst I had ever seen. Participation in the Marine Corps Institute (MCI) education program was at record highs in CBIRF because it led to fast-track promotions which ultimately meant you would be transferred out of that awful shit-show.

I loved everything about the Marine Corps until they fucked me and put me there. My physical fitness scores were solid, my marksmanship was expert level, proficiency and conduct were in the highest levels of the Marine Corps standards. I was not a shitbird; I was highly motivated and born and bred to do this, literally, as I would discover later in life. Incredibly, the Marine Corps was not done fucking me yet.

In one of the rare instances, we were "allowed" a day or three of field training –usually when first sergeant fireman was coordinating with FDNY to bring in trainers for us- we did a night FX (training exercise). I was learning to operate the new encrypted field radio that night as all new guys are required. During this field exercise, a pop-up flare went up and I failed to close my eyes and became blinded. I continued moving forward and fell into a fighting position. The weight of the radio and my gear twisted me awkwardly. I had made a Fucking New Guy (FNG) [stupid] mistake and the end result was I had torn my meniscus in my right knee. I kept my mouth shut for as long as I could but when I couldn't finish my PT test's run in time, I had a problem. I was put on light duty and moved into the administration office. I became a clerk for the fireman first sergeant. The guy was an unbearable, condescending prick who never treated his subordinates with any semblance of respect and especially disdained infantry Marines. I witnessed him disrespect our company commander, an infantry officer, behind his back after he left our office on countless occasions. I hated the fireman first sergeant and the longer I was in that office, the more I radiated that energy, and |I am sure he became aware of it.

For a year, I underwent physical exams, reflex & mobility tests, and prescribed GI candy i.e., Motrin 800 mgs. Finally, an MRI at the naval hospital on base revealed I had a torn meniscus in my right knee and needed surgery. That never happened. Before that surgery happened, I began waking up with stiffness and cramping in all of my muscles. Eventually, it got to a point where I couldn't stand up straight. At one point, I felt my heart racing and honestly thought I was going to die. The staff sergeant in our company office drove me to the emergency room at the naval hospital early one morning. After hours of testing, I was notified I was suffering renal failure. My creatinine, protein and B.U.N levels were skyrocketing.

If you think that Ole Uncle Sam can't fuck you more than once, twice, or thrice then you are sadly mistaken. At first, the doctors kept me in the hospital stating that I surely had to be "abusing" the GI candy they were prescribing me for the past year. That is, the prescription strength 800 mg of Motrin, 3 times per day, over a 12-month period for pain while they slow-dragged their feet to perform routine testing to ascertain what the issue was e.g., x-ray, MRI, etc. Unbeknownst to me was that the Marine Corps was secretly hiding a scandal in which chemicals had contaminated drinking water on base. It began in the early 1950's and was supposed to have stopped. It was attributed to an increase in certain types of cancers and kidney failure was also an issue. Best part…I was living in one of the areas of the base identified to be affected. You can't make this shit up. But it gets better. After lounging in a hospital for 2 weeks, drinking water from an area that was not affected, my kidney function improved, and I was discharged. Discharged from the hospital and then hurriedly discharged from the Marine Corps. The Marine Corps claimed it was because of my knee injury but –wait for it- we will never know because my nephrologist "lost or misplaced" my medical records. Ole Uncle Sam slipped his dick in again…no vaseline. Years later, I learned about the scandal and was told that I was not eligible for a portion of the settlement because it was corrected before the time I was stationed there. My reply is simple… bullshit. An investigation was done by Criminal Investigation Services Camp LeJeune and every sailor [officer] who touched my medical records blamed someone else or feigned ignorance. So much for integrity.

So, dad was right; the Marine Corps and Uncle Sam will fuck you and don't expect the VA to help you when you come home. Especially if you can't prove that what happened to you is from your service. In later chapters, I am going to discuss how the United States Army discharged tens of thousands of soldiers with "personality disorders" who were suffering from post-traumatic stress disorder (PTSD) and traumatic brain injury (TBI) in order to avoid paying their retirement benefits. Uncle Sam saved a lot, but the damaged veterans paid dearly for the "fuckery" because the stigma of a "personality disorder" -that was never diagnosed previously in life- stigmatized them from employment prospects and stigmatized them from reintegrating into society upon their return home. Thank you for your service? What I am going to show you is that our government is full of tyrants. Tyrants run our government and fill positions in every agency and branch, and the more you read, the more you will see examples of it.

CHAPTER 2

THE BEGINNING

In order to understand how I got where I was it is necessary to understand the circumstances that brought it forth. I do not believe in coincidences; I don't believe that G-d plays dice with the workings of the universe, no matter how irrelevant or miniscule the details might appear. G-d does not "do random".

The paint on the stone floor is old, worn and peeled off in most places of my cell. I'm stripped naked and given a green padded garment that use Velcro to hold it in place. It's called a "turtle suit". The turtle suit is used for suicidal inmates who might pose a threat to themselves. In this instance, I repeatedly denied any homicidal or suicidal ideations or intent. Yet here I was sitting on a concrete floor in a jail cell that can be most succinctly described as a medieval dungeon. It's not a far stretch to call it that because the prison is over a hundred years old. The conditions have been the subject of many local news stories in the local newspapers. I did not know this until later, but I can confirm its horrific state.

There is a one-inch green mat that sits on the cement floor of my cell. In the far opposite corner there is a camera mounted on the wall to record and view my cell at all times. Water drips down on my head from the leaking ceiling and the showers directly above my cell on the next floor. The paint, plaster and stone of the ceiling is crumbling, stained yellow and black -perhaps moldy- and I wonder if it will collapse on me if I try to sleep on my mat.

My thoughts are with my pugs; Geno, my seizure alert dog and his younger sister Isa (ee-za). I last saw them after hugging and kissing them before I went outside my home. For years, my pugs were a source of joy and support for combat injuries that the United States government neglected. The government never offered any support to pay for their training.

The alarms on my phone are piercing and going through my head. I have had no medication for my PTSD for weeks nor any medication for migraines I developed after I suffered a TBI in Iraq back in 2003. The sunlight makes it worse and I was outside cutting grass in a piercing sunlight which only served to aggravate and exacerbate my headaches. I live in the countryside, a rural community south of Millville, New Jersey. I have nearly an acre of land that I cut with a push-mower. Its late September, but it's hotter than normal and despite the rain the evening before its muggy and humid.

I slowly gather myself and check my Samsung 6 smartphone to view the alerts. I loved my Samsung phone and kept it even after I switched cellular providers and received a phone with that new provider. Basically, I kept the Samsung 6 as an internet-use-only phone. I had downloaded the ZMODO home security app onto that phone and inserted a hi-capacity micro-SD card. ZMODO retains video for 30 days, but I installed the micro-SD card to transfer and store videos for my records and future review. I have four cameras on each corner of my residence. They have night vision and motion sensor recording which automatically triggers a 14-second recording clip of whatever source of motion activated it. In most cases, it triggers when cars drive past my home on the country road directly parallel to my residence, NJ 718.

I look at my screen and am perplexed; there is a car sitting across from my home. I can't see who is inside, or how many occupants it contains. It's odd and given recent circumstances, disturbing, at this new residence of mine. I have only been living here for less than 6 months, but I have had many disturbing occurrences which ultimately led to the installation of those same cameras. On three separate occasions I had feared for my safety and well-being of the pugs. First, the tire on my riding tractor which I used to cut the grass was flattened. Second, the tire on my car was flattened without any apparent cause. I would say lastly, but the most notable up until this point, was one which required me to call 911.

On that last occasion, I was sitting in the bedroom watching tv and was startled when a loud banging was occurring on the wall immediately outside and opposite from my seated location. It was as if the source of the noise knew I was sitting directly opposite that wall though I can never prove that. Immediately, my pugs went ape-shit. Not knowing what was outside my home, I called 911. I did not like using my cell phone from my home because the remote location of it was, essentially, a dead area with no cellular coverage. Regardless, I called 911 and spoke to the dispatcher.

I informed that dispatcher what was occurring and that I was in my home, armed, with firearms and would be forced to take action if there wasn't an expeditious response by law enforcement. The dispatcher told me not to leave my home and that police were enroute. An African-American state trooper arrived in my driveway as I saw him from a small window above my kitchen sink. He had his M4 assault rifle up and at the ready. His presence activated motion-censor lights in the driveway, and it helped bring his complexion and uniform into focus and view. I tell the dispatcher to inform the trooper that I am coming outside to meet him. The dispatcher advised me not to but to leave my firearms inside which I did. The trooper did not discover any source of that banging on the side of my home, but this 911 call was recorded.

Fast forward to September 20, 2017, and I am looking at an unknown vehicle sitting across the road from my home. Normally, I wouldn't give something like this so much thought, but after the KKK fliers began appearing on my lawn and driveway, things changed. I believed the placement of those on my lawn and in my mailbox, as well as the three aforementioned incidents, warranted such scrutiny and were not necessarily equivocal with "paranoia" or "psychosis". I would imagine it would most aptly be described as a justified state of hypervigilance.

"Joe, I don't want to see you get jammed up." the voice on speakerphone calls out with a tone of concern in their voice. It's a male voice with an Italian-American accent.

"Vince, how long have you known me for? How many legal battles have we fought together? I know what to do; ask for my lawyer and don't say anything" I reply.

"Joe, don't answer any questions or go anywhere. No arrest warrant or search warrant, you don't invite those fuckers in." Vince continues.

"Vince, I got this. I know what to do. Trust me." I reassured my trusted lawyer and friend of nearly 15 years back in central Pennsylvania.

"If you get jammed up, use your one phone call to call me and I will refer you to an attorney locally as soon as I can find one for you. It'll depend on the situation as you know," Vince continued reminding me he had a summer, beach home in Brigantine, New Jersey.

"I know. I got this, Vince. Trust me." And immediately thereafter ending the call. This phone call occured after 1 pm on September 20, 2017, just hours before I am alerted to the unknown car's presence.

The car leaves and I spend the next 45 minutes texting and calling friends and family. At 10:18 a.m. on September 20, 2017, I emailed a political op-ed / letter to the editor to major news outlets in New York City and Philadelphia. This op-ed is later described by the United States Attorney's Office as "beautifully articulated" and "magnificently written" which the district judge later concurred. That letter was a summary of my less-than 6 months living in the 2nd congressional district of New Jersey and its representative in Congress. The email was carbon copied to the VA liaison for that congressional representative. It is important to note that not one person at any media outlet whoever received an email communication from me [ever] reported feeling "threatened". None of the recipients -including employees of that representative's office staff- called police; they did not shelter in place, nor was their conduct of business altered in any shape, way, or form. I have no doubt that it made the representatives feel "threatened" as it related to their current positions & careers. I was a "threat" to their privileged positions of power -whether real or perceived- and my phone call with the congressional representative's chief of staff the day before was what initially sparked that fear. A fear of exposure and a "threat" to be exposed. It was never a "threat" of violence.

"Joe, hold on the line, I have the chief of staff here in the office" the VA liaison exclaimed.

"Mike, you've hung up on me multiple times. I called the office in the capitol just as the congressman told me to do and EVERYTIME I've been told to hold, only to be hung up on after minutes waiting!"

"Joe, I am putting him on now." He replied.

"Hello?" the Chief of Staff answered. A tone of arrogance typical with the political elites.

"Do you know who I am and why I am calling?" I asked.

"No, I have no idea other than what I've just been told now." the chief replied.

"4 months ago, your boss, the congressman, told me to reach out to you specifically to schedule a meeting with him through you. He told me to do this if I had a problem with the VA or with his staff. So… I am calling you now." I informed the chief.

"Well, I know nothing about this meeting or whatever was promised to you. I wasn't privy to that phone call." the chief replied. In the coming months, he would claim he was [actually] on that May 2017 phone call between myself and the congressman only to recant that when the U.S. district court endorsed a Rule 17c subpoena. A rule 17c subpoena typically, and in this case, would mean that the congressman's office, his staffers, and anyone who had any record of electronic or written communication with myself be forced to turn these over. I requested the subpoena after showing that the United States Attorney was not being completely forthcoming in disclosing what could be deemed exculpatory or impeachment evidence. Through my court-appointed lawyer, I produced email communications that brought greater context into my interactions with the congressional office. The scope, nature, depth and duration of my interactions. Ultimately, the Rule17c subpoena forced the government to withdraw one count of its [initial] three-count indictment.

"Okay, well I am telling you what I was told to do. You can check with him. I am having problems with BOTH your staff and the VA. Your VA liaison stopped assisting me and the VA has sent my bills to collections." I continued on to the arrogant and clueless chief.

"Well, again, I know nothing about this so it's not going to happen." The chief laughed back.

"What the fuck could you be laughing at? What the fuck is so funny about what I just told you?" I shockingly asked.

"I'm not laughing." The chief replied while audibly laughing. It's important to note that I could hear no one else on the call. There was no echo typically associated with a call placed on speakerphone. Believing that this call was being recorded, I now pulled an ace from my sleeve.

"Listen here you motherfucking cocksucker…Yes, I know you're a peter-puffer. Quite frankly I don't care that you "putt from the rough". I could care less. I spoke to Mike immediately after speaking to the congressman promised me a face-to-face meeting…Mike told me specifically 'Joe I know the chief of staff very well and once he takes ONE look at you he will be MORE than eager and willing to help you'. I mean, what the fuck else does that say about you if it doesn't say you're a cocksucker?" I finished this statement and the arrogant laughing was now absent from the other end of the line.

"Mike didn't tell you about that, did he?" I asked the chief.

"No, he did not." The chief hesitantly replied.

"Did he tell you about how he would call me from his cell phone on the way to work because there were things he couldn't say on the phone in the office? Were you PRIVY to that, sir?" I asked the chief again, in a more adversarial tone.

"I was not privy to that."

"Mike told me a lot of things including his own suspicions on the failures and obstacles to the VA paying medical bills for veterans it can't see in a timely fashion." I continued on, the silence from the other end was deafening.

"I did not know about that either." the chief replied.

"So he didn't tell you about the picture message I received of 'Mike FR in Mays Landing' holding his crank?" I now dropped the bombshell. After homosexual inuendo suggesting some sort of gay quid-pro-quo was disgusting. I blocked all mediums, including his congressional email address.

"I did not know about that." the chief now mumbles quietly.

"I'd love to show you a screenshot of that message sometime." I replied.

"How can I help you, Sir. What can I do to make things better?" the chief asked. Long gone was the arrogance present when he first got on the line. There was no more laughing, there was only trepidation. I could imagine the chief's mind moving at a million miles per second as to the implications of my disclosure, and how to nullify it. This is what these types of slimy, career sycophants do, and this guy had a history of latching on to potentially promising politicians and filling that time in between working for liberal fake newspapers.

"I would like the meeting I was promised. I want to share with your boss my problems that I've had with both your staff and the VA." I resolutely replied.

"That's not going to happen… but how can I help." the chief defiantly replies.

"Listen, I want to be very clear. I am not threatening you. People like me do NOT make threats. From my experience, I hold to the old maxim that people who make threats do so out of fear and from a position of weakness. I am neither. But I have written op-eds for numerous newspapers. I am prepared to go public with everything I have received and gleaned from your staff and local district office. I don't want to do that. I think that might cause some veterans or patriots to take rash actions…" I explained to the chief. Months earlier, and in the wake of the Republican softball practice shooting by a Bernie Sanders supporter, a local democrat operative began posting a hastag #huntrepublicancongressman on social media. I did not have social media at the time and despise it. BUT…I did take a link to a news story and forward it to the district office. The democrat operative in NJ was providing detailed steps of how to use social media to track the whereabouts of republican congressmen. It detailed noting their patterns, details of themselves and the places they frequent. The operative further explained how using Google Earth could allow would-be assassins to scout the terrain and features of places they never visited before, thereby allowing them to further plan attacks.

"I am not threatening you and want to be clear about that. But I am worried about repercussions if I go public. I am trying to be responsible and handle this privately yet professionally with the congressman. I think that denying me this promised meeting would ultimately result in career suicide for your boss, you and all of your staff, if not something worse in line with that. I even emailed my concerns about this, and Mike told me the congressman thanked me for notifying him of the news report.

"How can I help you, sir? I want to help you, Sir." the chief asked.

"I just want the face-to-face meeting, I told the congressman I would travel to Washington with my service dog and meet him there for HIS convenience." I stated, now offering the arrogant elitist a way to save face and out of the situation.

"That's not going to happen, sir." the chief replied.

At this point in time, I realized I was talking to the chief of staff for a congressman who was essentially a term-limitless tyrant. The congressman had been in office for 12 CONSECUTIVE terms…24 years! He was a career politician. My thoughts flashed through my mind thinking about this immovable fact and its impact on the demeanor of the person I am speaking with on the other end of the phone. I was rapidly, in fractions of a second, speeding through my thoughts and what was paramount to me that I handle this situation wisely i.e., with wisdom appropriate to this situation. As a Jewish man, I immediately thought of King Solomon, son of David who slew the Philistines Goliath. I thought of the passage from 2 Kings, when Solomon confronts another career politician Avyatar the Cohen. Avyatar made the mistake of wagering his continued political and religious prospects by proclaiming his loyalty to Solomon's brother who was attempting to usurp Solomon on the throne following the death of King David.

In 2 Kings, chapter 2, verse 26, Solomon confronts Avyatar and tells him "He's a dead man and that although he deserves death he will not kill him but rather send him back home to his ancestral lands. Solomon's wisdom in this instance was brilliant. Solomon knew that the greatest punishment for the types of people who thrive and live by their privileged positions of power is to remove them from power. Solomon believed this was worse than death. I concurred and had previously expressed this same sentiment and the wisdom of Solomon to the VA liaison. Perhaps it was time for a change in that congressional district.

I even suggested to the congressman's VA liaison that I might challenge the congressman myself. I informed him I had volunteered for Ron Paul's campaign in 2008 and was a paid campaign employee for President Donald Trump in 2016 in the state of Delaware. Initially, I was a volunteer, but I busted my ass and after losing my job for wearing a Trump for President shirt to my place of employment on a dress down Friday, the campaign brought me on full time for a week to push for the rally planned in Harrington Delaware. My firing was complete bullshit; for weeks I watched employees come to work on Fridays with socialist Bernie Sanders shirts and Hillary Clinton gear. I was fired in retaliation for wearing my Trump shirt on dress down Friday, I was informed by my feminazi supervisors that I was expected to work late and the next day (Saturday)…on the Holy Sabbath. When I arrived at work wearing my kippah and blue jeans my supervisor reacted with disgust. I was notified of my termination the following Monday. One of the reasons cited was my unprofessional dress on Shabbat and that my supervisors did not want to work with me. I was the only white male working at that company. The staff there couldn't call me a "nazi" because they knew I was Jewish but their disdain for me materialized regardless. I was happy and grateful for the opportunity the campaign gave me to make money in that situation. The congressional staff were aware of this through the VA liaison's emails and phone calls with me. I also made it known that many conservative voters in the district perceived the congressman to be a R.I.N.O. -**R**epublican **I**n **N**ame **O**nly- and out of touch with the America First movement. It was true, in fact, it was well known that the congressman had made disparaging remarks about President Trump prior to the election and after. There was no love lost. My expressions citing these facts and opinions further alienated me with a VA liaison who was increasingly inappropriate with his remarks toward me in our phone conversations.

"Well then, I have made it clear to you that I am not threatening you but…well, you're a dead man then." clearly referring to my 'career suicide' remarks earlier. I thought, now I've told this guy THREE TIMES I am not threatening him so he can't possibly twist that. In my mind, this call is being recorded and the context is clear. An hour later I forwarded an email with the original news link regarding the potential for political violence that I spoke of earlier. Hours passed before I received a response and when I did…it was from the VA liaison. It was odd because once I had blocked him from communicating with me, especially by cell phone, he backed off. Now, I am getting an email in which he, TOO, is asking me how we can fix the situation and move forward.

It is important to note that neither the chief of staff nor any of his staffers called the police. They did not shelter in place and when the district office manager was shown the email sent after that phone call, she would testify a year later saying that she saw the email and that "she thought nothing of it" and that "business continued as usual". While these facts are consistent with my claims of the context of the remark and conversation that day, that same district office manager would later be exposed for sharing her testimony during my trial with the chief of staff. She deliberately lied to the jury, at the behest and questioning of the Assistant United States Attorney, to falsely claim that it was my interactions with their office that prompted more than ten thousand dollars worth of security upgrade. These upgrades were made to the district office and the congressman's home. There was one problem with that claim; the upgrades were made a month before I moved to New Jersey and two months before I ever had any interaction with their office. I couldn't possibly have been the catalyst for those upgrades because they didn't even know who I was at that time.

A day after the office manager testiLIED (lying in testimony) to the jury, the chief of staff testified and disclosed to the USAO that her testimony was inaccurate. Even worse, the lies were discovered because these two government witnesses shared their testimony while (supposedly) under sequester by the district court. They should never have been sharing their testimony. When it was disclosed, the jury was in the jury room and had not entered the courtroom. When they did take their seats, the AUSA began with the chief of staff as the first witness and briefly revealed the shared testimony and that it was "inaccurate". This did nothing to nullify the impact left on the jury the day before and when they went home with that information in the forefront of their minds. As you read, you will find that many of the versions of events changed & evolved only to be outright refuted by factual evidence. It didn't seem to matter to the jury and in other instances in which my counsel tried to present impeachment evidence to the jury, the district judge refused permission for it to be shown.

I did not reply to any of the emails from the congressman's VA liaison that night. I tried texting my ex-girlfriend about the situation and that I was concerned about it. Later, some of these text messages would be shown as evidence against me. Text messages in which I was using voice to text applications because I couldn't type well as a result of the fine tremor syndrome I suffer from due to my combat TBI. I made the mistake of trying to use voice to text to convey what happened and my concerns while it was raining. The rain hit my screen and further impeded my messages content. One of these texts was presented as evidence but the immediate text message after stating the difficulty I was having using voice to text and the rain hitting my screen was not allowed to be shown to the jury. How could that be allowed by a supposedly fair and impartial jurist? Think of how many times you -the reader- has sent something using voice to text and how badly it mistyped what you actually said! This is a common occurrence with closed captioning. I should know…I'm hearing impaired from my service in Iraq as a machine-gunner. I wear hearing aids in both ears and the VA healthcare system would not provide the hearing aids for me. I have service-connected disability ratings for tinnitus and have repeatedly failed hearing tests but I could not get the VA to help me purchase hearing aids. You might ask why or how this happens and I just revert to the facts involved in my case and the historical evidence of my prosecution to include official VA medical and disability & compensation records. There is something bigger that must be conveyed here. ALL of my phone calls are taken on speakerphone. And, because the cellular service was so bad inside my home, I often took my calls outside the home on speakerphone…in the presence of my security cameras that were recording it all. So, in my Samsung 6 cellular phone, there existed a recording of the phone call I would later be charged with making a "threat to murder" the chief of staff. But not JUST the chief of staff, the government argued it was a threat that applied to ALL staffers at the office. Even people who I never met or spoke to and who were not privy to my communications with the office. On July 16th, 2018, the district court ORDERED that my Samsung 6 be turned over to me to obtain this data. Today, more than five years later as I write this, I never got it. My court appointed counsel only sought a forensic extraction of the call logs from the month of September 2017 and never requested a complete extract of the device. Even still, my lawyer informed the district court that there were discrepancies in phone calls appearing on the device, but not on the records. That would mean that my cellular records were altered. The judge said it must have been "tower issues" but even one second calls or calls with a call time of zero seconds (a hang up) were appearing. The Rule 17c subpoena produced the congressman's VA liaison's congressional cell phone making lengthy calls to my cell phone. This refuted his initial 302 sworn statement to the FBI. The most disturbing aspect is that my AT&T phone records had clearly been altered and the judge couldn't have cared less. If my device, and the congressional cell phone records showed calls between our phones, why would my records not show them? It was because someone was trying to remove any evidence of those phone calls and never thought the judge would endorse a Rule 17c subpoeana for those congressional cell phone records of the

VA liaison. And when it showed these discrepancies that could only be the result of evidentiary tampering, the judge wrote it off as "cell tower issues". Thirty minutes of phone calls -on ONE day alone- is not a cell tower issue. That's deliberate!

My cell phone contained the screenshot of the message I received and recordings of the charged call and what followed on September 20, 2017. It's inconceivable that any defense counsel would not request the full content of the device, especially in light of my claims of the evidence it contained. I found out years later, during a 2255 filing, that my trial counsel never even requested it. It made sense; this was because I specifically remembered him telling me that he could never review that volume of evidence with me because "he did not have the time."

That phone call on Tuesday, September 19th, 2017, resulted in me writing that "beautifully & eloquently written" op-ed. I never left my house except to go in the opposite direction of the congressional office to get cannabis. I was now -more than a month- without my required seizure medication because the VA failed to refill it timely and, when they did, the sent it to the wrong address (repeatedly) because they could not update my address from Dover, Delaware to Millville, New Jersey. Both of those address fall under the umbrella of the Wilmington, Delaware VAMC.

That same phone call with the chief of staff on Tuesday September, 19th later helped me write one of the best op-eds I ever wrote. On Wednesday, September 20, 2017 at 10:18 am, I emailed it out to several major news outlets and copied the congressional office. It was the catalyst for, and what precipitated, my phone call with my attorney Vince. It is how I found myself staring at the screen of my Samsung 6 looking at a strange car parked on the shoulder of the remote country road that ran parallel to the front of my residence. Despite my warnings from Vince, I thought I had everything covered. Multiple safeguards in multiple digital forms would protect me and show that the congressman, who had a veteran light himself on fire in protest, could be exposed for making deliberately false statements in press releases to the public. The Rule 17c subpoena would later confirm what I already knew.

The Northfield New Jersey clinic (CBOC) was in the congressman's district, and it was one of the worst I ever visited. The congressman knew it and could not do anything to fix it, even after the self-immolation of one of the veterans who attended the same clinic as I just a year earlier. The average person accepts that politicians are expert liars skilled in the arts of semantics and deception. Attorney Sidney Powell once wrote that they (politicians) are better than stage actors or Hollywood's best because they love the camera more and are better actors in front of the camera. I actually had proof and, because of it, I had to be crushed.

CHAPTER 3

BUREAUCRATIC TYRANTS

At this point in this book, it's safe to say that the car parked across from my home on September 20, 2017 was law enforcement. It was an off-duty NJSP detective. Aside from the three incidents I previously discussed, it's important to understand the totality of my interactions with the NJSP, specifically, the Port Norris New Jersey Station and how it relates to my interactions with the Veteran's Health Administration (VHA). Due to my rural location south of Millville New Jersey, designated law enforcement for my residence -with regard to responding to calls- was, for all intents and purposes, the Port Norris New Jersey State Police Station designated station A100.

In January 2016, I received a threatening and retaliatory communication from a VA nurse who worked at a Community Based Outpatient Clinic (CBOC) under the umbrella of the VA Medical Center (VAMC) Wilmington, Delaware. I later submitted these threatening communications in a civil suit I filed in United States district court. These communications stemmed from a secure, electronic messaging system that veterans can use to contact their care team. It is aptly referred to as the VA secure messaging system.

The basis for these communications was that the Veterans Health Administration (VHA) was not, and could not, update a veteran's contact information and physical address. The VHA repeatedly demonstrated this inability and, when questioned, it was explained by multiple VA staff that the system for maintaining information is not shared from state to state or VAMC to VAMC. This means that despite being a federal agency, one VA CBOC in one state would not notify the other of a change of address. This is astounding and contradicts most people's perception of an organized federal agency. Despite this massive bureaucracy, the VHA cannot update addresses promptly (or correctly) if a veteran moves between states e.g., from Pennsylvania to New Jersey to Delaware, etc. I had been seen in all three of these states; the Lebanon Pennsylvania oversaw my care and the Wilmington Delaware VAMC oversaw BOTH Delaware and southern New Jersey. The two facilities were notably different in their standard of care as well as patient relations. Wilmington VAMC was one of the worst facilities as rated by employees and veteran patients during the time I was enrolled in that system.

The events that I am about to relay are substantiated by my federal VHA medical records. In late January 2016, after briefly being treated at the Northfield New Jersey CBOC, I moved to Dover Delaware. Unknown to the average citizen, the Northfield CBOC was forced to the forefront of notoriety when a veteran patient lit himself on fire after not receiving care he needed from the CBOC. The congressman of New Jersey district 02 came under increased scrutiny, but it was short lived. It was not a total surprise, as I have already presented that his chief of staff was intertwined, through past employment, with some of the major news outlets in the country e.g., the Los Angeles Times. Instead of the "media" and "journalists" holding federal officials to account for a breakdown in medical care that ultimately resulted in a veteran lighting himself on fire, these "journalists" acted as a propaganda mouthpiece in defense of these officials and agencies. Sometimes, they maligned the veteran's mental health issues as the root cause of the problem.

Predictably, these officials express outrage and quickly their statements evolve to the need for more funding which they ultimately blame on what political party is in power. The congressman at the heart of my criminal case was a member of a committee for Veterans Affairs as well as the House Select Intelligence Committee. This congressman used the plight of veterans as a "plank" in his re-election campaign platform(s). He used it to cite what he wanted to do and then later used it in press releases to boast about his accomplishments regardless of the veracity of his proclamations. And the "media" and its "journalists" were absentee in their self-professed responsibility to hold government accountable.

Upon moving to Dover Delaware, I updated my address and contact information with the Dover CBOC via secure messaging and telephone calls. I was reluctant to engage in telephone calls with VA staff for a couple reasons. I suffer from a combat hearing impairment which led me to speak in a louder tone than what people might expect. VA staff would label this as "yelling" at them whenever I reported problems with getting care. After the Phoenix Arizona VAMC "deathlist" scandal, VA employees were under intense scrutiny as to handling appointment scheduling. In an act of CYA (cover your ass), any complaint about not receiving timely care of medications was immediately depicted in clinical notes by VA staff. Any time there is a written, electronic, or telephone contact, the VA staff member will summarize the encounter in typed notes that become a part of the veteran's medical record. These petty, bureaucratic tyrants depict the interactions as unfavorably as possible to paint the veterans as disgruntled and / or impossible to deal with. I began requesting and reviewing medical records and noticed these changes. Any veteran who disagrees with the staff characterization of a phone call encounter has no recourse to dispute the staff member's narrative. I decided to keep all of my communications in writing i.e., letters, faxes and secure messages. If needed, I would fax or had my fiancé Dana handle calls.

Despite my best efforts to notify VAMC Wilmington, my contact information was not updated correctly. It is important to remember that both the Northfield New Jersey and Dover medical facilities fall under the umbrella of care of the VAMC Wilmington. VAMC Wilmington served BOTH south New Jersey AND Delaware. Now living in Dover Delaware, I was not receiving appointment or medication notifications via postal mail because of the inability to update my address. The lack of communication did not end there; I was scheduled to be at appointments in the Dover CBOC while simultaneously required to be at an appointment an hour away at the Wilmington VAMC. How incompetent are the VA staff that they can't even correctly book appointments? How insulting and unjust to then penalize my inability to attend one of the appointments as a "no-show". "No-shows" are a derogatory note in a veteran's medical record which VA staff use to blame veterans for not receiving timely care. In this particular instance, it was a joke and demonstrates the incompetence of VA staff as well as their weaponization of veteran's medical records to insulate themselves from any investigation or accusations of misconduct.

Later, in late January of 2017, a Dover CBOC team nurse assigned to my care threatened to revoke my secure messaging privileges. This would've been catastrophic for my ability to ensure my communications with VA staff were clear, concise and indisputable as to content and context. The team nurse continued her threat and blamed the United States Postal Service for not delivering VHA communications to my correct address. I responded to that secure message by questioning her threat to terminate my secure messaging and attaching a file to my reply containing a photo of the letter I received. That photo, submitted in my criminal case and later civil suit, clearly demonstrated the VA's inability to perform basic clerical work and type the correct address on the letter sent to me at the wrong address. This team nurse simply replied that the address on the letter was what the VA had in my file. Unbelievable. I responded by stating I was contacting the Patient Advocate -a VA employee employed to address veteran patient complaints- to correct my contact [mis]information and to report the threat by the team nurse. I explained it was a violation of the VA's Healthcare Bill of Rights, specifically to be treated with dignity and respect. Having no justification for her actions or messaging her threat to me, the team nurse immediately reported ME for "abuse". Meanwhile, I repeatedly contacted the patient advocate to no avail. I left voicemails on the patient advocates extension; later, his mailbox was full and could not take more. When I reported the patient advocates lack of response and full voice-mailbox, VA staff would transfer me to an extension that would ring endlessly -in some instances for longer than five minutes- until disconnecting.

Less than two weeks after receiving a threatening message from the team nurse, I received a written letter from a Dr. Washington of the VAMC "Disruptive Behavior Committee". I was notified of MY responsibility to not "abuse" staff, make threats, and that a copy of the letter was added to my medical record as well as sent to VA police. Unreal. I was threatened for disputing the false assertion of my personal information problems and my expressed statement to contact the patient advocate was now deemed "a threat!?" You cannot make this up and copies of these documents are a matter of the court's record. In response, I replied in writing -via certified mail with signature receipt- disputing the claims of Dr. Washington and notifying her that I perceived her letter as an act of intimidation to discourage me from utilizing the patient advocate as a resource in addressing issues I was having with the VAMC. I sent copies of the threatening secure message chain as well as Dr. Washington's retaliatory letter to the Office of the Inspector General (OIG) for violations of my rights as a patient. I received a letter from the OIG confirming receipt of the complaint -also sent certified mail with signature receipt- sent to Washington, D.C. The letter stated I would not be informed of any actions taken (or not taken) as well as the details of the investigation. Essentially, there was no accountability or oversight for these tyrannical bureaucrats…until President Trump signed the VA employee accountability act months later. Incredibly, after my arrest, Dr. Washington sent another DBC letter to my address telling me I was banned from all CBOC's and could only use VAMC emergency rooms for care. The reason listed stated that I had threatened VA officials on social media!? Even the USAO never accused me of doing this and no one ever presented any evidence that I WAS on social media. I showed this letter upon my release from federal prison to congressman Christ Smith of New Jersey. I was directed to the East Orange VAMC whom assumed my care when initially transitioning from the FBOP. I was immediately placed in community care because I stated I didn't feel safe going to VA facilities and that there was a history of retaliation and abuse. The community care director concurred and approved my request for community care placement while adding that he believed this letter -also signed by the VAMC director- to be illegal.

I had had enough of the Dover clinic and in late March of 2017, I moved back to southern New Jersey. The absence of care for my migraines, seizures and PTSD exacted a tremendous toll on my relationship with Dana. I moved back to New Jersey -closer to her- but we were living in separate homes for the first time in 3 years.

Upon my arrival in southern New Jersey, I (again) updated my personal information and requested appointments. By this point in time, it had been more than 2 years since I saw a mental health professional and 6 years since I saw a neurologist. Considering the seriousness of my diagnoses, this was unacceptable by any standard of care in third world countries. There was simply no justification for the VHA's dereliction of duties, threats, and retaliatory administrative actions. It was no surprise that I met tremendous resistance in acquiring appointments. The inability of VHA facilities from one state to another state was evident (again) in that the Wilmington VAMC attempted to schedule my mental health appointment back in Dover Delaware. My frustration was only exacerbated by the fact that phone contact was severely impeded by a weak cellular signal at my new home. I soon sought out the congressman's assistance with inquiring into getting care. After all, this was the same congressman who was making the plight of veterans a "plank" in his re-election platform.

In late April 2017, I was invited to attend a meeting with Vineland New Jersey CBOC personnel. The congressional VA liaison would also attend and be present for this meeting. The meeting was presented to me as an opportunity to present issues and obstacles I was experiencing while trying to get care. I have a 100% service-connected disability and compensation rating from the Veterans Benefit Administration (VBA) arm of the Department of Veteran's Affairs. VHA provides the medical treatment and assessments that VBA uses to determine VA benefits. Quite simply, there was no sound justification for the roadblocks, obstacles, and open hostility I was experiencing. I attended the meeting with my service dog, Geno, and was repeatedly shot down, interrupted, and talked over when I presented issues and detailed events of specific instances of misconduct by VA staff. I was told that those things "were in the past" by the clinic manager and that the purpose of the meeting was (now) a plan for moving forward in my care. At this meeting, I explained to all present about the lack of cellular service at my new home. I further explained that this only increased the need to utilize secure messaging. I even provided the clinic staff present (my team nurse, nurse manager, etc.) a copy of a fax sheet sent to the congressman's office days prior to include my fax number to receive written communications. I would actively monitor my secure messaging account, and also set email notifications to my email address whenever I received a secure message. The VA CBOC would never use this fax number and insisted on calling a cell phone that would not ring because of a lack of service. Despite being informed of this lack of cellular service, the VA would continue to call with important appointment and medication information. Not receiving an answer, the VA CBOC began calling the police to conduct "wellness checks" due to me not answering calls that I was ultimately not receiving in real time due to a lack of a cellular signal.

In May of 2017, I received a dental appointment with a VA Choice Program affiliated provider to perform an extraction of a molar. I had a root canal done prior to my initial deployment to Iraq and a filling was also performed. In combat, one of the many concussive events I experienced while serving as an infantryman, this filling was knocked out. I can recall spitting it out of my mouth into my hand. No one should be misled or underestimate the sheer force and power behind a concussive event or if it can result in what I've described. The VA Choice Program was instituted in the wake of the Phoenix Arizona VAMC "deathlist" scandal. Choice was designed to give veterans a "choice" in selecting healthcare services in the community when the VA was unable to provide regular care or care within 30 days. The problem itself was just another extension of a deadlocked bureaucracy inability to address problems. The VA routinely failed to pay the Choice providers for the services they provided the veterans. The Rule 17c subpoena resulted in the release of emails between top VA officials discussing "the failure to pay 17,000 veteran's Choice bills in South Jersey" which ultimately resulted in the veterans receiving collection letters. VA employees amusingly referred to the problems as "black hole billing" and "an inability to receive payment within 9 months… if ever." The average citizen would think (perhaps) an investigation should ensue. Over the course of my discussions with the congressman's VA liaison over the next several months, we discussed the VA's inability to pay Choice obligations in addition to not processing travel pay reimbursement to these appointments. No investigation happened and in the years that followed, reports of embezzlement and misappropriation of VA funds became public knowledge. The program, in and of itself, was an extension of the VA bureaucracy, a major impediment to care and disservice to veterans whom later took their lives after being overwhelmed with medical bill collection notices. The Rule 17c subpoena resulted in the release of emails in which congressional and VA staff [improperly] shared my personal identifier information in the subject lines of emails. In one instance, after dozens of emails doing so, the congressional VA liaison admonished the VA CBOC nurse manager for doing so. The liaison stated he "could not open that [email]" as it was titled on his email server. Clearly, there was an awareness that this was inconsistent with protocol established in the wake of numerous instances in which VA negligence resulted in the improper disclosure and acquisition of veteran's personal identifier information. Recipients of sensitive veteran information, e.g., home addresses, next of kin family members identities, phone numbers and diagnoses, included nefarious actors such as the Islamic state in Iraq and Syria (ISIS).

The improper use of VA email didn't stop there; the congressional VA liaison improperly shared my personal email address with CBOC staff. I specifically requested he NOT do this, but he did it when VA staff would claim I hadn't acknowledged or responded to secure messages in a timely enough fashion. Remember, my secure messaging account was already set to trigger my personal email address when a secure message was received. There was absolutely no basis or justification for the congressional VA liaison's disclosure of my email address. There is no justification or basis for doing so -as a VA employee- unless you were aware of prior complaints against VA staff through secure messaging. That is, unless, the VA staff wanted to have a medium for communication outside normal messaging while thinking they could not be compelled to turn over these emails if asked due to their origin from federal email addresses i.e., va.gov.

I became aware of the liaison's improper disclosure because the Vineland CBOC nurse manager used it to email me at 7 a.m. to schedule a meeting with Wilmington VAMC director Vince Kane. The tone of the message was perceived by myself to be hostile; I expressed concern that I would not be able to present problematic concerns inhibiting my ability to receive care similar to what occurred in our April CBOC meeting. Only this time, I would be sat down and scolded by the VAMC director personally. Not happening.

What complaint could I have possibly presented? Simple. The Choice dental procedure I had done was long overdue. An infection has spread through my gums and required a regimen of strong antibiotics. That was the state of neglect the VA left a 100% service-connected disabled veteran. It's inconceivable that the VA's response would be a failure of CBOC staff to ensure delivery of these needed antibiotics. Consequently, I suffered a 102-degree fever and a seizure that followed. The record in my criminal and civil case details the failures of the CBOC staff to arrange a local pharmacy to provide the medications as well as the VA pharmacy sending any by mail. The Vineland VA's CBOC staff negligence caused additional undue, and unnecessary, suffering.

There are people in our government and contemporary society who mock anyone who mentions "The Deep State" yet I have just provided you with a glaring example of such. The bureaucratic tyrants entrenched in the department of Veteran's Affairs are unelected, lifelong appointees/employees whose federal employee unions make any possible disciplinary action -including termination from employment- impossible. That is exactly what the Deep State is; it exists as an administrative branch of government not sanctioned by the United States Constitution and incompatible with the rights and provisions it entails. The mere existence of this cloaked branch of government has been empowered by the courts who have delegated their authority to these bureaucratic tyrants and the Code of Federal Regulations (CFR). The reasons for this abdication of judicial responsibilities has set an unlawful & unconstitutional precedent. It subverts the will of the American people who pay for the salaries of all government employees. It is the people from whom they get their positions of power, yet these petty bureaucratic tyrants wield it indiscriminately against those same people who empower them. Bureaucratic tyrants exist as the foremost existential threat to the average American citizen's way of life. These petty tyrants will be, if left unchecked, the catalyst for a second civil war.

CHAPTER 4

AGENTS OF TYRANNY: TAX COLLECTORS

At the time that I am writing this, the talking heads on television are reporting on alleged differences in the criminal justice system. Some argue that there is a two-tier system of justice. There are many who will claim that it is racist and there is no doubt that racists DO exist in the system. However, having experienced it firsthand, I can provide a unique & differing opinion as to what is the root source of this apparent difference.

Having experienced the very worst of the federal criminal justice system, i.e., the prosecutors, judges, and line officers within the Federal Bureau of Prisons (FBOP), I contend that it is not simply racist. To label it racist is an injustice to everyone who belongs to a different race or ethnic group that is not possessing the current "victim" label in the fakestream media. I contend that this is a system that is biased against the poor and uneducated, regardless of race, color, or creed. If true, it is the antithesis of what is enshrined in our Constitution and what our founding fathers intended.

The current criminal justice system, having experienced both the state system in New Jersey and the United States federal system, is one that is dominated by the wealthy elite. Those who lack funding [the indigent] cannot afford to hire good -or even decent- counsel to defend themselves. The prices are exorbitant, and it relegates the poorest of society to public defenders or court appointed counsel. I am not going to allege that these lawyers are the "bottom of the barrel", "bottom feeders" or anything that could be perceived with a negative connotation. What I will say is that it has become a disservice to those they represent. Public defenders are inundated with hundreds, if not thousands, of defendants. They are assigned these cases with little resources and even fewer attorneys to provide adequate counsel. The public defenders go into a case, regardless of the facts or adversarial evidence that could be presented in their defense and seek to get their clients to agree to a plea deal. Whenever someone enters a guilty plea, they swear an oath to testify and enter their plea under oath admitting guilt. My problem with this, as an observant Jew, is how do you swear an oath under G-d if you're admitting guilt to a crime that you KNOW you didn't commit? How? Is it because someone pressures you? Or is it because someone who possesses a higher education and greater degree of understanding of the system tells you that [this] is your best option?

Far too many times people who are innocent enter guilty pleas. They swear an oath -under G-d- that the plea they are entering is a sincere act of contrition. In reality, they are overwhelmed and ill-advised, almost threatened, that if they exercise their constitutional right to have a trial by a jury of their peers, that they will endure the "trial tax". The trial tax is what prosecutors and judges utilize to discourage the accused from taking their case to trial. Regardless of their expressed guarantee of such rights, the accused are quickly informed that if you exact that right you will [later] be subject to greater sentences and even sentencing enhancements that can add increments of a longer sentence onto the baseline sentence for the offending acts. This dilemma is only further exacerbated when prosecutors dump on additional counts of crimes, most that they likely could not obtain convictions for through the process- but that they utilize regardless to provide leverage against the defendant to accept their plea deal. The uneducated, or anyone uninformed and untrained in law, will not understand and experience an overwhelming sense of defeat. I experienced this trial tax and had a sentencing enhancement applied to my federal sentence for "obstruction of justice". The prosecutor argued, and the judge concurred, that because I testified in my own defense against the eight NJSP government witnesses, that because the NJSP were found to be more credible, my testimony was not credible, false, and equivocal with perjury.

Essentially, I was punished and given greater time for exercising my constitutional right to testify against my accusers and in my own defense. The records and transcripts in my case are replete with evidence that undermines and refutes the testimony of the New Jersey State Police who testified in pre-trial evidentiary hearings in my federal prosecution. Their testimony contradicts each other, incredibly, and was further undermined by their own CAD abstract. The CAD abstract is a computer-generated report of all radio transmissions of any responding officers that is interlinked with their police vehicles via GPS. On my direct appeal, the Court of Appeals for The Third Circuit would opine that they were "wary of such an enhancement when there is no concrete evidence that Mr. Brodie testified untruthfully or committed perjury" and that "the application of this enhancement is based upon testimony that opposes the government witnesses." Think about that for a moment; you can be enhanced and given a greater sentence for merely providing your version of events against those of your accusers. The Court of Appeals said that although they were "wary" of such an enhancement they lacked the jurisdiction and ability to overturn the enhancement because they did not sit as the trier of facts in those proceedings…even if they would have ruled differently as the triers of fact. That's a powerful statement and admission by a Court that is supposed to ensure that injustices do not occur in the lower courts. To admit that they are powerless to reverse such an abuse of judicial discretion, while admitting there was never any evidence of perjury, has sanctioned the criminalization of exercising one's right to testify in their own defense. When I see people exercise their Fifth Amendment rights not to answer questions due to a fear of possibly incriminating themselves, I longer equate that action as a tacit admission of guilt.

I think it's important that we have addressed these moving forward as they will provide a basis and foundation for what I will now lay out. My critics will argue that anything I say is not credible because I was enhanced for "obstruction of justice" and "not testifying truthfully" but I will argue that the government NEVER presented -and the court never cited- any "concrete evidence" that I lied under oath. Essentially, I was branded a "liar" and "perjurer" based solely on credibility findings of the Court, whose jurist, I was increasingly becoming suspicious of being biased and prejudiced. Unlike the government or Court, I later acquired evidence that was either improperly withheld from me or that was not available to me at the time these proceedings occurred. Perhaps the worst example is that I later acquired evidence -after my conviction and direct appeal- that irrefutably demonstrated the USAO disclosed an altered version of my VA medical records immediately after my arrest. These VA medical records are, in fact, FEDERAL RECORDS subject to 18 U.S.C. § 641 & § 2071(b) which criminalize "any act to alter, modify, or delete such records for profit or gain". The USAO disclosed a 17-page record sample from the night of my arrest when the actual content was 59 pages. More than 2/3 of my medical records were deleted to facilitate the government be able to ask leading questions and suborn the perjury of the NJSP. The NJSP perjury was elicited to deny any invocation I made of my right to counsel after my arrest and to eliminate evidence which contradicted the government's basis for denying bail. The government can argue that someone is a flight risk or a threat to society i.e., self, others, or property. In my case, not having a passport or financial means to flea, I was designated a "threat". This was the entire basis of my arrest and prosecution: I was a "threat" to others and it was what the government rested it's entire case on. It was imperative that the government removed any evidence, interview notes, clinical assessment after my arrest which could undermine my argument against pre-trial detention. Had I not been detained pre-trial, I would have been able to acquire the evidence (such as true and correct copies of my VA medical records) that my [overwhelmed and incompetent] defense counsel could -or would- not.

The criminal misconduct of the government was discovered one month after my direct appeal. I acquired a certified copy of my medical records from the hospital I was taken to post-arrest. The facility was NOT a VA facility but a hospital nearby that later transferred the 59 pages of medical records from various assessments conducted on me to the VA for reimbursement of service fees. Remember, I was a 100% service-connected, combat disabled veteran who had full healthcare rights through the VHA. The facility would submit these records as justification for payments of services rendered. Once I possessed the hospitals original [complete] records from the night of my arrest by the NJSP, I was overwhelmed and disgusted. The records disclosed by the USAO to my defense counsel in reciprocal discovery had the header of each page of the hospital's records removed and a "VAMC Wilmington 09-21-2017, Joseph Brodie ****" (social security number) in its place. The NEW header also included "Page 1 of 17" and continued in sequential order for the following pages totaling 17 pages. The incompetence of tyrannical bureaucrats that plague and infect our government like a virus is that they forgot to remove the page numbers at the bottom of each record page! One page began a section of clinical notes to assess the threat of self-harm, risk of danger to others or property and was clearly marked 1 of 20…for that section alone. This means that my FEDERAL medical records were altered to remove 19 pages of clinical notes. 19 pages removed in comparison to the 17-page total record disclosed by the USAO. There is no way to reconcile this evidentiary tampering.

The USAO has a duty to "disclose true and accurate records of any evidence they intend to use against the accused, [or] which might be perceived as impeachment or exculpatory to the defendant in discovery." Clearly, the government did NOT do this because what was removed was documented evidence that existed both as impeachment evidence AND exculpatory evidence. Quite simply, the USAO could not have that information contained in it because it would have undermined their narrative. It was also highly critical of the VHA and something the VHA did not want introduced into the record in United States district court. Again, these are well documented and exist in the record for anyone to see, yet the jurist who ruled on my civil action denied any misconduct by the government. That jurist also denied an evidentiary hearing to re-cross examine those NJSP as well as a certificate of appealability to seek appellate review. Let this sink in…the jurist who oversaw my criminal case -and later oversaw my civil action related to that case- would completely exonerate the government of disclosing altered federal records despite the irrefutable admission of "concrete evidence" of prosecutorial misconduct and violations of multiple Rules of the court by the USAO. To add insult to injury, the jurist opined it would not have made a difference in his credibility determinations as it pertained to the admission of evidence at my criminal trial and further stated it was "just a continuation of Mr. Brodie's fabrications and lies to this Court."

I agree that it would not have made a difference in the court's credibility determinations; but that is only because my initial suspicions of the court being unduly influenced, biased, and prejudiced against myself. Sydney Powell famously wrote, "What the government claims is proof & fact, and whatever evidence the defense submits that undermines their narrative is perjury, obstruction of justice, etc." I couldn't agree more with what she wrote in her book." In order to appreciate the seriousness of my evidentiary submissions, I have to discuss my encounters with the NJSP and elaborate how the evidence withheld from me contributed to my wrongful conviction.

The alarms on my phone were going off shortly after 9 pm on August 25, 2017. Motion sensors recorded two NJSP cruisers in my driveway. Both of my pugs were alerted to their presence and began the typical pug bark, also referred to as "the aroo". I push to keep them at bay inside while I slip out the front door to greet the first trooper.

"Is there something I can help you with gentlemen?" I asked, confused but more irritated at their arrival.

"Are you Joseph Brodie?" the trooper asked.

"The one and only. What's this about?" I replied, with a slightly increased tone of irritation.

"We were called to come out here and check on you. The VA said that you did not attend your appointment and we came out to perform a wellness check." The second officer inserted.

"You know, guys, I've told the other troopers that you have to stop coming out here and doing this. You're coming out here NOW, after 9 pm, for an appointment that was cancelled weeks ago and you're doing so hours after the close of the clinic. You're annoying me with these "wellness checks" and you're upsetting my neighbors." I stated to all.

"We didn't know that you cancelled it. We are just doing what we were called out to do." the first trooper continued. The first trooper was younger and clearly the trooper with less seniority.

"Well, I am alive and well and in no need of a 'wellness check' so late in the evening. The fact that this appointment was cancelled via multiple mediums and yet the VA deemed it necessary to dispatch you anyway is either incompetence, but more likely retaliation for filing another OIG complaint. It's been my second OIG complaint against the VA in less than 6 months." I press on, still irritated.

"Can I just see your ID so I can confirm you're okay for my logs." The young trooper asks.

"Smith, I'm going to head back. You good here?" the second trooper asks.

"Yeah, I'm good. I'm just gonna get his info and then head-out myself." Smith replies. I already knew his name having see his nametape. Paying attention to detail has been a habit of mine since my days in the Marine Corps. I hand Smith my drivers license while I watch the old guy leave.

"This is bullshit, you know? I cancelled all appointments weeks ago. I sent emails, certified mail, and notified the local congressman's office. There is no reason why you guys should come out here." I tell Smith.

"Well, we knew none of that. We just know you didn't show for your appointment and that you didn't answer your phone when they called you...so they called us." Smith continues.

"That's funny because they know I don't have service out here and that my phone doesn't ring when ANYONE calls it. What's worse is that when I cancelled my appointments with them I did so IN WRITING and reminded them to communicate with me only in writing…but preferably not at all." I told Smith while shaking my head in disgust.

"Listen, I am a veteran myself. I know how shitty the VA is when it comes to healthcare. I have had many of my own problems with them." Smiths shares with me.

"Well, I didn't see a neurologist for more than 6 years. I had a TBI in Iraq and I am supposed to see a neurologist every 3-6 months. I was sent to a community provider at Inspira in May, but the VA never paid them. I received my third collection notice a couple weeks ago and cancelled all remaining appointments because of that. When I contacted Inspira about the bills and collection notices, the billing manager called me back with their attorney on the line to apologize." I explained to Smith after taking a nice deep breath. I know I am talking to a veteran who knows what I deal with…that level of bureaucratic incompetence that manifests as its own type of tyranny by default.

"I feel ya man. That sucks. Are they getting things straightened out?" Smith asks as he hands me back my drivers license.

"I doubt it. I had been in communications with the congressman's office to get it resolved. His VA liaison was sympathetic but would call me sometimes when he was out of the office and says things that he couldn't say in the office, but that provided a better picture of what he thought was going on." I told him while unlocking my cell phone and sitting down on the front steps to my home. Smith's cruiser has been running with the lights on, but the pugs had settled down. They've taken up a chair near the window and are watching Smith and I talk. The pugs can read my body language and have relaxed, evident by the diminishment of the infamous 'aroo' bark.

"What do you mean by that?" Smith asked, his body language intrigued with the toes of his work boot on the lowest step to my porch.

"Well, that's just it. The VA hasn't been paying a shit-ton of veterans Choice Program bills. Do you know what this is?" I interrupt myself to make sure Smith understands me.

"Yeah, I do. I've heard about it. It's supposed to ease up on the delays." Smith adds.

"Well, yeah. Supposed to work that way but it takes time to get into the program and it takes longer to get them to reimburse the Choice providers. It's a fucking mess. Everything with the finances of the program is fucked. Even the travel reimbursement. It's a total shit show." I tell Smith while shaking my head.

"So that's why you stopped going?" Smith asks me with his eyebrow raised.

"It's not just that. They can't even update my address since moving here from Delaware. They have sent my medications to the wrong address. I had to contact my old treatment in Pennsylvania just to get them to send me my meds. They agreed to do it but only on a limited basis until Wilmington VA unfucked itself. That was in May…I haven't had my meds for PTSD or my seizure & migraine meds for more than three weeks" noticing now that Smith is listening as if something is clicking in his head. I can see the light bulbs turning on.

"Well that explains why they wanted a wellness check. They must know you don't have your psych meds." Smith added.

"It's PTSD…it's not psychosis and they know I have no history of any type of psychosis or self-harm. For fuck's sake, I worked in mental health for over ten years and have a masters degree in the field. I don't want to sound paranoid, but the VA is more about covering their own asses now since I filed those two OIG complaints and got the congressman involved." I explained.

"Well, I heard he's real big on helping veterans. Hell, everyone around hear knows that. He promotes himself about that publicly on the regular." Smith adds.

"Listen, I talked to the guy on the phone one time. In the end of May… he called me personally. He's a nice guy but I don't think he has any clue what is going on or what the problems are. He told me I could call his chief of staff to arrange a meeting if I had problems with the VA or his liaison. He seemed sincere but when I got my second collection notice in July, I asked for that meeting and was informed he wouldn't attend. I can't sit in a room with any VA employees anymore. I just don't trust them…or his liaison." I explained. It was obvious to Smith that there was something behind this statement and more than what I had disclosed.

"What do you mean by that?" Smith asked

"That's too long of a story and you've already been here longer than you should." I retorted, declining to say more than what I have.

"Listen, I'm Army too. I'm having problems with the VA and you seem to be much more knowledgeable of the inner workings of the system. I'm going to do something for you," Smith adds while reaching back to his breast pocket to pull out his little notepad he had earlier used to record my information.

"What's that?" I ask.

"Here's my cell number. I will let the guys at my station know what is going on with you and the VA. A lot of them are veterans… mostly national guard who exaggerate their service record. But I've been deployed just like you and I can identify with what you're going through more than they can. I'll make sure they know of the problems with your cell phone and the collection notices. This way, if they get a call to do a wellness check, they'll know how to respond. Preferably not at all." Smith tells me. He seemed sincere and sympathetic to my plight. It was obvious to me that he had some personal experiences with the VA… none of which were positive.

"Alright man. I'll do it. And what I will do is I am going to fax your station documentation of this so they can see it themselves. I'll send it to your attention. I know you guys are just doing your jobs, but this is not the first time this has happened. I hope it's the last though. Besides, there's some information I received from the VA and from their Choice provider that doesn't add up. I'd feel better if law enforcement had it and since you guys are -technically- my local police…you guys can take a look at it. Just be ready. I sent it to the U.S. Attorney in Wilmington, Delaware but, I never got a response." I added.

"No shocker there. I have no faith in our government to do the most basic tasks anymore. My deployments really opened my eyes to that. And maybe you can refer me to the congressman's poc for help?" Smith added.

"Listen, that's a wasted effort. No real power there to change and the way the system is structured in combination with the shady shit of the VA, I think you'd be better off passing on that 'resource'" I tell Smith, while now making air quotations in the air while saying resource.

"Alright man. You're gonna have to explain what that means to me sometime. You have my cell phone. If you need anything or if I can help, just let me know. We're veterans. We're brothers." Smith smiled.

"Sounds good. I'll fax that stuff out to you tomorrow. It's getting late and my dogs are starting to whine…just be ready for what I am going to send you." I add while standing up off my steps.

"Alright, I'll make sure to pass the world around the station so the guys know." Smiths smiles while shaking my hand.

Smith walked away that night which would be the first of many visits to my house that he would end up making before my arrest by the NJSP less than a month in the future. In the next 26 days trooper Smith and I would text 1,039 times. I know this exact number because I had my cell phone records subpoenaed by my public defender on my state charges the following summer. The records were incredibly long; 25,003 pages of text and call records complete with the originating number and the terminating number. The cell phone towers are recorded and even calls that are dialed and hung up before ringing show on the records as calls lasting 0:00.

On July 24th, 2018, while the final pre-trial evidentiary hearing is occurring, a third party digital forensic expert is conducting an extract of my cellular phones in an office above the courtroom on the next floor. The USAO stalled in allowing us to access the phone. The USAO claimed that, despite their best efforts, the FBI was unable to "crack into" either of my devices. I steadfastly maintained that there was a recording of the phone call in that device because it was on speakerphone in front of my home security cameras. I also claimed that the testimony the NJSP had given regarding my arrest on September 20, 2017, was rife with deliberate instances of perjury in order to conceal my invocation to have a lawyer and see a warrant from NJSP when they first arrived to arrest me. Eventually, the USAO delayed ever further while telling the Court in one proceeding that they "lost" my device in transit sending it to another lab to "crack it". It was complete bullshit, one of many deliberate lies made to the Court to stall and delay any of the phone's contents until after the evidentiary hearings were completed and the Court made its ruling on evidentiary issues. I have never hated anyone as intensely as I did the assistant U.S. attorney by that point. This woman had been leading the NJSP in her examination of them in those evidentiary hearings in a very specific manner. The AUSA was very careful and precise on what she said and how she worded it; always giving the NJSP a free-pass on any perjury charges in the future by asking if the "knew" "could remember" or "could recall" what happened. It seems irrelevant, but lawyers do that to provide an evasive answer "opening". After all, if they're deliberately lying (committing perjury) and are exposed in the future…they can always say their memory or recollect faulted them and thereby…it was NOT deliberate i.e., perjury. The degree of semantics that this woman used was sickening. I openly wanted to vomit in many instances when she would begin an argument to the Court and the jurist would seemingly finish her statement for her when she appeared too stupid to spit the rest out. In summary, the AUSA was a "brilliant idiot" and I wondered how she got into that position. Most importantly, I realized that she was dangerous…she was the epitome of evil, corruption, and injustice.

Later, in the federal detention center in Philadelphia where I was being held before my trial, I met another inmate who was prosecuted by her in his prior case. He, remarkably, also had the same defense counsel as I did and reported the same laissez-faire attitude with his defense as I was witnessing play out before me. That inmate went to trial and lost; at one point he (purportedly) answered a question in cross examination to which he replied he was innocent and that she (the AUSA) was "dirtier than a back-to-front wiper." It didn't help him any as he was convicted and sentenced heftily. He was now brought in on a violation of his supervised release. While I laughed at the thought of that (and agreed), I became increasingly apprehensive about my defense counsel. In the weeks prior to the first of my three pretrial evidentiary hearings, he did not visit me to prepare. My trial lawyer also did not acquire my phone records or locate my phone to arrange getting the contents. It was my state lawyer who was appointed to represent me on the overlapping state charges who subpoenaed and acquired those records. Incredibly, in defense of ineffective assistance claims, he would argue to that Court that he acquired these records. He didn't…and he didn't visit me for the 7 weeks prior to these crucial evidentiary hearings. I really began to wonder if he was tanking my defense or if he just didn't care about my situation. Either way, I became increasingly distrustful of my own defense attorney as I was confident in the AUSA's absence of integrity.

Simultaneously, fear and doubt crept into my mind from my accusers and the person who was supposed to defend me from them. Most people don't ever experience this type of situation but when you're going up against the United States government -with all their power and resources- with decades in federal prison at stake…most people begin to pray. Like people I shared foxholes with before, and those that I shared jail cells with then, people always turn to G-d when the task at hand seems insurmountable. G-d helped me survive the first time…what about now? I would have no chance of Divine Intervention if I pled guilty to a crime that I knew I didn't commit. I couldn't give in to the devil incarnate across from the defense table and expect as much. Later, many people would ask why I didn't just take a plea deal while aware of their ridiculously high conviction rate & the looming trial tax. This is how I would explain it to them: I would be no different than the others who came before me and succumbed to that nor would I be doing anything to expose the madness & injustice of this system for those who came after me. I wouldn't be worth such Divine Intervention, and I could never reconcile swearing an oath to G-d while confessing guilt to a crime that I knew I didn't commit.

CHAPTER 5

DISSENT AMONG TYRANTS

"You home?" the SMS from Smith read.

"I'm stopping by" another followed. I was in the shower when these came through, but my pugs alerted me to a visitor. I rushed out of the shower, threw on some clothes to see who or what spooked the pugs. Sometimes it was just wild turkeys passing through my property and crossing the road in front of my house. I checked my phone having not heard the alerts and, sure enough, Trooper Smith was exiting his marked troop car with a bag of food from the local Wawa. Wawa makes awesome subs and sandwiches and having one two miles away -in this otherwise-remote location was a blessing. I quickly threw on shorts and a t-shirt and made my way out to greet Smith.

"You don't answer your texts?" Smith said with a smile on his face.

"I was in the shower, sorry. What's up?" I asked. At this point were standing in front of my house and his troop car is parked in my driveway. My driveway extended from the road in front of my residence -NJ 718- down along the right side of my residence and I would typically park my vehicle in the rear of my home. It would look like no one was home. I don't know why I did this but after having my tire flattened, I decided this was closest to my bedroom where I was sleeping and could (perhaps) allow me to intervene or stop any further vandalism. The driveway was roughly 75-100 feet from NJ 718.

"Not much, I was in the area and taking my lunch. I figured I'd stop by." Smith replied extending his Wawa sub and small bag of chips.

"You want something to drink with that?" I asked.

"Nah, I got something in my cruiser." Smith shrugged off the offer. Isa and Geno sat in the window at the front of my home just curiously watching and occasionally barking at the visitor. The pugs were accustomed to visits from the police by this point in time… late August 2017. Having filed multiple OIG complaints &submitted numerous collection notices to the congressional office, the VA would deliberately call me on a phone in which they knew I had no service. When I didn't answer, they would request a "wellness-check." Smith's visit the previous night was one such check despite the fact that I had cancelled all appointments with the VA weeks earlier because of their failure to pay Choice bills.

"So here…I wanted to show you this. So you can say you actually saw the emails that I cancelled all future VA appointments." I said as I extended a handful of email printouts.

"There's other good stuff you might want to take a look at toward the bottom. It'll give you a heads-up of what to expect when dealing with them and if you decide to involve the congressman's office." I invoked an intonation when saying that which was somewhere between skepticism and alluding to something more puzzling.

"What's this?" Smith asked.

"Those are emails I received along with a letter from Inspira legal counsel. The other emails are from the Wilmington VA medical center in which the director is [personally] telling me that my bills were paid and, as proof, he submits that those are [allegedly] the payment authorization numbers. The problem is, when I called and spoke to this lady, Mary, who is the billing supervisor… she told me that what I received from the director is not even the correct format or length of characters." I explained.

"So…what does that mean?" Smith asked.

"Well, apparently, it means that the director of the Wilmington VAMC is giving me authorizations which aren't in the proper format. According to the VA, these bills were authorized and paid by the VA. And…according to 'Mary' AND their legal counsel…they haven't been." I continued.

"So, who's telling the truth?" Smith asked me.

"That's a good question. I don't know. The VA says its in the books as paid but the vendor hasn't received payment and issued me these collection notices." I continued to explain to Smith whose interest and expression changed enough to shift his energy from devouring his Wawa sandwich to interpreting these documents.

"Here's what worse…look at the date of the email from the VAMC director. It's from August 16th, 2017. I reached out to 'Mary' before and after that date about these collection notices. This next sheet here is a transcription of a voicemail and conference call I had with her and their counsel. Mary explained to me that I should never have received these notices and that it was a mistake." I continued to explain to Smith while allowing him to shuffle through the documents.

"And then this came…" I continued as he flipped to a subsequent collection notice from August 25, 2017.

"Look at the date. It's after the phone calls with the Choice provider and their counsel… AND after the email from the VAMC director with the otherwise-bogus authorization codes. I took that latest notice from August 25th and sent it to the congressional office the day before yesterday. The VA knew that I had cancelled my appointments after my second collection notice, but when I took this 3rd notice and sent it to the congressional office, they sent you out here to do a wellness check for missing an appointment that was cancelled weeks before." I said as I pointed specific dates out to Smith when he flipped back and forth through the documents.

"So… who's right? The Choice provider or the VA director?" Smith asked, confused, and puzzled.

"That's my point. The VA director sent this on August 16th. This notice is more than a week after that. Obviously, the billing supervisor was correct when saying these codes meant nothing in their system. Maybe it is in the VA's system, but it doesn't mean a payment was made in the bigger picture. So, if you ask the VA… and according to their books, it's paid. If you ask the Choice provider, it isn't paid… either way I shouldn't be getting these notices." I explained trying to emphasize the inconsistencies and contradictions between both.

"So, they're cooking the books?" Smith asked in shock and dismay with a fucked up smile on his face.

"You said it, not me. The truth is…I don't know. When I sent this third notice to the congressional office I did it to refute the claims of the VA director. I mean, either this guy is utterly incompetent and unqualified to be in that position or he's just gaslighting me and the congressman. Either way, it gets worse because when I emailed it to the congressional office, I ALSO sent it to Inspira. I followed that up with a phone call directly to their legal counsel asking why I was still receiving this after our conference call and their apology letter." I continued to explain to Smith while emphasizing the 'also' to show I was following through on both ends and to further illuminate the glaring inconsistencies in the VA's account and the Choice provider.

"What did their lawyer say?" Smith asked.

"He told me he was no longer representing them." I told Smith with a bit of finality.

"What!?" Smith asked even more puzzled than before.

"Yeah. He abruptly got off the phone with me. I could tell he had me on speakerphone when he answered because of the echo in the background, but I can't say who was privy to that call." I added, matter-of-factly.

"Dude, this is so shady. It makes me want to stay away from the VA altogether and not even try to wade through this bullshit." Smith said shaking his head.

"I agree. You gave me your cell so that I could give you a heads up and help you navigate the process and I want you to see this. I am going to give you a copy of these." I continued holding the printouts and documents in my hand while extending the papers toward him.

"Yeah. Who else did you show these to?" Smith asked.

"Well, back in June I was having phone calls with the congressman's VA liaison. He was telling me that a lot of problems were happening with the VA paying anything, let alone bills. I had this problem, specifically, when trying to get my travel pay reimbursement for traveling to Choice appointments. The liaison would call me from his cell phone or another blocked number. He was telling me the reason for this was that there were things he 'couldn't say while in the office' and that was why he would call me that way." I explained in greater length to Smith.

"And…?" Smith asked.

"He told me that he, himself, was having problem getting reimbursement payments for his own appointments and that it was well known something wasn't right in the accounts payable department." I continued.

"And then what?" Smith asked.

"Well, at first, I became suspicious and the fact he was calling me 'off-the-record' as he was describing it ultimately gave it some credibility." I explained.

"No shit!" Smith s replied making more of a statement than asking a question.

"And then I just stopped talking to him." I cut short.

"Why?" Smith asked.

"Well, when I reminded him of the call I had with the congressman in late May, I reminded him that I was told to request a meeting if I had any problems with the VA or his own staff…and that all I had to do was reach out to the chief-of-staff to schedule it." I continued.

"And…? So why didn't you?" Smith asked, wondering where this was going.

"The liaison told me that he knows the chief VERY well. He said "he would take one look at me and be more than happy and willing" to schedule an appointment for me with the congressman." I said shaking my head and looking down at the ground.

"What the fuck does that mean?" Smith asked disgustedly.

"I think it means he's a peter-puffer. He putts from the rough." I replied shaking my head.

"WHAT⁉?" He really said that to you?" Smith exclaimed.

"Yeah man. I only met him in person one time. He didn't strike me as a homo himself, but maybe the chief was…I don't know, I never met him. But then…" I continued.

"Then what happened?" Smith asked.

"On a Saturday afternoon in June, I got a weird message from an unknown number telling me it was Mike FR from Mays Landing. So I assumed it was the liaison because that was where the congressional office was and I didn't know any other 'Mikes'" I continued.

"What did he say?" Smith asked.

"Not much after that. I just got a pic of someone holding their crank." I said still shaking my head.

"Get the fuck out!!!" Smith exclaimed. I think he thought -at first- that I was fucking with him been then realized I wasn't when I immediately responded,

"I took a screenshot and saved it. Here… look!" I said while looking through my phone and finally extending my screen toward him to see.

"No, fuck no…I don't want to see!" Smith explained turning his head away,

"It wasn't from the same number as before, but I didn't know what to make of it. After that, I blocked his cell and later his email for some time. It was really fucking weird, but based on his remarks about the chief being 'more than eager and willing to assist me' it just seemed like some type of gay quid-pro-quo…that to get help with the VA there were expectations. I figured… fuck that. I refuse to [literally] suck someone's dick to get what I'm owed…" I explained to Smith who is just shaking his head now.

"I heard he was a homo." Smith mumbled, shaking his head in disgust.

"Who, the chief?" I retorted quickly.

"NO! The CONGRESSMAN!" Smith exclaimed.

"Well, I don't know about that. He's married -I think- and I never got that vibe from him. I never met the chief of staff so I can't say for sure there either. I definitely do not think that the congressman is a homo. I just think that he has people working underneath hm using AND abusing the power that comes with the position" I continued.

"This is so fucked up. I don't blame you for not pushing more. And it seems that there is some shady shit going on with the VA and I wouldn't want to be involved in that…when the federal government is involved and anything goes upside down…" Smith continued.

"Oh I agree. I was worried about me inadvertently exposing something. I wrote for newspapers and did some investigative journalism, and this is not an area to delve into without some trepidation. Knowing that, I took a precautionary measure and sent these documents to the U.S. Attorney's Office in Wilmington Delaware… certified mail with the green signature cards" I explained to Smith who was still reeling from these revelations. I think if he didn't see it, he would never have believed it but the fact that I had some physical and digital evidence to corroborate my remarks it made him visibly uneasy. I am sure he was thinking about his own prospects for progress in addressing the VA. Remember, Smith was an Army veteran who was deployed to Iraq in the years immediately after my own deployments.

"And what happened then?" Smith asked, alluding to the USAO.

"Nothing yet. I never heard back, but I figured since the source of these problems was the VAMC based in Wilmington, I sent it to that USAO in Wilminton." I rationalized to Smith. Smith's whole demeanor changed. He started to pick at his sandwich and opened the small bag of chips he had purchased with it.

"Are these your only copies? Smith asked.

"Yeah, you want a copy?" I replied.

"Yeah, this way I can show it to the guys at the station so they know what is going on here. This will help them understand what's going on if the VA calls in another 'wellness check'." Smith explained.

"Okay, well I will fax them to your station… to your attention… if that works for you?" I asked.

"Sure, I'm going to keep a file on this." Smith continued. I actually felt reassured and validated having shown it to a state trooper and that it piqued his interest to the point where my interpretation of these events could not be misconstrued as some type of 'conspiracy theory'.

"Consider it done. I have your fax number from earlier this year. I got it from the NJSP headquarters when I called to ask about registering my firearms in New Jersey. I have a lot of questions about that and they told me to take them to your station in Port Norris but they're back in storage in Pennsylvania along with my ATV. I didn't want to drive into New Jersey with them after reading articles of people who did the same and ended up with felony charges." I explained and made it abundantly clear that my firearms were not going to be moved until I had a plan of action.

"Do you think you could help me with my guns?" I asked Smith whose mind was obviously still on what I told him and showed him.

"Sure. Just make sure you send me that stuff so I can read through it." Smith replied.

"I have more you know…" I added to Smith whose was visibly disturbed by this.

"More of that!?" Smith said with a combination of disgust and shock.

"Yeah. More stuff. The email chains of that I received from the liaison and my exchanges with those same people individually. They don't match up…their stories, that is." I continued.

"No shit." Smith said disgustedly.

"Yeah, there's more. You can see the collection notices from June, July, and August and when you look at them, you can see that they retroactively changed the bills to insert payments that were definitely not made. THAT happened after the Choice provider's lawyer got involved. It's so fucked up. You can see it for yourself." I continued trying to assure Smith what I was telling him. I was at a point where I didn't need to produce any more evidence, but I could tell that Smith wanted to see it. I think, as a veteran, he had his own issues with the VA, but this would provide insight to something more disturbing.

A split-second later, a car flew down the road in front of my house. The speed limit on that road in the area was 35 or 45 mph and this car was doing about 60. The driver definitely didn't see the marked cruiser in my driveway until it was too late. By the time the driver saw him, Trooper Smith was hurriedly moving toward his troop car.

"Send that stuff to me, I gotta run." Smith hurried to his cruiser. He soon peeled off out of my driveway. I went inside and faxed the documents to the Port Norris Station A100. It felt good to be taken seriously, and for someone other than myself to validate what I was seeing and experiencing. Most importantly, I felt that by sending it to the NJSP and Smith's attention, it provided another safety outlet like the precautionary measure I rationalized by sending copies to the USAO in Wilmington, Delaware. I did not want to get 'jammed-up' by inadvertently stumbling into something. As far as the other bullshit with the congressman's staff…I couldn't have cared less. In reality, things only got worse when the congressional office got involved and began their inquiry. The fact that they couldn't get their stories straight was disturbing, but I already knew that the VA was a bureaucratic beast with a fair share of scandals in the past, financial, or otherwise. The added suspicion of the person trying to help me from the congressional office, both as a staffer and a veteran himself, lent credence to that impression.

I think my situation became more concerning because that same summer, 2017, President Donald Trump pressed congress for legislation to hold VA employees accountable for criminal behavior or negligence. A high percentage of veterans and their families believed it was decades too late, but better late than never at all. The VA used to be a dumping ground for low quality medical "professionals" who couldn't compete in the private sector. The benefits of working for the VA extended well past mere financial and healthcare benefits for themselves and their employees. VA employees understood that once they were hired, it would be nearly impossible to be removed [fired/terminated] from their employment. It basically gave the bottom of the barrel job security they didn't deserve in positions designed to help individuals whom nothing BUT stellar care was expected, earned, and deserved.

Now… there was a president whose party had a majority in congress and could pass legislation to shake up that bureaucracy. It was what the former president repeatedly described as 'draining the swamp'. I think it's an apt description of the messy situation that exists as our federal government's expanding bureaucracy. But I also think that people should never underestimate or form a preconceived notion of what these people are without accepting them as creatures of that swamp. Creatures that dwell in a swamp can be described as ones that stealthily stalk their prey before striking without warning. They lie in wait for a vulnerability to exploit. It immediately conjures images of a snake constricting its prey after an ambush attack, an alligator's sudden strike, but I believe the bureaucratic tyrants are much more like stalking alligators. They lurk beneath the surface, their own survival is paramount, and they strike stealthily on any being that dares trespass its turf. Swamp creatures are incredibly dangerous, and people should be forewarned that this extends to our bureaucratic tyrants. As government size and employees rapidly increase, most people believe that it won't affect them or not in an adverse manner, at the very least. This is a common misconception; once the apparatus is in place, it can be weaponized against anyone. At the time of this writing, I have watched hours of federal employees testifying before congressional committees who have suffered retaliation for reporting conduct that should normally fall under the category of whistleblower protections. It's currently an era where the Catholic church "should be" covertly infiltrated to arrest persons who possess pro-life ideologies. It's the time of FBI agents sitting in on PTA meetings between parents and school officials where they express concern for Marxist indoctrination occurring under the guise of curriculum. Those same FBI agents lurk in the parking lots afterwards taking down license plates of persons identified as "problems". Sexual education was once reserved to the grades in which adolescents began puberty, now the 'alphabet mafia' wants to expose grades K-4 to LGBTQ+ story telling. I think it speaks volumes that when news reports cover these contentious issues, the materials reportedly being shown cannot be shown on the news broadcasts. If the material is THAT explicit, why would we ever show it to young children? If you disagree…the feds will take note. Of course, it is possible that they won't take notice or, maybe, they will just send the IRS to your home to audit you and demand entry into your home without a warrant, informing you that they don't need a warrant to enter your home. The violations of our Bill of Rights in each of these possible scenarios is egregious but it doesn't stop the tyrants from perpetrating them. Think about that.

CHAPTER 6

TYRANTS & FALSE FLAG ATTACKS

Tyrants across the world have the tendency to resort to false flag attacks. That is, an attack that is staged against their regime by an enemy -real or imagined- in order to justify a campaign of retaliation. These attacks are used to incite nationalism, a particular identity, or… to foment the rhetoric of a potentially once-obscure ideology. Conspiracy theories allege that 9/11 was such an attack. Others speculate that the apartment building bombings in Russia were used to begin a military campaign against Chechnya. Even more recently, radical leftists have perpetrated false flag demonstrations for the sole purpose of alienating their opposition with negative images later broadcasted 24/7 in the fakestream media. The LGBT+ alphabet mafia used the notion of intersectionality to evoke reactions after Jussie Smollet faked his own homophobic, racist, "pro MAGA" hate crime. Incredibly, he never went to jail for more than a few days and the district attorney's office failed to hold their own accountable when the situation evolved into a free pass for Jussie.

The 383 SMS messages between myself and Trooper Smith are a matter of record and exist as an evidentiary exhibit in the civil action I filed to challenge the basis of my conviction. Remember, the subpoenaed phone records corresponding to my cellular phone showed I spoke of and entered as an evidentiary exhibit…1,039 TOTAL SMS between us. That means 656 messages were deleted. Also evident in those subpoenaed phone records is that my phone was being used for phone calls and SMS messages after my arrest -and well into the following day- when I sat in the 'dungeon' at Cumberland County Prison (CCP). My state public defender successfully subpoenaed those records when my derelict absentee counsel in my federal case did not in the month preceding my criminal case's pretrial evidentiary hearings. My then-attorney was reserve Army colonel Jeffrey Klavens. Col. Klavens thought I was getting railroaded and tried to help me in areas that my federal lawyer failed. It was my state public defender who identified the last originating number on those records as belonging to a NJSP landline.

"You home?" Smith's sms read.

"Yeah, did you get my faxes?" I text Smith back.

"That was some interesting reading lol." Smith replied, immediately texting after saying he was "stopping by. He wasn't far away because he arrived at my home within minutes. My residence was barely 2 miles from the A100 station, so it wasn't inconceivable that he had just left there to go out on patrol.

When trooper Smith arrived at my house we stood outside on the front lawn like before. He parked way down into my driveway stopping short of parking parallel to the side of it. This would be the common procedure for one of many stops he would make to my house in the next 4 weeks before my arrest. Smith had assured me that he took my faxes and put them in a casefile that he was holding for safekeeping. Smith also texted me telling me that he had "posted things around the station so these guys know what is going on." We discussed those faxes and the sketchy inconsistencies between what the Choice provider, the VAMC Wilmington Director, and what the congressional VA liaison had all communicated to me in those emails, voicemails, and letters. Their stories were irreconcilable; essentially, there were three different stories and EACH was pointing the blame at each other.

"Did you know he's a former cop?...your VA liaison?" Smith asked me.

"Yeah he told me. 14 years ago or 14 years total, I cant remember. Either way, you would think that he would know not to send those messages to someone he hardly knows. IF he is the person who sent it. But then again, the remarks he made about my appearance and the chief of staff lead me to think the whole office may be a bunch of closeted homosexual republicans that we see get exposed every so many years on the news!" I joked, laughing out loud at the bizarre absurdity -yet possible irony- of the situation.

"I heard he was a homo, so anything is possible I guess." Smith smiled back.

"I don't know. I don't think he has any clue what his staffers are doing." I replied into an awkward silence that followed.

"So…what was this I heard about a marijuana plant out here on your property? You gotta tell me about that. When I was talking to the guys around the station about you, they said you called us out here because you found one growing out back," Smith asked sounding a bit skeptical but probing for the details. Apparently, his fellow troopers weren't that open with him. I was surprised they didn't tell him the extent of all their visits to my home other than the "well-being" checks.

"Well, did they tell you anything else? About the flat tires? My tractor? My car?" I asked.

"No, not a word. What's that about?" Smith asked.

"Well, I was out on the riding mower cutting grass and I decided to go back further -into the tree line- because it was a jungle. When I started getting further back, I ran over a few plants and then stopped in time to see more. I didn't know what to do, and I was paranoid thinking I might be implicated because I had a medical script for cannabis. So I called your station and asked them to come out. I showed it to the trooper, Ciaurelli, and he took it with him." Laying it all out for Smith.

"Shortly thereafter, the tires were flattened. Someone was banging on the outside of my house in the pitch-black dark. Crazy shit was happening. It started to die down and I reflected to contemplate if it was because I called you guys out here?" I continued.

"That was it?" Smith asked.

"Well, I thought it was, but then I had another idea. Something worse. I could tell you about it, but I'd rather show you. Hang on…I'll be right back." I reluctantly stated, pausing before I left to go inside to fetch something.

"Here we go again, last time you went inside and brought something out… it fucked up my day and perception on a lot of things. Is this more of the same?" Smith half-jokingly asked.

"I don't know. You'll see…you tell me." I replied disappearing into the house with the pugs greeting me with the infamous "A-ROO's" and subsequent kisses. I quickly gave them their loving hugs, kisses, and belly rubs. I ducked into the spare bedroom and returned out -at half a trot- with some papers in my hands.

"Here," I said reaching out with more papers in my hands. They were not visible to Smith at that point.

"What's this?" he asked and, instantly, his demeanor changed. I watched his eyes scan over the papers. Flipping them over to see the front and back.

"Where did you get these?" Smith asked.

"That's the thing…someone has been leaving them in my driveway and mailbox. My cameras cover 220 degrees… they have night vision too, but the trees in the midpoint of my driveway obscure that area at the end of my driveway near my mailbox. I tried to decide what to do with it. Putting it in my mailbox? Not sure that's a crime? Leaving them on my lawn, doubtful anything wrong there…AND, I certainly didn't want to call you guys to come out and take a look at it. I figure between the pot plant -in combination with the VA shenanigans- that you guys didn't need another stop out." I explained. I watched as trooper Smith's eyes scanned over the papers. I had handed him fliers for the Ku Klux Klan (KKK) in south Jersey. Apparently, it had migrated from Maryland into south Jersey. At that time, there were many news reports of these fliers being distributed in neighborhoods as far as Lakewood, in central jersey. It really freaked out some of my brethren when they found them in their neighborhoods. I don't think it was to intimidate, but rather a reflection of the ignorance of the people involved that they didn't know the demographics of the locations they were targeting for recruitment. It's a "toss up" for me still to this day.

"Well, its unsolicited…and its littering if they're leaving it on your property, so you could've called but I get what you're saying." Smith countered, emphasizing that it was a crime.

"I just hoped it would go away, but its been pretty consistent and regular." I added.

"It's nothing to be worried about though, it just looks like they're trying to recruit some rednecks out here in the country." Smith added as if dismissing the potential threat that it could pose.

At this point in time, I did not tell Phil that my "on-again, off-again" fiancé was Jewish…despite living two hours away and [still] making visits to check in on me and to let our pugs have playdates. It seemed like the amicable thing to do especially since our pugs had bonded into a "pugpack" (a wolfpack for pugs) complete with its own hierarchy. I certainly didn't tell him that I had Israeli flags flying on the property when I first arrived or that she was Jewish herself. I held these bits of information back because I had experienced antisemitism just two years earlier while living near Atlantic City, while I was going to that awful Northfield NJ VA CBOC. The worst part of it was that when the police responded to a hate-bias incident I experienced while walking my dog with a kippah on, the local police dismissed it. They really didn't care to intervene, and we certainly didn't feel better about living there. Dana made a point of telling me how stupid I was for wearing my kippah outside, and that those types of incidents were why she hid her Jewish identity. I was never one to cower in fear after what happened to me as a young teenager, but I was beginning to see her point. And that brings me to 20 years earlier in central Pennsylvania.

In November of 1993, I was in eighth grade at Shamokin Area middle school. At this point in time, I was living with my mother and playing sports for every season of the year. As football season came to an end, I was preparing to move on to the next sport…basketball. Basketball practice started and I walked home from after school practices in the dark. I had heard rumors of a gang of skinheads being founded in this "G-d-awful economically depressed area" that was once a bastion of anthracite coal mining. I couldn't understand why skinheads would want (or need) to be present… in an area predominantly of white Christians. There were movies being released in the period, and I thought it was just a fad or phase that would die out. I was wrong.

One of my teammates was walking home in the opposite direction from me and, for whatever reason, was violently attacked from behind by three of these "wanna-be" skinheads. My teammate didn't know what hit him. He was listening to his compact CD player and had his earphones blasting to the point where he never heard their approach. This was ten years before cell phones and texting became mainstream but, even still, the word spread. Our friend had to go to the hospital for a head injury. He suffered a laceration and concussion but wasn't sure if he was hit by a bottle or a fist. The next day it would be revealed that the attackers approached from behind on bicycles adding to their speed and stealth. When they reached striking distance, the main attacker commenced the attack by "popping a wheelie" into the back of our friend's skull. He never knew what hit him and the beatdown commenced shortly thereafter.

The next day in school, the attackers were identified, and the entire football and basketball team waited outside the junior high school for one of the attackers. He was in his 2nd [or 3rd] repeat of a middle school grade. Essentially a "senator" in a middle school that required half as many years as his current "term". While everyone was crowded outside in front of the school, the "jocks" began yelling obscenities at a small group of shaved heads wearing black combat boots with white shoelaces. They all wore black flight jackets with orange color lining the inside of their jackets. The two groups never crossed the street toward each other, but the skinheads were clearly outnumbered. While all of this happened, several "female skinheads" were compiling a list of names that would later be described as a "hit-list" by local media news outlet nearby. WNEP Newswatch 16, based in the Scranton & Wilkes Barre area of northeastern Pennsylvania, picked up the story. A Pennsylvania State Police (PSP) sting operation quickly ensued and made the headlines.

It seemed the two events were related and to this day I am not sure. I can tell you that the police department in Shamokin (or neighboring "Coal Township") were ill-prepared to handle any type of anti-gang intelligence or deterrence operations. The PSP had more resources and launched their own. The PSP sent an under-cover, African American trooper, [in plain clothes] to loiter in down-town Shamokin…alone. I can remember (literally) three black people living in Shamokin -at the time- so this trooper 'stood out'. Downtown Shamokin, even in my teenage years spent living there, was renown for cars from the surrounding areas "cruising" the main drag, Independence Street. Friday and Saturday nights would bring incredibly large crowds to the otherwise unremarkable "city". The Shamokin skinheads had taken up several street corners and other areas on the fringes on that main strip, but their presence was still recognized. Even more recognizable, was the sole black man who was quickly eliciting some disparaging racial epithets that could be heard from one end -to the other end- of this half mile drag. The situation escalated and the skinheads moved in to hand out a stone-cold hate crime. They beat the trooper enough until every other state trooper in the entire county [and nearby task forces] came out of every car, crook, and crawlspace to apprehend the skinheads. It was an arrest, but it wasn't the end of the Shamokin skinheads either. If anything, it reinforced the phrase 'there's no such thing as bad publicity' and as bad as it was…it put them on the map throughout the state.

So it wasn't a shock when I was informed that a "hit list" of 8th grade students at the school was comprised in response to the outrage of my teammates beating. Actually, it was a shock; I was called out of class and into the principal's office. It was the principal's voice and he was instructing me to report to his office. At this point in time, I was first in my class and never a disciplinary problem. I was the quarter-back of the freshman football team and one of the starting five for the 8th grade basketball team. Noteworthy was that the 8th grade basket-ball team accumulated 118 straight wins earning coverage on ESPN in that same era. To be honest, shocked wasn't the right word. I was shitting in my pants with my heart pounding through my chest as the adrenaline shot through my veins when I walked down the steps several floors to the principal's office. Each step I took, it felt like my heart was going to burst through my chest on the next step.

The principal was waiting as soon as I went through the set of double doors. He told me to go back to his office with him and that he wanted to talk to me. Mike Leshock was our principal and he seemed fair, but was relatively new to the position. His ability to reach an insanely maniacal scream at students was renown, but rarely heard. What I knew of Principal Leshock was that he was childhood friends with my mom's (only) younger brother Harvey. When they were children, they built a "raft" to navigate the creek that flowed through the city of Shamokin. Euphemistically referred to as the Shamokin "Shit crick" (crick is coal region dialect for "creek"). It was called this because at one point in the early 20th century people's home sewage flowed into the creek. The creek dumped into the Susquehanna river and ultimately into the Chesapeake Bay, a state away. This was all well before the creation of the Environmental Protection Agency (EPA). The story of their raft was told [and retold] by my maternal grandparents. I was reminded of it when my grandparents learned Mr.Leshock became principal. The story was as brief as their voyage, but incredibly funny. The raft failed and my grandmother observed the two boys, a young Leshock & a young (uncle) Harvey, emerge from the water after their raft "catastrophically malfunctioned." The two boys had no chance to salvage their raft and exited covered in shit. Maybe it was really shit or [maybe] it was just iron oxide runoff from the coal mines that washed into the creek? I wasn't there -and I don't think that they people who were there- could give an exact approximation of what percentage of filth covering them was what.

This story flashes quickly in my mind as I walked behind the front counter in the front office. Principal Leshock invited me to sit in the chair immediately adjacent to his desk. He didn't seem pissed, but I was still shitting in my pants.

"How's your mother doing?" the principal asked.

"She's good. Busy… but doing well." I timidly replied while getting a feeling that this was not a disciplinary visit.

"I told your mother that I would sign off on your request to redshirt for football this year as long as you were NOT going to be a problem for me. So far, you have not been a problem for me, so I have no reason to regret that." Principal Leshock continued. I was seriously wondering why I was here if he just confirmed my suspicion that this was not to give me demerits or detention for some misdeed.

"I gave you my word, sir, and I always keep it." I replied.

"I heard about what happened to your friend, Warren." Principal Leshock added.

"Yeah, it sucks, but he will be okay." I replied.

"Do you know of any retaliation or anything coming down the pipeline?" Principal Leshock asked.

"I don't know. And whatever that raucous was this morning, I want you to know that I was not involved in it and was not in the crowd outside. Although I did watch it from a window on the third floor. Better view I suppose." I conceded such after proclaiming I was doing what was consistent with my obligation to NOT be a problem for him.

"Okay…well, the reason I ask is this…" Principal Leshock paused after sliding a piece of paper with writing on it. It was obvious to me that it was a girl's handwriting because it had feminine, bold loops. I noticed the cursive writing, that seemed engrained in the DNA of young teenage girls, who expressed their dramatic personality attributes through their handwriting. It was, in some sense, a measure or written indicator of a teenage girl's femininity.

"What the…" I breathed out as I saw it. I was a numbered list but there, clear as day at the very top of the list, was my name.

"It's a list of names of you and your friends. Even Warren who was attacked the other night. One of our teacher's confiscated this list but apparently there are copies circulating within a certain element sympathetic to Warren's attackers and eager to see more." Principal Leshock added, holding nothing back.

"Any idea why you and your friend Ricky are number 1 and 2?" he added.

"No. I don't. I wasn't there. My home is in the opposite direction from where Warren lives and where he was walking when he was attacked. I wasn't there this morning, so I don't have a clue." I was lying. It was a lie, and I am pretty sure to this day that Principal Leshock knew it was a lie. Ricky Brugger was the only [openly] Jewish student at our school and I was a suspected/unknown/closeted Jew whom people suspected because I didn't celebrate Christmas but never gave any more information than that.

"Well, I had to ask you. I will be calling a lot of these names in to ask the same question. I would appreciate it if you don't mention to any one of them why you were here. The student who had this, described it as a "hit list" and has been suspended from school." Principal Leshock added noting that this was more serious because of an out of school suspension versus the in-school suspension which was essentially all-day detention.

"I won't say a word. Some of them visit my grandmother with me and they know that you and uncle Harvey are friends from childhood. I'll say it was about that." I replied. That was not a lie as I could just state that, while at the same time, not revealing to the principal that most of my closest friends knew he went on an ill-fated "cruise" down the shit creek with my uncle as a child.

"Okay. So be careful. Be mindful of your surroundings. I have talked to your coach, and I understand that you will all be encouraged to get rides home with parents... or to carpool if needed, just until we can get this straightened out."

"Makes sense." I said while clearly my mind was running a million miles per second just thinking about the list I just saw. I was, legitimately, in fear now.

Principal Leshock was correct; that was not the only list made and it would be confirmed in the (very) near future. Basketball practice went exactly as the principal said it would with everyone getting a ride home if needed. The following day was a home game against Tamaqua. When I arrived for the game, I noticed an overwhelming police presence. The city police chief was "undercover" standing outside the entrance to the gymnasium wearing an inspector gadget-like trench coat. He looked ridiculous...like the pink panther detective. I remembered thinking how someone who was, once a "tunnel rat" in Vietnam, a police detective would know how to better camouflage himself. He looked ridiculous and conspicuous. It was not raining, and it was not the appropriate jacket to wear for the weather. Newswatch 16 was at the game that night. They took some footage of the game -including me hitting a turnaround jump shot from the free throw line- and made sure to interview the principal about the hit list. To his credit, Principal Leshock did everything possible to minimize any potential fear or bad press this could mean for the school district or city. In recent years, Daniel Tosh named Shamokin as "shit-hole of the week" in his sketch comedy show *Tosh.0* that aired on *Comedy Central* for 13 seasons. As bad as that was, the skinhead press coverage from Channel 16 was -by far- the worst. It put Shamokin on the map for more than the [suspected] inbreeding and the resulting Cro-Magnon mindset; It appeared to millions of viewers that Shamokin was a place where even the children were not safe from being targeted by white supremacist gangs who had no real racial "enemies" to lash out at. Newswatch 16 only exacerbated it by showing the hit list on their ten-p.m. broadcast. I saw the footage they captured, happily smiling at my nailing a turn-around jump-shot, only to feel a sense of dread and panic when they showed the list without it being pixelated. They showed the list without protecting our names. Anyone and everyone, with bad intentions or sympathetic to that movement, [now] saw my name (and those that followed) as the camera panned from top to bottom. Soon, the phones were ringing from one parent to another. The parents were horrified that the news station did not censor the names out to protect the identity of these MINORS. They redirected their rage at the news station, and Newswatch 16 ensured that the 11 p.m. broadcast -as well as any future images of the list- would be pixelated. For me, the damage was done: I was terrified of Neo-Nazis, I lost the image of competent police officers, and hated the news media whom I felt would sacrifice children JUST for a good story.

I never recovered from those events. The next week entailed me having marked and unmarked city and state police cruisers parked outside my home until the remaining skinheads could be brought in on charges. The father of my only Jewish friend, (Ricky) #2 on the list, came over with their enormous German shepherd dog on a few nights. My mom and dad were divorced, and it was thought I was more vulnerable because of that and… being number one. My friends teased that Ricky's dad was trying to get a "side piece" by hooking up with my mom. In poor taste, sure…but that's what pubescent teenage boys did to make light of any aspect of an otherwise-terrifying situation. These events scarred me for life, and all flashed before my eyes at a million miles per hour as I stood on my front lawn in the late summer of 2017 showing the KKK fliers to trooper Smith. I kept that to myself because that fear of trusting an incompetent cop was still there, and I was more guarded as a result. It was probably a good thing that I didn't go into detail with trooper Smith because I honestly didn't know what to make of him. The things that he told me over the course of the next three weeks shook me to my core. Some of his remarks to me in SMS messages reinforce that uncertainty I have with regard to him. One of those messages was NOT deleted and can be viewed by anyone. What ensued in the following weeks was both incredible and equally disturbing. In an era where distrust of law enforcement is at an all-time high, the revelations that I am about to make (and previously made to my legal counsel) will reverberate long after the ink used to tell this has dried. In fact…events, in the years since, will only support what I relay.

CHAPTER 7

ILLUSIONS OF TYRANNY

*"Everything appears to be a cover-up. I'm not a conspiracy theorist…
but when you look at the information and intelligence they had, the
military had, it's all watered down. I'm not getting intelligence, I'm
denied any support from the National Guard while we're under attack,
for 71 minutes…could there possibly be actually…they kind of wanted
something to happen? It's not a far stretch to begin to think that. It's sad
when you start putting everything together and thinking about the way
this played out…what was their end goal? If I was allowed to do my
job as the chief we wouldn't be here; this
didn't have to happen. Oh yeah,
the crowd was filled with federal agents."*

—Steven Sund,
Former Chief of the Capitol Police
Tucker Carlson Today, April 2023
Http://www.newsmax.com/politics/steven-sund-tucker-carl-
son-jan-6-2023/08/03/id/1129581/ns.mail_uid=e40f24e9-
9a90-4a68-9763-da6da1322d5b&ns_Mail_job=D-
M508272_08042023&s=acs&dkt_nrb=010102focsr8

In May of 2023, FBI director Christopher Wray testified before congress. One of the questions posed to Wray was how many undercover
FBI agents were present at the Capitol on January 6, 2021. Wray

said he wasn't sure and that he did not believe that any "undercover" agents were present. "Believe". Next, Wray was asked how many FBI "assets" were present. Wray said he could not give an exact number of how many Confidential Human Sources (CHS) were present. Wray was asked about identifying these "assets" [CHS] to allow full disclosure via video recordings from the Capitol. This was because in the same month, senior FBI analysts were told they could not review certain recordings from the Capitol riot to identify rioters because it could endanger or identify their sources. Congress pressed further questioning to ascertain if these individuals incited the individuals who acted violently that day? Were they committing acts of violence themselves? Director Wray appeared offended and incredibly defensive for someone who had done nothing but answer evasively. Consider the impact of revelations that FBI assets incited [or perpetuated] riotous acts. You cannot have full disclosure if you withhold videotapes.

This testimony was the result of Special Counsel John Durham's investigation into the FBI investigation regarding Russian interference and "treasonous" acts by President Trump. The report was scathing; it stated the FBI did not adhere to the interests of justice and letter of the law. It further added that the agents involved were so "anti-Trump" that "confirmation bias" dominated the prevailing modes of thought at the heart of the investigation. Confirmation bias is when you go into an investigation with an idea of the crime and then -selectively- utilize evidence that helps confirm suspicions to "connect the dots" to how the crime was perpetrated. They are, essentially, choosing evidence that [confirms] their bias. Criminal investigations are not supposed to reach a conclusion first, then find the information and evidence that helps support that theory. Criminal investigation is [supposed] to be more like that of the scientific method. Because the FBI was plagued with confirmation bias, they ignored and dismissed exculpatory evidence.

This testimony was corroborated by the testimony of two FBI agents turned whistleblowers. One agent testified that instead of treating the Capitol riots as one singular event in the District of Columbia, they treated it as acts of "violent white extremism/nationalism" and used the states of residence for anyone who visited D.C. between January 5th and 7th to then export instances and "membership" in these "extremist" groups as proof of its presence in [all] 50 states. It's incredible to know that the federal government was 'cooking the books' and manipulating statistics -per the FBI whistleblowers- to redirect FBI resources AWAY FROM child sex predators and human trafficking investigations. It is the same concept with labeling parents domestic terrorists because they want to have a say in the curriculum of public schools teaching their children. The rationale here is to never let a crisis go to waste. What if it is a manufactured crisis? How could you reject offers of additional security and national guardsmen only to cry how understaffed law enforcement and security were after the fact. The Speaker of the House of Representatives and the D.C. mayor refused and rejected offers. The FBI director refuses to (or cannot) answer how many of their assets were present or what their roles were in the rioting. The director's responses were a tribute to the very best of semantics and word play. Devil's advocates could argue that they denied extra security and used FBI assets to incite a riot so that a former president could be criminally prosecuted in the future…just not after the events but rather wait until he announces his candidacy prior to the next presidential election. All of these actions, especially attacking whistleblowers, are inconsistent with our fundamental American principles. Those who are in power fear one thing…losing their power. A manufactured crisis or event helps justify the suppression of civil rights to battle an entity (or ideology) that the ruling class perceives as a threat. I am going to offer you insight into something similar but what I believe to be worse.

My SMS messages with trooper Smith are a matter of public record. Anyone can view them on the civil docket I filed after my conviction and sentencing. There is one more visit trooper Smith made to my home in September 2017, prior to my arrest. Trooper Smith sent one of his text messages announcing his intent or imminent arrival at my home. In this one particular instance, I had video of a vehicle that I believed left a KKK flier in my mailbox since our last visit.

"So, I have something I need to show you" I told Smith as he exited his car and walked toward me on my front lawn.

"Uh oh, now what? No dick pics please." Smith replied with a chuckle.

"Check out this video from the other night around 2 am." I said as I handed him my cell phone. My ZMODO app was open and there was a night-vision 14 second clip that was surprisingly clear. As the distance increased, footage would become more "grainy" but in this case, because of the lighting, it was possible to identify the approach and departure of the vehicle in question. It wasn't an old pickup truck with a confederate flag flying from a two-by-four in the bed of the truck. It was remarkably similar to an unmarked police car…identical to the one parked opposite my home around 3 p.m. on September 20, 2017, the day of my arrest. Smith focused on it and kept replaying the video in its entirety.

"I can't see a plate." Smith said with an air of dismissal.

"Well, I actually have the flier here. I called the number and it was a voicemail praising the driver who ran over that woman in Charlottesville last month. I said I received the flier and was interested in learning more about membership." I told a visibly stunned Smith but ensuring that he was aware that more was to come.

"I received a call back. Given a number of a guy to call. I ended up talking to some young guy who visited my house. He's in the army reserve and goes into detail telling me about the memberships in like-minded groups. *Hammerskins*, a skinhead group based in Atlantic city was mentioned and he discussed the proximity of a local biker bar near his home frequented by members of The Aryan Brotherhood." I continued.

"Why the fuck would you do that?" Smith asked.

"Because I want to know who's been fucking with me and why. Know your enemy…Sun Tzu…some shit like that. But it gets worse, bud" I said as I watch the entire demeanor of Smith's face change as if he is anticipating what I'll say next.

"This guy, while telling me about these other groups begins to give me samples of the group's members. He tells me that it's not just rednecks and hillbillies. He tells me that there are professionals, cops, prison guards, and many other different types of people affiliated with these groups. I was repulsed hearing what he was telling me and did my best to hide it and keep my demeanor and facial expressions as that of interest more than disgust." I explained.

"When was this?" Smith asked.

"The other night. The kid, he's a young kid in his early twenties, was bragging about this and his involvement in it. I used my army service to foster some trust and camaraderie in addition to drinking beers right here in the same spot where I talk to you." I stated matter of factly. Smith looked like he saw a ghost. His face turned white and he was expressionless. It appeared as if he was experiencing one of those moments where his mind was moving a million miles per hour. Finally, Smith sighed and it appeared as if he deflated to half his size.

"It wouldn't surprise me. I've heard rumors long ago from the 1970's and they still exist today." Smith candidly spoke now but with some shame.

"Dude, this is not 1970's KKK, this is 2017!" I countered with an emphasis on the varying demographics of membership.

"I know but it's something that always comes up. Especially with Hispanic or black troopers. They always say how they KNOW that there are still white supremacists in the state police here." Smith continued although more skeptic and dismissive of it. I was fucking stunned at what he just said. I was thinking he would tie it into the congressional response to my VA problems, but his mind completely skipped over that and went to discussing a controversy within the New Jersey State Police.

Unbeknownst to me, the NJSP had some serious problems with real or imagined bias perceived by the public. I later discovered it reached a flashpoint before, during and after the race riots in Camden, New Jersey. Racism and prejudice, it turned out, were long-standing problems in the public's perception of police and the state police, specifically. In March of 2023, ABC Philadelphia reported that a NJSP detective posted photos on social media of his heavily tattooed torso. Someone took a closer look at it and identified it as tattoos worn by white supremacists. REAL white supremacists. The detective was placed on administrative leave while an investigation was conducted but I was never able to find a report detailing the findings of that investigation. It was not the first time. In the summer of 2019, another officer posted pictures on his social media at a Proud Boys event making gestures that some argued were white supremacist gang signs. I never knew of this, but as I am listening to Smith speaking and revealing these things to me, I am now thinking about my own childhood trauma and combining police WITH neo nazis. The fact that I am hearing this directly from the mouth of state trooper is what is most disturbing. I wanted to hear what he would say next but, at the same time, fearful of what he would say next. All I could think about was how much that car looked like an unmarked, police cruisier. Local police didn't cover the area where I lived; it was policed by Port Norris station A100.

"There's this one guy at my station. He's a loudmouth, Hispanic trooper. He goes on and on at the station talking about how he KNOWS that there are white supremacists in the ranks of the NJSP. He says that black and brown drivers are "targeted" by white troopers and explained when he worked patrolling the Atlantic City Expressway, how he would deliberately stop white drivers in retaliation and to "balance" it out," Smith continued fluctuating his voice for emphasis on the trooper's knowledge and certainty of racists in their ranks while using air quotes to emphasize the reverse racism of this trooper's remarks and behavior. I did not know his name at this point, but would later be able to identify him from testimony in my pre-trial evidentiary hearings.

Trooper Rivera-Guzman answered evasively twice as much as any of the other (8) troopers during these hearings. Rivera-Guzman's testimony is a matter of record. Guzman stated he could not remember, recall, know, or was sure no less than 37 times. It helped that the AUSA was asking leading questions with those dog-whistle words of evasive testimony to solicit the response she needed from them. At one point, my absentee lawyer objected to leading the witness and the jurist [incredibly] sustained it. I said incredibly because the docket is rife with objections or motions being denied and overruled, while the government had only (1) motion denied in-part throughout my entire prosecution. Why is Trooper Guzman's mention so noteworthy? He wrote the investigation report for my arrest with a rookie trooper before turning over the investigation to detectives. Every aspect of his testimony and details of the report were inconsistent with his own CAD Abstract. The totality of testimony, not just Guzman's, was the most incredulous shit-show I could have ever imagined. The troopers who testified contradicted themselves on nearly every key detail. As I listened to trooper Guzman's testimony after introducing himself -in which he was the trooper who admitted to patrolling the AC Expressway prior to working in port Norris- I understood his motivation.

"Then what makes it worse, is that there is a detective at my station who denies any and all of it. This guy denies any police racism or racists in the ranks. I wonder if he's a closeted neo nazi because of his passion to dispel what he considers lies. So… I have to listen to these guys go back and forth only for as much is necessary and then I'm out of the station." Smith continued.

"So, you don't get involved or add your two cents?" I asked skeptically.

"No, and I'll tell you why. A lot of these guys talked about the military service and exploits only to later learn that these guys were all bullshitters and lying about their service. They were lying, not just exaggerating but just flat-out fucking lying." Smith said shaking his head.

"Stolen valor?" I asked making a reference to an act criminalized as a felony for individuals who claim military service or decorations that are patently false and done so to gain prestige or gainful employment and or promotions.

"Totally. After that I stay out of listening to what they say. They're all full of shit. And when it goes into white and black stuff, I don't want to be a part of that conversation." Smith added.

"That's fucking unreal. Not what you said but how these guys are supposed to be the state's finest, yet they have these types of conversations that sound like arguments, mind you. No wonder there's such a bad public perception if this exists between the troopers themselves.

"Yeah, tell me about it." Smith said shaking his head.

"You know, if I didn't have this conversation with you, I wouldn't have given as much consideration to the possibility of what this kid was telling me…and it doesn't dispel any creeping thoughts I had about that car in the video I just showed you and how much it looks like an unmarked cruiser" I replied with angst, clearly indicating that I was not dismissing anything and that anything was possible.

"Yeah, well fuck it. I have to get going." Smith said while looking at his phone.

"Gotcha. This kid's mouth moves faster than a duck's wet ass. If I hear anything more I'll let you know. I swear I think he's a meth head and that's all he talks about when mentioning the biker bar" I told Smith as he's walking in front of his cruiser toward his troop car.

"Great. Keep me posted. Like I told you, the more information I have, the more I can post around the station and let the guys know what is going on." Smith said before getting into the driver's seat. The one thing I can say with great certainty is that Smith always left his troop car running. It's engine was whisper-silent but it was always there like background white noise during these talks.

Over the next two weeks, I would text Smith with more information. I stated that as a journalist, I previously shared tips with police while living in Atlantic city in 2015. I even mentioned -by name and rank- the chief of police and captain that I would share tips with and told him to reach out to them to verify my credibility. The most disturbing part of my text messages with Smith is not the things he actually says -although he says some incredulous things that a well-informed public would not appreciate to know exist in the mind of a uniformed state trooper with such prevalence- but it's what is missing. Remember, only 383 SMS existed on my device while my subpoenaed phone records demonstrated that an addition 656 existed, but were deleted. Those records also show phone calls and text messages to and from my family after my arrest and calls from a NJSP landline while I was sitting in prison. Again, they never had a warrant to go into the phone and deleting evidence on it would be obstruction of justice. It's not [just] me claiming these things happened…the evidence submitted into the record in my civil suit indisputably proves it and refutes any statements by the USAO or the court attempting to gaslight me or my supporters.

CHAPTER 8

A CONFLICT AMONGST TYRANTS

Up until this point in this book, I have taken you through flashbacks to different times in my life as well as different times during these events. Some authors do this time-flipping travel to and from because flashbacks play an integral role in their writing style. I am a firm believer that this can be an effective style, but in my writing, this is a tool. The pieces of machinery and players involved in the entire situation that led to my wrongful arrest and conviction involved so many different factors that flipping back and forth helps you perceive the events from a firsthand account allowing for greater context, understanding, and meaning.

Over the first two weeks of September 2017, I had another significant encounter with trooper Smith that plays into this story. I had reminded Smith how I had acquired the Port Norris station fax number by calling the NJSP headquarters in Trenton. I explained to them that I had to register my firearms in New Jersey from Pennsylvania where they were being stored. Storage units can be difficult, and their policies change with time. My storage unit was expensive and because it contained my firearms there, I didn't see it as wasting money because I was in no hurry to bring any firearms into New Jersey. I was an NRA member and had taken classes on gun safety and home defense. I even took a course in December 2015 while living near Atlantic City and was forewarned about my situation. I was told not to bring my firearms unless absolutely necessary. If I had firearms that were illegal under the draconian gun laws of New Jersey, I would have to turn them into the police, put them in a gun-trust, or render them inoperable. It could be expensive, laden with bureaucratic tape common with socialist states like New Jersey, and the entire process could be incredibly frustrating and confusing.

Dana went with her parents to Aruba to celebrate their 50th wedding anniversary. We were not together and often not even speaking to each other civilly, but I seized the opportunity to take my pugs to her home to housesit and pug-sit her two pugs. Geno and Vin Diesel had been together since Diesel was 8 weeks old and helped Geno get through a tough time after losing his only other pug companion, a 12 year old "Bailey" who was named after the alcoholic beverage. Dana had added another pug to her family, Axl Rose, a rescue from Los Angeles. Dana had been aware of the problems with the VA, the inability of the congressional office to budge, as well as the inappropriate homosexual passes, I was perceiving and receiving. It was at this time that I also learned that I would not be able to store my firearms in storage. The policy was changing to ban storing firearms, ammunition, or any flammable items. Before leaving to housesit at Dana's, I let trooper Smith know that while I was away, I would be making arrangements to have the weapons shipped in a truck with my ATV. He had offered to help me with the process of registering and or surrendering.

I don't know why but when I was away there, I received a text, then phone call from Smith to answer my phone. When I finally got on the phone and called him it was apparent that he just needed someone to vent to as he was having problems with his ex-wife not having his son sent off to school wearing a clean football jersey. At this point in time, we were acquaintances heading toward a full-fledged friendship. Our service in the Army and deployment to Iraq made the sense of brotherhood that we shared a strong anchor point to build a solid friendship upon. Smith wasn't infantry like I was, but he was a combat engineer. Combat engineers have a dangerous Military Occupational Specialty (MOS) and I had encountered them frequently in my deployments.

Once that conversation died down, I reminded him that I was having those items delivered to New Jersey at my home and would need him to stop over when he was working to advise, and or confiscate. I told him there was no way that I was getting in my car with firearms. If I was stopped, it could land me in prison and was a semi-frequent occurrence in the world of gun owners simply transiting through the state. Smith and I had made a deal; he would help me, and I would teach his son to ride an ATV. Smith's son was a pug fanatic and had told his father he would love to meet my pugs. This would provide the opportunity and give him a chance to learn how to ride an ATV. Full disclosure, there were many times in which Smith would ask me to go out for a beer, stop over his house to hang out and meet his girlfriend, or just to hang out and have a beer at his house. The distance from my house was not far but it was certainly not something that I wanted to drive if I was drinking. Sorry, not sorry…it wasn't happening. Truth be told, I didn't know what to think of Smith at this point in time. I still didn't completely trust him, and I knew that he was sharing information I was gleaning from the kid at work. It would be an opportunity for him to move up the ranks, it facilitated me being a great source (which was something I always enjoyed when doing journalism), and a chance to get some peace with that knowledge or to just move!

The remaining text messages in my phone between Smith and I track the events at the time. Some don't make sense though because they seem incongruent with the conversation at the time and that is because some of them were deleted. I distrusted police enough to know that I couldn't trust a guy who might just befriend me only to betray me. Another reason I never took him up on hanging out other than him stopping at my home was some of the remarks he made in texts that are still in evidence. One occasion he replied "f'in A" to being told white supremacists were planning to thwart an event (riot/ mostly peaceful protesting) by ANTIFA in the coming weeks. He seemed to equate President Trump to white supremacists and admittedly supported Trump. Considering this was the same guy who told me about white supremacists and race retaliation in the NJSP, how the fuck did I know that he wasn't one of them? However unlikely I thought that might be irrelevant. I had to keep my guard up. I can assure you though he was aware of my Jewish heritage as well as Dana's. We exchanged pictures and I sent him a picture of her from Aruba, tanned and decked out for an evening dinner there. Incredibly, I also mentioned it to the VA liaison in one email while inquiring about what religious protections extend to precluding a service dog (Geno) from entering a Muslim establishment. Geno was denied entry in which the employee told me that my rights under the Americans with Disability Act (ADA) could not supersede his right to religious observance. Apparently, Geno was "dirty" and associated with Jinn (demons). I later saw this email in discovery and specifically mentioned that I had my Jewish ancestry traced back on my father's side. Many Jews converted to Christianity in early America, but a spiritual conversion does not remove the DNA we carry. I had good reason not to trust Smith, and the former cop VA liaison for the congressman. Later, they would eventually collaborate to produce a news release by the USAO describing me as a white nationalist and white supremacist. This was deliberately done to taint the jury pool in the event I possessed any notions of going to trial. The USAO claimed that I possessed white supremacist literature when a search warrant was executed on my home. The fliers that had been placed on my driveway and shared with trooper Smith were now my own. The NJSP deliberately staged the materials in their crime scene photos and took a hunting license off my .22 caliber small game rifle so that when they showed the pictures to the jury, they could make it look more like a sniper rifle… like Remy from the 1995 motion picture *Higher Learning* played by Michael Rappaport. The photos that were shown to the jury at my trial were not exactly as they were found and, again, this was done to further inflame the jury.

Guns in New Jersey are despised and seen as evil and unnecessary. New Jersey has some of the strictest, if not THE strictest gun laws in the nation. It is a Marxist-socialist state run by white liberals who prioritize social justice, Diversity Equity & Inclusion (DEI), and re-write history in an attempt to rid themselves of their own "white privilege". They are opposed to a merit-based society free from any consideration given to a person's demographic factors. I don't want to be judged as a Jewish, white male and I don't think the questions should be on job applications or involved in any hiring process. I believe as Justice Antonin Scalia did when he opined in dissent to the affirmative action rulings. Any system in which favorable actions & decisions are predicated upon race, color, or creed…you ultimately create a racially discriminatory system some dubbed "reverse racism". Since 2017, fortunately, the Supreme Court rejected and overturned the decision because Asian American students were claiming they were being biased by awarding acceptance slots in admissions to lesser qualified students who were Hispanic or black. The Supreme Court agreed and affirmative action as a guiding factor for admissions in colleges and universities is no longer legal. I have served and shed blood, sweat & tears with people of all colors in the Army and Marine Corps and I am a firm supporter of a color-blind society.

Eventually, I did speak to Smith again at my home.

"What's up, dude?" I asked Smith who steps out of his marker troop car with a ear-to-ear grin on his face.

"Not much. What happened to your four wheeler?" Smith asked. I felt bad because that was my part of the process to assuage any type of inconvenience I might cause him by getting him involved in taking/registering my firearms.

"It would not fit in the truck that I paid for. My brother is letting me keep it at his house for now until I can try again. All hope is not lost," I continued with a reassuring smile on my face.

"Okay, lets get to it. Where are they?" Smith asked. It was afternoon so I wasn't sure what shift he was working and if this was his lunch break or just a business visit.

"I have them inside. They're laid out on the bed in the bedroom. I would say condition 4 but they're not even assembled. I wanted no problems or confusion." I said as we got closer to the door and the pug's "a-roos" became increasingly more audible.

"Good to go." Smith replied as I stopped ahead of him.

"FYI, before we go in there, my dogs might jump on you up until your knees so I apologize for any pug hair they get on you… it's summer hot still and they are shedding badly." I said as Isa and Geno jumped out of their window to greet us at the door. The door opened and the "a-roos" went on for a solid minute or two until they went and got toys for Smith to throw. He did and then we all moved to the bedroom where the firearms were laid out.

"Holy shit, is that an AK!? That's definitely not legal. You'll have to turn that in or put it in a trust like I explained to you before." Smith said, surprised and with a look of all-business on his face.

"No, its not an AK. Its an SKS but I figured that all the same. The other one is a .22 caliber and I'm not sure of that one after reading and re-reading the exact language of the New Jersey law. I figured it is likely it might be banned, but I don't know. The other one is my .22 caliber Remington small game rifle…and of course my Glock and other pistols." I said pointing from one to the next in the layout before us. The pugs came over, dropped their toys at our feet, and were waiting for more play. Isa was 7 months old and pug puppies at this age are notoriously playful. I was worried thinking about how much the NJSP uniform color is similar to the United States Postal Service worker's uniform. Don Geno had initiated hostilities with the USPS mail carrier in his first year of life. He was now 4 ½ and passed that onto his younger sister. Thankfully, they did not make a mistaken connection, and this thought quickly dissipated from my mind.

"Okay, this one definitely has to go. I'll check out the other one. Your hunting rifle is fine you can keep that." Smith said flipping over the hunting license attached to the trigger guard by a gigantic safety pin.

"Alright. I just want you to take them. I do not want to go through a gun trust, and it just seems simpler if I surrender them to you guys. This way there will be no question as to the location or legality of these weapons." I said extending my arms out in front of me with my palms out. It was as if I was literally shoving away any liability associated with the weapons.

"Dude, are you sure you want to do that? We'll keep them and if you ever move you can get them back, but you might get it back after a couple thousand more rounds have passed through it. It will likely be a more-used rifle then than it is now." Smith seemed to want to counter my decision. His logic was simple; he knew other troopers would take my firearm out of storage and take it to a range to fire themselves. They would never clean it and likely beat the shit out of it with no regard for the owner.

"I thought about it and this is what I want to do." I insisted.

"Alright. Cool deal." Smith replied.

"Do I help you carry these out? Are you putting them in the trunk?" I asked Smith nodding at the disassembled rifles spread out across the bed.

"Nah. Not today. I will check on this other one for you and come back when I am working this weekend. I can stop back then and take both if I have to. This way I wont have to make two trips. Then on Monday, you can come down to the station and sign the paperwork." Smith added making it an issue of convenience for both of us.

"Okay. Well, I don't want to get in trouble until then" I cautiously added.

"Dude, I am the only one who knows they're here. I will be back in a couple days. Just keep them disassembled and locked up at all times when you are not home. Do NOT put them in your car or drive anywhere with them." Smith advised placing an emphasis on the transporting them via my privately owned vehicle.

"It'll never happen. I'll either be with them 24-7 or when I am away, they will be locked. I am not taking them anywhere and will be anxiously awaiting your return her to get this one if not both" I reassured Smith while pointing back down to the SKS. I really didn't have a choice other than to give it up. Some people would have been against this but, then again, not too many gun owners of this rifle would have ever considered moving to New Jersey because of its strict firearm legislation.

"Cool. Nothing to worry about. I'll take care of it this weekend." Smith replied as we moved toward the front door, pugs closely by and visibly wondering what the hell had happened to the game of fetch they were expecting to continue. I was sure to continue the game after Smith left because Geno had a propensity to be a spiteful urinator if he perceived something as a deliberate insult. I admit, it's hilarious but having had my shoes pissed-on too many times and remembering the sickening feeling of obliviously putting my socked foot into a pissy-wet shoe was always enough for me to avoid anything even close to offending the pug mafia Don. It was something I didn't want Geno teaching to his younger sister, Isa.

To my dismay, Trooper Smith never came back that weekend. I texted him to remind him and his replies were sparse and indecisive. The weekend passed and I only learned from a text message that he was "super busy" on calls. It didn't feel right. I had actually arranged for the kid to come over and be here Friday, then again that Saturday, nights so he could get eyes-on this kid feeding me information. It never happened and I was alarmed by the fact he never stopped back. Something in my gut was killing me and I could almost here alarm sirens going off, but I just attributed this to my distrust of police and paranoia from having read the penalties. I would receive a phone call from Smith the morning of September 20th, 2017, that creeped me out even more. I was increasingly speeding toward a situation that could most aptly be described as FUBAR…fucked up beyond all recognition. It ultimately ended up being worse than FUBAR.

CHAPTER 9

AN OMINOUS WARNING

Early in the morning on September 19, 2017, I received a text message from trooper Smith telling me,

"U need to call me"

It didn't seem that pressing and in the event Smith was having another meltdown over his ex-wife sending his son to school with a dirty football jersey on then it could definitely wait. I texted Smith back and told him I was jumping in the shower and would call him after. Before that text came in, I had been discussing the drama that was surrounding college football after Robert Lee, an Asian American sports reporter for ESPN, was removed from a broadcast at Virginia Tech's football game because his name was identical to the former confederate general. In the text immediately prior to Smith's urgent message to call him, I had expressed how I was glad I did NOT have social media. I think this is important (again) because it demonstrates in another facet that I did not have social media to "stalk my victims whereabouts" in order to plan an attack. The USAO and FBI, in all of their claims, never produced one piece of evidence from any social media accounts that I owned or accessed from any of my devices because I simply didn't have them. I have seen the damage it has done and how it destroys people's lives, relationships, and employment. I stand by my decision to remove myself from that garbage. One would think that some shred or "scintilla of evidence" demonstrating I was doing so would be necessary to demonstrate "intent to carry out treats". The government couldn't produce that but it's okay…the Court still awarded the government the enhancement because I owned firearms. My firearm ownership and military training in knowing how to use them was used against me. My Second Amendment rights were unconstitutionally criminalized. That's like me telling my neighbors who argue with each other that because they possess a butcher knife in their kitchen knife block, that they have intent to stab each other after a heated argument. It's asinine but that was how my (supposed) "fair and impartial" jurist ruled. I can't make this shit up, I'm not making it up, and all anyone has to do is see the evidentiary submissions made to the same jurist in my civil action to overturn the conviction.

An abundance of evidence was submitted, but judge's have notoriously huge egos and hate to admit they made a mistake. Especially judges who refuse to recuse themselves for alleged political bias and justify their refusal to do so by citing their confirmation vote in the United States Senate 98-0, with votes from both parties. Considering that those 98 individuals possess an approval rating of less than 20% (collectively), that wasn't saying much. And I made sure to tell my judge that in response to his boast of bipartisan support. In retrospect, it didn't help me and made his hatred and animosity for me grow exponentially. The enormous egos do not like it if anyone comes into a case and expects to have their constitutional rights respected. It's even worse if the person recites them and self-advocates in furtherance of those rights. The federal criminal justice system is an assembly line used to warehouse human beings and (now) punish political opponents. Justice is not a concern nor the intended goal of that system.

For example, my judge once clerked for federal judge Mary Ann Trump (Barry) whom at the time was making publicly disparaging remarks about her brother, President Donald Trump. Because interns clerk for judges that they most identify with, and often become products of their school of thoughts later in their own careers, I was incredibly concerned that my outspoken support, volunteer work, and employment with the Trump campaign in 2016 would result in prejudice and bias. The other elephant in the room was the ongoing and very-public animosity between President Trump and the former congressman at the heart of my case. Finally, it's important to remember that 95% + of DOJ employees donate to democrat party candidates. That's astounding and, in and of itself, a grave concern for anyone who openly displays or professes a libertarian or conservative ideology. The "deck" could not have been more stacked against me, and it only got worse as my prosecution evolved. I was TRULY fucked.

"What's up? I just got out of the shower. It sounds important." I said to Smith who picked up before his phone could ring a second time.

"You need to be careful. Do you hear me? Be careful!" Smith warned me with a shaken voice.

"Why?…What's going on? You told me not to worry that you would take care of them." I replied back to Smith obviously thinking this was about the firearms that he never came to pick up. It WAS Tuesday and our original plan was to have them picked up that weekend and me go to the station the day before (Monday) to do the paperwork. But because Smith never stopped by the previous weekend when he said he would, I obviously didn't plan on going to the station on Monday.

"I'm not talking about that. What you're doing, you need to be careful. I gotta run." Smith said abruptly hanging up without saying goodbye.

I was fucking terrified at what that meant. Was it something with the VA? The congressional office? The documents I sent to the USAO in Wilmington? Smith had copies of everything. Or was it my worst fear? Getting information to share with Smith. Had I been exposed. It was possible if not probable after what happened the preceding Friday night.

"I have to go to my girlfriends to use her printer before she leaves" the Kid complains on the other end of the line.

"Why not just take whatever you have to Staples and get it done there? I have someone coming over here that I want you to meet. I got some beer too." I told the Kid, knowing he likes to drink beer and hoping to have him at my home when Smith would arrive for the rifle(s).

"Dude, this is not something that I can take to fucking Staples or the G-d-damned library!" the Kid continued,

"I have no ink in my printer, and I need to get these copies made this weekend!" the Kid was (clearly) emotionally charged by this point.

"Fuck it dude, bring whatever you got over here, and you can use my printer to scan and make copies. It even has a fax if you need it…" I said while laughing to deescalate the Kid's growing frustration.

"You have a printer?" the Kid asked quickly in response to that statement.

"Yes, a fucking good one. I have an all-in-one and its good to go. Don't sweat it, just bring over whatever you need to." I continued trying to soothe this Kid in order to get him over to meet Smith.

"Fuck it. That'll work" the Kid replied, now audibly calmer.

"Yeah, I got a 30-pack and a friend is probably stopping over I want you to meet. Don't worry though, he's cool." I tell him alluding to Smith and that he shouldn't freak out when he sees a uniformed trooper come. The Kid didn't know that, and I wouldn't reveal that until I knew Smith was on his way over. He said he was working all weekend so I knew it would (most likely) be Friday or Saturday.

The Kid had a problem with pain killers. I noticed him popping them when he last visited. I noticed two things from this habit of his; the first was that it helped his mouth move like a duck's wet ass. The Kid could not stop talking if his life depended on it. The other thing I noticed was that he was easily agitated to a near violent state of mind in an incredibly short amount of time. The phone conversation only confirmed that, and with beer in my fridge I figured he would be quite talkative. Smith could hear it for himself, and I would not have to worry about my credibility. Smith could now get his intel from the source. I knew enough to know that I did not want this kid to keep coming over my home or having anything to do with him at all.

The kid showed up before dusk on Friday September 15th. The sun was setting over the pine trees across the road from my house and it would be dark within an hour. New Jersey is known for the Pine Barrens and the Jersey Devil is said to reside there according to local legend and modern folklore. Like a great portion of the state, my home was near these giant pines and the horned owls that would often swoop down out of them beginning at dusk. Isa was not quite eight months old and neither her nor Geno were allowed out at this time of day for this reason. If they did have to go to the bathroom, I took them on a leash.

I immediately asked the Kid what was so damn important that he needed copies that urgently. I had a beer in hand waiting for him when I saw him pull into my driveway. He reached into his pocket and pulled out a twice folder piece of paper that fit perfectly into the back pocket of his Levi's jeans. He handed it to me and I was ill-prepared for what I was about to see.

"What the fuck!?" I said, opening up the folded paper with one hand, shaking it loose as I held my own beer in the other hand. I had a cooler of beer on ice right next to the front steps to my home.

"I told a guy at the bar I would get copies of this made for him and give it to him Sunday when I see him. I owe him a favor," the Kid went on. Later I would learn that this was the biker who was also his supplier for the pain pills that he popped like Pez candy. I was doing my best not to show any emotion to what I was looking at. The Kid brought a flier for the National Socialist Movement (NSM) that proclaimed to be the only white "civil rights group." I had never even heard of these guys or this group at all. It was abundantly clear that I was looking at a recruitment flier and notice of a meeting for prospective members for a group of [legitimate] American nazis. Holy fuck. I had to keep it cool and downed the beer I was drinking. I reached for another that I would drink in two large slugs just to help ice my nerves.

"Dude, I never even heard of these guys. I'm not a fan of socialists or communists myself, so I'm not sure this is something that I would be into. But fuck it, you can use my printer. I have plenty of ink and paper. Lets just wait a bit because my pugs will go apeshit when you go inside with me and jump all over you." I tell the Kid, clearly wanting to stall as long as needed until the beer can kick in and further ice my nerves.

The Kid wasn't far behind me either; he was chugging beers pretty damn fast himself. My mind started to wander off thinking about my past experience writing op-eds for various newspapers and the notion of shifting to writing an actual book about what I was learning. What I learned from my childhood trauma was that these groups hate public exposure; it stops them from operating in the shadows, on the fringes of society, but it was the best way to make them go away. I always wanted to write a book and had previously wrote a manuscript for a book covering my tours in Iraq and service in the military. That seemed like a safer alternative, but I could not stop thinking about the potential for a book on this to go viral. The idea, and proof, that these groups were operating in a liberal blue state in an increasingly more brazen way would be a good story to tell…especially if their ranks were swelling with sympathetic professionals and people in law enforcement that could run cover for them. I kept flipping back to this as the kid was bragging about his involvement and knowledge in these groups. At some point I opened another beer and finished that too. The Kid's voice was white noise; I wasn't even listening to him, but focused on my thoughts of writing a book. And I had Smith's text messages, although he became increasingly guarded in saying things to me in text messages. Smith even texted me to stop bringing it up in our messages. Most importantly, Smith was adamant that I never call the station for him. By that point though, I have more than enough to [at least] demonstrate potential sympathies and resentments Smith (himself) possessed. I only snapped out of it because the pressure on my bladder was rapidly escalating to the point where I couldn't hold it anymore. I would have to go inside to piss and use that opportunity to get him his copies. I was secretly hoping that the Kid would be so inebriated that he would leave the original on the glass inside the printer so that I could show Smith. If not, I would have to ask the kid for a copy of myself and that might raise suspicions since I already discounted the group as socialists "who are nothing more than commies."

"Watch your step coming up." I tell the Kid as I begin to walk up the first step.

"Gotcha" he slurred back.

"I'll hook you up with the printer and get it started for you. Then I'll piss while that's getting done and come right back. Don't mind the pugs." I led him to the first room on the right upon entering my home. It was the room with my modem and all-in-one sitting on top of two storage containers. I flip up the glass and had put his heavily creases paper onto the glass inside; if I didn't, it would likely have gotten stuck in the machine or shredded. Both of the pugs are barking more excitedly than normal. Pugs are great watchdogs; they alert you whenever they hear a noise, they are constantly on watch, and have an innate ability to detect someone's demeanor and intent. Because my pugs were barking so ferociously, I figured that Geno was able to detect that this guy was under the influence of something and a potential threat. Aside from that, Geno was a renowned "Jewpug" and had his own Kippah with Chasidic curls that he wears for Chanukah. I'm sure the stench of nazi sympathizer on the Kid infuriated him and Isa joined in following his cue. I hit start on the printer and told him I'd be right back.

The pugs followed me to the bathroom but quickly retreated back to their guard duty watching the Kid. I broke the seal and took one of the longest pisses in my life. I had essentially chugged three beers just to ice my nerves and already had a slight buzz. I could faintly hear the printer in the background noise which was very likely giving the pugs something more to bark at. I can't explain what it was, but something similar to what most people describe as a "sixth sense" kicked me in the chest like a horse… instilling a sense of panic and fear in me. I felt it ride down into a pit in my stomach and my adrenaline was coursing through my veins. I quickly returned to the small office only to confirm my sixth sense.

"What the fuck is this? You're a fucking Jew!" the Kid asks while he's standing by the printer. The printer was on top of stacked contains and the container on top was a clear plastic container. He was holding my Israeli flag in his one hand and Talmud in the other. A lot of antisemites own the Star of David flag, if only for the purpose of burning it or otherwise disrespecting it. In this case, there was no way I could explain the Talmud with Hebrew lettering on the cover.

He didn't even care about grabbing his copies. The Kid looked enraged and my hopes of not setting him off was long gone. My pugs were going apeshit now, and Geno was in front of me in a protective posture. The Kid took a step forward swiftly and Geno let out a cry I had never heard from him. The bastard stepped on his paw. He stumbled backwards and then swiped his leg at Geno's face in a flailing fashion. He didn't connect the kick with Geno's face, but it got his attention and he retreated to bark from behind me where Isa was caught between anger and fear.

It didn't matter at that point. I remember it all happening. Like so many times when I was deployed and you encounter an imminent threat, you reflexively fight or run in what is known as the fight or flight response. I stopped being afraid a long time before and anger always dictated my response. It was not always good to go into a firefight with anger as your prevailing emotion because it impairs your ability to make decisions and respond effectively. This situation was not one of them. The anger was flowing through my body like an electric current. It felt good and I enjoyed feeling my body utilize its adrenaline to this extent that resulted in a rush of endorphins saturating my brain, creating this addictive rage.

I moved swiftly but decisively. The Kid didn't have a chance. Even if he wasn't as inebriated as he was, it would not have mattered. The space between us was minimal and cramped with storage containers. I jabbed his chin followed with an overhand left that devastated him. Before he could fall backwards again, I swept in and wrapped my arms behind his thighs, beneath his ass, in a double leg takedown. I used my momentum and the centrifugal force of my rapidly spinning body to shift him further off balance. I snapped him around mid-air and slammed his head into the floor at the base of the doorway into the room. His eyes were wide open, and I saw him blink in a daze but his face was otherwise emotionless. While some people might recognize this as game-over and stop fighting, it just caused a great surge in those endorphins. I wanted to punish him. Geno is standing on the far side of the room outside the small office/

storage area. Isa had run and hid somewhere, and I couldn't see her anymore.

I whisked the Kid up and used his head to hit every doorway and door to exit my home. The steps that I had previously cautioned him over were now insignificant as I launched him down them. I tossed him with my left hand on his throat and my right hand in his belt loop. I heard the denim rip as I did so, but it did nothing to impede the throw. If throwing antisemites was an Olympic sport, I'd win gold.

I wasn't done either. I don't even remember my feet striking the surface of the steps going down my front porch. It is possible that I just skipped them or glided over them. I'm not sure and I wouldn't be surprised if I "supermanned" the steps because I felt like I had super-hero type strength. My anger was being reinforced with fear; fear from my childhood neo nazi trauma and fear from what would happen now that I was compromised…and this guy knew where I lived. That fear reinforced and synthesized itself into and out of my rage as I quickly assumed a full mount on the Kid's back. I was soon landing looping downward punches to the sides of his temples. I stopped a few times to grab his face while in this position so that I could smash his face into the ground in between punches. The Kid just brought his arms up to the side of his head using his biceps and forearms to buffer the blows. I don't know how many times I hit him or smashed his face into my lawn. Out there, in the country and a rural area like that, he couldn't possibly hope that someone would hear this and come to his aid. I remember grabbing his head from behind and feeling my fingers push into his eyes. He screamed awkwardly and, realizing that I had his eyes, I pressed harder. Fearing that I would have to move now and revisiting the anger I felt from being helplessly waiting for a police response when my home was vandalized in the weeks and months before, I continued to punish him.

"Stop! Stop! Stop! Let me go!" the Kid said with his screams muffled in the dirt and grass of my front lawn. I realized I had to snap out of it, or I could kill this person. I had to check on my pugs. Where were they? Did they run out the door during the scuffle? They couldn't survive in the country with the wildlife here if I didn't get them safely inside. It was the thought of them running away into the country in terror that ultimately stopped me. My love for my pugs was the only force in the universe that could've stopped my rage.

I DID let him go but it didn't help him much. His nose and mouth were bleeding. His eyes were bruised from my attempt to gouge them out from behind. The bruising was quickly evident. He stumbled upwards and away from me and it was then, during this spin, that I caught a glimpse of my work. He had knots, hematomas, on blood sides of his head and a larger one on his forehead. His Levi's were ruined now; the busted beltloop was the least of his concerns due to the grass stains on both thighs from landing the way he did on the front lawn. I stepped closely to the front door realizing that the Kid was no longer a threat. I saw both pugs were inside the house. Both of their tails were down between their legs and their ears were back indicating they were in a state of fear, if not all-out panic.

"You're fucking dead Jew boy! You're fucking dead!" the Kid mumbled out of his mouth as he stumbled back to his car. It sounded like he had marbles in his mouth, and I wasn't sure if it was his state of inebriation or that I knocked some teeth out with the overhand left from inside. It was a combination of both.

I never replied to the threats. I was incapable of speaking at this point. Everything, all of my movements and thoughts were instinctual, and communication had shut down in response to the heightening of other bodily impulses. My limbic system was in high gear and because communication was not required, my body didn't expend energy on it. I went in and looked at the pugs. I slid down onto the laminate floor and Geno came over to me. Isa poked her head around the doorway from the room opposite of where the printer was shaking in fear. She soon got her courage back and joined Geno near me on the floor. Finally, my speech came back to me. I spoke to Geno in Russian to calm him, and baby talked Isa at the same time while petting each of them intermittently. I saw my cell phone laying on the base of the wall behind me. I went over and grabbed it. I checked the screen to see a crack on it that must've happened in the takedown. I was certain it was in my front pocket. When I opened my phone,

I saw his car STILL in my driveway. I quickly closed the phone and told the pugs to "STAY!".

I got up quickly and went out the front door. For all I knew the Kid had a gun in his car? What the fuck did I know? I started a brisk glide toward his car with my right arm extended pointing away from my house. He was screaming something in his car, but I couldn't hear him or make out what he was saying. His car clicked and shifted into gear, and he backed out of my driveway hastily in an attempt to show his anger while retreating. I walked back inside to the pugs.

The next day I woke up with bruises on my legs and hip. It was likely from the takedown slam and my phone. The bruises lasted for 2 weeks; they were deep tissue bruises and a purplish-black that screams pain at the slightest touch. I didn't venture into the room with my printer because I didn't want to see any more damage. I was afraid I would just see a shitload of damage and get more upset and angry. I consciously avoided it for days. I spent the day Saturday reassuring the pugs and giving them a lot of love. I felt bad that they had to see that but Geno and Isa both saw the lengths I would go to protect them. It was a quiet day and I laid in bed waiting to hear from Smith to no avail. Needless to say, I would not be able to get the Kid to comeback and meet Smith. But I did have his copies that he wanted to make and that was enough. I didn't sleep well that Saturday or Sunday night and expected retaliation. I was glued to my cell phone's screen to view my cameras while the pugs slept on my chest and in between my legs. By the time Monday had rolled around, I was confident that I could breathe some more, but I also knew that I could not get complacent with my security. It wasn't paranoia, it was a heightened state of mind and hypervigilance.

I did not have an episode of violence like that until (almost) 2 years later, to the day. In the Federal Detention Center in Philadelphia, in between my trial and sentencing, I had beat another white supremacist to a bloody pulp. I went to the hole for 6 weeks afterward, but it was worth it. I had to send a message. A few months earlier I went to the Special Housing Unit (SHU) or "the hole" over some bullshit. The officer on my block decided to have my cellmate pack up my personal belongings to ship them to the SHU. Normally, the officer on duty is supposed to do that, but laziness is extremely common in correctional officers. My cellmate took Dana's home address and wrote extortion letters to her while I was in the hole. Because I couldn't call or email, there was no way for me to communicate with her. The letters she received were extortion with implicit threats of violence and worse. When I finally had an opportunity to "fix" that problem, I didn't hesitate to do that.

I don't like being in that state of being. Caution is thrown to the wind, and I could be an extremely dangerous and efficiently violent person. It kept me alive in combat, but I swore that I would never take a person's life once I left theater. These two incidents were flashpoints of my destructive potential, and they scared the shit out of me. Only certain things scare me, but that state brought utter dread into my conscience that overwhelmed me and caused literal panic.

The fact that Smith didn't respond to any messages, calls, or stop by that weekend that I thrashed the Kid started making bells go off in my core. I saw it as a red flag. Smith never told me he was one of THOSE troopers, but he certainly said things in person and in SMS that exposed his sympathies. I questioned how far those sympathies went and if his absence was somehow connected to the Kid's beating. It was incredibly disturbing when I finally did hear from him on September 19, 2017, for only a few moments to warn me. The prevailing question in my mind was who [or what] did he mean?

It would be later in that day that I had my phone call with the chief of staff. The call occurred just before 2 p.m. This was just hours after Smith's cryptic warning. It was a major reason why I told the chief that I was NOT threatening him. I reiterated it and got off the phone telling him no less than three times that I was not threatening him. Later in court, the AUSA would ask me "if you weren't threatening him, then why did you keep telling him you weren't threatening him?" as if to imply that because I kept repeating myself that it was, in and of itself, a veiled threat. It wasn't, but I was incredibly paranoid after Smith's warning. I was dealing with serious issues in multiple areas of my life and was not taking chances anywhere. I did not have my medicine for PTSD in more than 7 weeks and I think that affected my limbic system's potential response to greater threats. Additionally, I had two stress induced seizures in as many months because the VA stopped filling my anti-seizure medication as well. I desperately needed to get my medications refilled and delivered to me and…I needed to move…ASAP.

CHAPTER 10

SEPTEMBER 20, 2017

Fast forward to September 20, 2017. I have flipped back and forth to provide greater context of the events that transpired on this day. They are permanently imprinted in my mind and memories of this event, incredibly, have grown more detailed. As time progresses, I attribute my recall to hours of daily meditation to deal with the ensuing traumas. The flurry of events and actions taken against me prevented me from reexamining the events. Whenever I tried to do so in the past with my court appointed lawyers, they dismissed me and the process [itself] began to ring irritably. Any attempt by myself to reconcile and recollect was dismissed by myself because whenever I ventured there in my mind, I was reminded of my lawyers saying it was immaterial and / or irrelevant. The negative connotation associated with this process was what prevented me from doing so prior to writing this book. I am finally in a place where I can provide my account of what happened. It all began on September 20, 2017; that day would change my life forever and irreparably.

Yesterday, I began my day with a vague yet ominous warning from Smith. With that in mind, I made a point of NOT "threatening" or saying anything that could misconstrued as a true "threat". Yet -as the day progressed afterward- I became increasingly worried that my words and the context they were used in would be deliberately misconstrued. At one point, I had been outside in my front yard texting Dana about this fear. I tried to convey this in a text as a sense of impending doom set in. The text message, via voice to text, erroneously printed what read like an admission of guilt. "I am afraid they say I'll threatened the chief of staff" vs "I threaten[sic] the chief of staff". I was unaware of the typo at first but upon reviewing it, I immediately text Dana to apologize and tell her that I was outside using voice to text. I also told Dana that to make matters worse, it was raining, and the raindrops were hitting my screen and making my texts come through erroneously. I spoke to Dana on the phone to CLARIFY that text message and that my fear was my words being twisted into a threat. I repeatedly expressed my intent was not that I DID threaten the chief of staff. Dana told me not to worry about it. Hours had passed and the congressional staff were still emailing me to find a resolution. No one called the police, the congressional staff did not shelter in place. These would have been procedures and protocol after the shooting at the republican party softball practice three months earlier. When people feel truly threatened, they take steps to report it and protect themselves. That did not occur and was not the case. In fact, it was the opposite. Finally, I believed the calls were recorded and that the context of my words would be clear from any recording

I ended up going to get some weed from my friend. The stress of the recent events could cause me to suffer a seizure. I had used medical cannabis two year earlier and found it to be incredibly effective for both seizures and PTSD. I was living in Spokane Valley, Washington in mid 2015, and sought out an alternative to prescription medications. I was fearful of the cumulative, long-term effects of the prescription medication on my vital organs e.g., my kidneys and liver. I wasn't concerned about drinking because I would only drink in the absence of medication. When I did drink, it was rare and used to minimize the withdrawals. Withdrawals from these prescription drugs were unbearable. Alcohol, in small doses, was able to reduce the severity of the fine tremors I was experiencing in my hands and jaw. Drinking to the point of intoxication was counter productive with PTSD, but using a small amount to help myself function was a reality. I would experience difficulty preparing food for myself or my pugs because of the shaking in my hands. I did not want to inter-act with anybody because most people would observe it and ask me questions that I wasn't comfortable going into. So, I ended up getting weed and relaxing a bit. I was reticent about how far I could lower my vigilance. I began compiling a political opinion editorial. The words were flowing again just as they had when I had submitted numerous writings to various newspapers over the past twenty years. I sent my rough draft to Dana in an email and she replied that she loved it. She thought it was long overdue and was exposing weak-nesses and problems with politicians who serve endlessly without term limits. Tyrants become too comfortable in these positions when their re-election seems unquestionably certain. I had been arguing for term limits on politicians and all civil servants of every level of government. There is too much room for abuse by the bureaucratic tyrants as there is corruption for the legislative tyrants.

My bruising was worsening as the days passed since body slam-ming the Kid. I slept more, but the sleep was not quality because I was waking up frequently. The PTSD medication reduced nightmares I would have by, essentially, wiping my memory clean of my dreams. I simply didn't dream when I took them, but I still wasn't getting the high quality of sleep that I needed and longed for. I have always had recurring nightmares since returning home from Iraq, but I also had dreams that would evolve and take on new events. My dreams were always combat-related in nature; spinoffs from my past experiences or anxieties associated with future events to come. I woke up that morning and I decided to send out my op-ed. Just as I had done the day before with the email the government labeled a "threat", I carbon copied various major media news outlets to my op-ed. I had been having discussions with a producer from ABC in Philadelphia since June. I also made sure that the op-ed reached the congressional staff. The silence that followed was deafening and unnerving.

I was working in the yard since sending the op-ed. It was hot and I was mowing the law with my push-mower because the tractor was still not reliably repaired. I had taken off my shirt and whipped it toward the front of my house in an area I had already cut. I had slip on sneakers because I had difficulty tying my shoes with the fine tremors in my hands. I was wearing North Carolina blue mesh shorts. Once I was finished, I then called Vince. Afterward, I kicked my shoes off and laid down on my bed. I dozed off until the alarms started going off.

Knowing how on edge I was, Dana reached out and called the Port Norris station to speak with trooper Smith. She was well-aware that we were acquaintances and that we both served in the Army. She reached out to ascertain what he knew and also to get him to come over and see me at my house. Dana did not reach Smith because he wasn't starting work that day until 5p.m. She does not know and was never given a name of who she spoke to. This phone call seemed to be the precipitating event for the arrival of the car parked on the shoulder of NJ 718 opposite of my home.

The NJSP knew that I had security cameras covering my property. I had given trooper Smith a demonstration of how it worked and streamed to my phone. The trooper who accompanied Smith in the last week of August also saw this demonstration. The SMS text messages that remained on my phone, the 383 of 1059, contained communications in which the NJSP were aware of my cameras and even took actions to evade their motion sensing capability. When the VA would call for a wellness check, I would always know before they could knock on my front door. The cameras had an incredible 220 degree, widescreen view. Within the hour, more troopers would arrive.

At 4:08:28 p.m. on September 20, 2017, a marked NJSP troop car pulled onto the shoulder of NJ 718. That troop car was opposite the already-parked unmarked car and on the shoulder closer to my home. The trooper who arrived -per the NJSP's own CAD Abstract- was Trooper Townsend. Approximately 57 seconds later, another marked NJSP troop car arrived and parked behind the first marked troop car. It was pushing the field of view on my cameras so I perceived this as a deliberate attempt to evade my cameras again. I am nervously watching these events unfold from the screen on my cell phone. I knew what to do as it was just freshly ingrained into my mind after speaking to Vince less than two hours earlier. I truly believed that once I hit send on my op-ed email that it would increase the likelihood of a visit from police despite the fact that it was innocuous. The second marked troop car contained Troopers Guzman & Galezniak. Five seconds after Guzman & Galezniak arrived, troopers Ciaurelli & Poeppel arrived at 4:09:30 p.m.

Dana would later disclose to me that when she called the Port Norris station that she did mention she wanted Smith to stop by and speak to me about what was happening with the congressional office. The troopers who arrived that day provided sworn testimony in Camden New Jersey federal court. They all swore that the purpose of their arrival was to conduct a wellness check of someone who owned firearms and that they had conducted "well-being" checks in the past. All of the NJSP who testified on behalf of the federal government did so on July 16th and July 26th, 2018. They all testified that they knew nothing about my interactions with the congressional office and that it was not the reason for their visit on September 20th, 2017. The troopers -collectively- answered more than 100 questions inconsistently with material evidence presented contradicting their testimony during those hearings. They testified differently about the order of their arrival, who was on scene, and who read me my Miranda rights and at what time they did so. There are three exhibits filed in my subsequent civil action known as Document 48-1 & 48-2 that examine their perjury in detail.

I was still shirtless and barefoot from cutting the grass earlier. I figured it would be best to go outside shirtless so that no trigger-happy trooper would claim I had a gun and shoot me. I remember Gerard Butler's character in the 2009 motion picture *Law Abiding Citizen* greeting police completely naked. I wasn't going to go that far, but I went with shirtless for that reason. I figured that if the responding troopers were aware of my knowledge of their questionable conduct -as relayed by trooper Smith- that such a mistake might present a prime opportunity to alleviate any concerns they might have of me sharing that information by shooting me dead.

I could see trooper Guzman and a young kid toward the end of my driveway closest to NJ 718. Guzman was smiling, "smokin' and jokin"…a phrase that was often referred to in the military. Clearly, he wasn't in a heightened state of alert and awareness. He had been present on another such visit and knew how it would end; I would tell them I was fine, to leave, and stop harassing me. In turn, they would reply they were "just doing their jobs" and it was because the VA called them for some reason, real or imagined. Trooper Townsend was midway down my driveway. I watched the plain clothes officer walk down my driveway toward the front of my house with troopers Poeppel & Ciaurelli.

"Guys, you gotta' stop doing this. Stop coming out here" I said as I exited my front door and quickly descended the steps of my front porch. The plain clothes officer whoever he was, was older and clearly senior. He stepped toward me, and trooper Peoppel stopped a few feet behind the plain clothes officer and slightly off to his side on his right. Poeppel was green; he was young with a distinctively round face. Poeppel was the fattest and least fit of the responding troopers or any trooper I had ever encountered up until that point. Poeppel had this look of arrogance on his face. He had (likely) been forewarned of my anticipated response, but his facial expression and demeanor radiated an arrogance that is common in police offiers who became police officers so that they could exact revenge on people because they had been shoved in lockers since their time in junior high school.

"Hey, how are you doin?" the plain clothes officer asks. Something wasn't right with this guy. It wasn't just that I saw him sitting outside my home for an hour before, since Dana called the Port Norris station, but it was just the energy and vibes he gave me. I felt like he was dangerous…and a killer or someone who wouldn't hesitate to kill someone.

"I'm fine. I keep telling you guys to stop doing this." I spit out with a tone of defiance and irritation that would make unsuspecting people cringe in awkwardness. Not this guy. Trooper Ciaurelli now approached the front of my house and stood by an old tree stump on my front lawn. He was in clear view of my cameras and to my right. He was even with the plain clothes officer and standing silently with his hands on his utility belt. I took a step back because Ciaurelli was pushing the limits of my peripheral vision and I wanted to keep these guys in front of me.

"Actually, we wanted you to come down to the station and tell us what happened between you and the congressional office and ask you some questions" the plain clothes officer said. Now my mind kicked into high gear. First off, there is no fucking way in hell that I am (voluntarily) getting into this guy's car and going with him anywhere. Something made me feel like if I took a ride with this guy that it would be the last ride that I ever took. Immediately I reverted to the trusted advice of Vince, my attorney. Vince had never lost a legal battle or stopped short of giving me the exact type of lawyering that the situation would dictate over the previous 15 years. I had no reason NOT to continue taking his advice.

"Do you have a warrant?" I defiantly retorted.

"No." the demeanor on the plain clothes' face immediately changed. Gone with his attempt to appear amicable and sweet talk me into taking a ride with him. I saw Ciaurelli's demeanor change to a stern look, but one that had a recognition or an "I told you so" moment going on within his own mind.

"You don't have a warrant and I don't have my lawyer. No warrant, no lawyer…no talkie, fuckface. You're trespassing, assholes." I continued as I stepped back and retreated up my steps and back inside my front door. The pug's barking was ongoing from the moment they parked their cars. It was background, white noise to me for the most part. They had continued to bark while watching from a chair in one of the front windows throughout this entire brief encounter. As I retreated inside, their barking faded back into my recognition once I had removed myself from this now-perceived threat. THIS is what Smith had warned me about. It would be nothing for a former police officer with 14 years' experience to call in a favor and snatch me up, detain me, and seize my devices containing evidence I had shared with trooper Smith. My suspicion and distrust of police -exacerbated by Smith's revelations- made it seem more likely. The stories of corruption within the NJSP were well-founded…and I would later discover they were alleged to be much worse.

I try to use my phone to call Dana and my brother to no avail. My phone was completely without service. Typical and I didn't expect it to work as I had metal roofing and historically suffered from this issue since moving in less than six months earlier. I can't call so I don't even try to text anyone. From this point on, I ceased to use my cellphone. It is important to note that there will be calls and texts made from my phone after I am in custody and when I did not have access to make these calls myself. I immediately went to my Samsung 6 to view my security cameras.

I watched the troopers back away from my front lawn and they huddled up. I couldn't make out what they were saying and couldn't hear them on my cameras. I knew they were not leaving because they seemed to be formulating a plan rather than chalking it off and leaving as they had before. Fearing this was the case, I flipped my Samsung 6 from the ZMODO app to its [actual] camera. I immediately knelt down in my front door and recorded the troopers. I knew that I wasn't supposed to narrate any videos that I was planning on using for evidence, but it felt important to explain what had happened during the recording,

"I just asked them for a warrant and that guy there told me he didn't have one. You can see they are not leaving." I was kneeling down because there were two pine trees in my front lawn and their branches hung down lower then head level. It provided some privacy but it this case it was blocking my view from their huddle. I had to kneel to see them and, while making my commentary, I zoomed in on the plain clothes guy.

I began to panic; I flipped from my video camera to pictures and snapped rapid photos. They would not have any narration and could be used as evidence. I wanted to give Vince the best possible defense or whoever he referred me to their locally. Suddenly, I saw the troopers pull their handguns from their holsters and switched to a two-hand grip in the ready position with their guns pointed at a 30 degree angle down in front of them. I used this approach when I was kicking down doors in Baghdad as a breach man. My years in karate as a child and year-round participation in sports enhanced the good genetics I was blessed with. It made me a pro for breaching doors and kicking them down. Sometimes though, I would kick the door and my foot would pierce through the poorly constructed doors. I found myself left hanging while balancing myself on one leg in a completely and utterly vulnerable position. Those moments brought panic because I was a sitting (or literally standing) duck. I was feeling the same type of panic because I could see what is coming.

My mind raced as to what was happening, but I felt my death would be imminent. They could shoot up my home and plant my own firearms on me after killing me. As they surrounded my home, I began to worry about a siege type situation in which they claim a gun was pointed from a window and they then go "Waco" just to "light-up" my house. The reason for this escalation was irrelevant; whether it was the congressman, the white supremacists in their ranks, or the fact that Smith had compromised them. Whether they knew I had the goods didn't matter anymore. The idea of a Waco situation made me most nervous. The pugs.

Whatever was going to happen, it didn't involve the pugs. They were innocent in this ordeal and didn't deserve to die with me. I shuffled them into my bedroom and they hopped up on to the bed. I knew it would likely be the last time that we saw each other. I immediately choked up and told them I would do everything in my power to come back to them…whether it was in this life or the next. I knew in my heart that Dana would adopt them and reunite their pugpack at her home two hours drive away. I hugged them both as tears poured down my cheeks. I didn't want to leave them; in that moment I felt the type of love for them that was amplified because of the sense of finality that accompanied it. This was goodbye and I knew it.

I looked back to my phone and the two troopers who attempted to surround my home from the side now turned their back and walked toward the front of the house. I could see them from my camera, but also looked out the window of my back door in the kitchen. It struck me as how stupid they were; they were (apparently) on the alert enough to draw their firearms but then walked back to the front of the house turning their backs on my home.

I grabbed the rifle that I knew Phil was supposed to take from me. I pushed the bolt forward, ensured there was no magazine with it and moved toward the back door,

"I'm coming out, I DON'T want to shoot any of you! Don't shoot!" I yelled as I pushed open my back door. The rifle I was [now] going to surrender to them was pointing at the ground. I held it in my right hand with the muzzle facing the ground. Trigger finger extended and off the trigger guard to make it clear I wasn't going to shoot. The type of rifle I had used big banana clips. The SKS is similar to an Ak-47 and the magazines for the SKS are even more bulky and awkward then the standard AK banana shape. Additionally, they are even more misshapen by an additional extension near the top of the magazine that snaps into place when inserted. If I had a magazine inserted, it would be ABUNDANTLY CLEAR to the NJSP. Smith had told me about their false bravado and stories exaggerating their deployments and, in some cases, their fictional deployments that never took place. These "wannabe commandos" now donning the uniform of the NJSP would [surely] know that this weapon was not loaded. The bolt was forward. The weapon was on safe. This is what we infantryman classify as a condition 4 weapon: Chamber empty, no magazine in the gun, bolt forward, safety on, and the [aforementioned] extended trigger finger off the trigger guard for good measure.

I stepped down off the deck of my back porch and placed my Samsung 6 phone down on the farthest corner of the back deck, right before I would turn the corner not knowing what [really] is awaiting me. I put my phone down to surrender and was blind for the first time in this encounter. NJSP crime scene photos will show it photographed in this exact same location. My car is parked in the driveway and, as I turn the corner, I remember that I have three flags hanging vertically on a clothesline that runs above my driveway. I park my car behind these flags to further shield it from view from anyone driving by on the road. One of the flags is of the Third Infantry Division "Rock of The Marne" and another is an American flag. I immediately realize that I emerge from these flags without real warning for them. To make matters worse, the sun is at an angle where it will block my ability to see them clearly. It is imperative that I announce my surrender. I am in the driveway directly outside the right side of my home. I make a deliberate effort to step farther away from my home because I know that my pugs are in the room directly opposite of my position. It was further imperative for me that I create as much distance between myself and the home so that no stray bullets strike anywhere near them.

"Please, I don't want anyone to get hurt." I called out as loudly as I could. I emerge through the flags and instantly WAS blinded by the sun. I immediately dropped down to two knees and could see the troopers and plain clothes detective less than 15 feet away from me with their guns drawn on me. The rifle remained vertical and as I dropped to my knees. I was sure to point the barrel toward myself and then away -out to the side- as I transitioned to holding it horizontally. While doing so, I placed my hands directly out in front of me like Frankenstein with the rifle now resting on top of my hands. It was on the back of my hands extended out in front of me. No human being is double jointed to an extent that they could flex their fingers (somehow) upwards to pull the trigger. And in the event one of these corrupt troopers would say I did, the barrel was point-ing away from them and at myself while transitioning from vertical to horizontal. This ensured that they could never say I pointed it in their direction.

Taking these steps and announcing my intention did nothing to alleviate the fear I felt while seeing their pistols all pointed at my head and chest. This was it, I thought. I slowly leaned forward and placed my hands -palm down- on the gravel of my driveway while the rifle rested over the top/back of my hands. I then slowly slid my hands across the driveway until I was completely prone. The pain of the gravel and stones tearing my hands was a good tradeoff in comparison to eight dozen bullets piercing my head and torso. As I lowered to the prone position, I felt that same pain extend to my torso because I was shirtless and barefoot at this time.

Trooper Ciaurelli stepped toward me telling me not to move. He drove one knee into the back of my neck while pulling my left hand to the small of my back. He pulled my right hand toward my left, handcuffing me, and placing his right knee into my lower back while torquing my handcuffed hands upward toward my shoulder blades. The tear in my supraspinatus rotator cuff tendon flared in pain. I kept my mouth shut from the moment Ciaurelli cuffed me and did his knee into the back of my neck until they started the troop car to take me to the Port Norris Station less than two miles away. There were five uniformed troopers on scene: Townsend, Guzman, Galezniak, Poeppel, and Ciaurelli. There was one plain clothes officer on scene. Three marked cars and the one unmarked car that arrived first.

All troopers testified that I remained silent as I just described. NJSP detective Matthew Hanlin also testified he was present on scene. The CAD Abstract for their response refutes his testimony. Hanlin wasn't on scene but claimed he rode to the scene with his boss. Incredibly, these two individuals were never on scene -per the CAD Abstract- at the time of arrest. They did not arrive on scene until 9:20 pm to execute a search warrant obtained through deliberate statements inconsistent with their own evidence and reports. Hanlin testified that I only came out of my house one time. Hanlin also testified that I never asked for a warrant or lawyer. Hanlin lied under oath in Camden Federal Court. Hanlin stated that he knew nothing about my interactions with the congressional office and that no one else knew. This is contrary to the information sent to me by trooper Smith in SMS text messages after acknowledging receipt of faxes containing details of my interactions with the congressional office. I understood why he was lying about this. The feds were planning on charging me federally for a "threat" crime -retroactively manufactured by the FBI & Capitol Police- while the state would charge me for unlawful possession of firearms. If I had invoked Miranda, as I did, on a duplicate state charge, it would apply broadly to any federal charges that would preclude what the FBI would ultimately have waiting in store for me. Hanlin wouldn't stop there; he altered a Miranda card later read to me by trooper Poeppel in my holding cell. I was officially read my Miranda rights at 1:15 A.M. on September 21, 2017…more than 9 hours after I was taken into custody. Hanlin would change the 1 to a 2 and place another 1 in front of the time written on the Miranda card next to half of my signature. It was done to alter the time it was read at 1:15 A.M. (five minutes prior to my transport to a local hospital) to 11:25 P.M. It was incredible as to the extent of mental gymnastics and semantic backflips Hanlin underwent to convince my judge that his A in A.M. was really a "P". He testified and apologized for his "sloppy handwriting". Hanlin was supposed to testify with the remaining troopers on July 16th, 2018, but the USAO said he would testify on July 26th, 2018, because he encountered a "family emergency". Doubtful. They needed to get their stories straight because on the 16th, trooper Poeppel slipped in his testimony and repeatedly said that it was he who read my Miranda rights to me -NOT Hanlin- and that he had done it at 6 pm when I was in the holding cell. No matter how inconsistent their stories were, my judge accepted it all. My judge would state that these minor details didn't matter, and that people often remember things differently under situations of extreme stress. For example, situations such as those that would require them to draw their pistols as they had done at my home. But that was at my home. These details were long after the fact and did not happen during an adrenaline-flushed situation. I was in their custody and no threat to any of them, so the rationale provided by the judge in my case was complete bullshit. What made it worse was that Dana sat outside the courtroom for sequestering during the first round of NJSP testimony on July 16th, 2018. The courtroom would be empty and only one trooper would enter to testify at a time. Even Dana couldn't be in the courtroom, so she sat outside in shock and disbelief. After the first two troopers testified inconsistently with each other, the USAO & FBI agents panicked in an impromptu huddle. Thereafter, the FBI agents started escorting the troopers in and out of the courtroom. During this process, Dana observed them sharing their testimony to have it consistent to the extent where their case would not be jeopardized by any of their blatant violations of my civil rights. Dana emailed my court appointed [absentee] lawyer and told her that the NJSP were sharing their testimony with each other. A good lawyer would have ensured it didn't happen (again) in the next round on July 26th, 2018, but he couldn't have cared less. It was a disturbing moment for Dana who had grown up thinking police and the FBI were brave heroes that told the truth and didn't lie or frame people. In fact, most of her childhood friends grew up to become police officers. It shook Dana to her core, and she continued to blame herself for calling Port Norris station that day as being the catalyst for the circumstances I found myself in.

Back in the Port Norris station after my arrest, trooper Smith arrived for his shift minutes before 5 pm and visited me in the holding cell at their station. He was in shorts and a t-shirt, holding his uniform on a hanger when he opened the door. I was not happy to see him. I was pissed. He knew something and didn't tell me. It was a miracle that I was sitting there in front of him. I was shivering in their holding cell. It was the size of broom closet. The air conditioning was kicked high because of the unseasonably warm temperatures for late September. I was shivering and shaking. My whole body was shivering violently.

"Who was the plain clothes detective? Is he the guy you suspect?" I asked him through chattering teeth. I wanted him to confirm whether this guy was the staunch defender against any claims of white supremacists in their ranks. Smith made him sound like J. Edgar Hoover disingenuously claiming, "there is NO mafia!" Perhaps the neo nazis in the NJSP had compromising photos of the detective in drag or hooking up with his "trusted deputy".

"He just happened to be in the area driving by that day." Smith solemnly spoke while not making eye contact with me.

"That's complete fucking bullshit and I'll be able to prove it" I angrily replied biting my tongue from my chattering teeth.

"I have to change for my shift, I'll come back in and see you before I go. I'll bring you a t-shirt." Smith added while slowly removing his body from the doorway to the holding cell and stepping back into the hallway.

"Can I get a fucking phone call? Can we take these fucking cuffs off, or at least loosen them? They're digging into my hands and my lawyer is expecting my call!" my anger with Smith and the entire situation was boiling over.

"I'll check with the detective and see what he says. He's in charge." Smith added when shutting the door.

"Oh great, my fate depends on the guy who lied and said he 'just happened to be in the neighborhood…'" I sarcastically yelled to ensure he heard it through the closing cell door.

Smith returned to the cell and handed me a 'Rocky Philadelphia' t-shirt that I would have my mugshot taken in.

"The detectives want the pin to open your phone." Smith said leaning against the door frame.

"I think we both know that is never going to happen." I immediately replied looking up at him to lock eyes. I wanted Smith to understand that I still had a lot of information in my phone that I am sure he did not want revealed.

Smith left and never returned to see me in the cell. I never saw trooper Smith again. Later, my state lawyer would go to great lengths to find Smith. Apparently, he was transferred to another station after my arrest. When he was located, he said his supervisor would not allow him to testify and that a subpoena would be required to make him appear. It was in striking contrast to the troopers who lined up to come to pretrial evidentiary hearings in July of 2018 to perjure themselves. And let me be clear, it's not me baselessly accusing them of prevaricating on the witness stand, its multiple pieces of physical evidence that undermines the veracity of their testimony. It was deliberate and with a specific intent.

A detective was most certainly on the phone at the time Smith had claimed. Dana would testify that someone from the Port Norris station called her cell phone and asked her to come in to give a statement. The detective told Dana that none of the NJSP wanted to see me go to prison. The detective convinced Dana that it was in my best interest to come inside and give a recorded statement about my mental health and PTSD. By doing so, Dana would be getting me treatment in a mental health facility instead of a penitentiary. It was complete bullshit, but Dana knew that I didn't have my prescription seizure and PTSD medications for more than a month. Dana was well informed of the problems I had with the VA and how they exponentially worsened when the congressional office got involved. Dana jumped in her car and drove the two hours down to give her statement. Hanlin would later testify that no one from the Port Norris station called Dana at all, ever. When my absentee lawyer presented him with Dana's Verizon cellular phone records demonstrating a fourteen-minute call, he denied it happened at all or that it was to elicit a false statement. He began stuttering like Porky Pig on the witness stand. His statement then shifted from 'a phone call never happened' to 'to my knowledge no one called' and that he was 'busy doing other stuff" and "it's possible that someone called" Dana as she testified. Despite Dana's Verizon phone records admitted as Exhibit A, Hanlin dismissed knowing it or that they elicited a deliberate false statement. Incredibly, the judge also dismissed the Verizon phone records with the fourteen minute call.

The Verizon phone records submitted as 'exhibit A' in the cross-examination of Detective Hanlin were not fake. They were hard material evidence demonstrating another questionable instance of sworn testimony that was exposed as false. Similar to the Miranda card's "A.M." really being a product of Hanlin's sloppy handwriting and that it was actually a "P.M," the judge in my case dismissed all of these instances of hard evidence. The CAD Abstract that showed Hanlin was lying about being on scene at the time of arrest was not provided during the days of the NJSP testimony. Instead, the CAD Abstract of my transport to a hospital for a mental health evaluation was waived around incessantly in Court during those hearings. They were immaterial and irrelevant to the perjury suborned by the AUSA while the Guzman CAD for the time of arrest was missing in action (MIA). Eventually, I would be able to demonstrate the CAD used for my transport and additional evidence to my evaluation would be altered in violation of multiple federal statutes in order to conceal the [suborned] perjury of the other troopers that testified. It would be used to conceal evidence that should've precluded their interrogation after 6 days in solitary confinement. I don't believe that the judge (himself) believed the rationale and justifications against the hard evidence of perjury. I could see the system in its most corrupt state. What was most upsetting is that my judge was the former chief of the

Public Integrity Division (PIN) in the department of justice. That division is an anti-corruption body that ensures no political interference occurs. Incredibly, I had first-class seats to watch its former chief betray those values associated with his former position. I lost all faith in a fair trial and the system. It was like I was in hell; gaslighting me while being told up was down and right was left. I had no idea just how bad my hell was going to get. And in the Port Norris station holding cell, my hell was only beginning.

A TORTUOUS HELL

The t-shirt did nothing to warm me up in that holding cell. The room was roughly five by five feet. The door to the cell was a solid wooden door two inches thick. It had a slot roughly five and a half feet up from its base that slid back and forth. It allowed the troopers to do checks on their prisoners. They could speak to me through it and vice versa, but after speaking to them during the transport I had nothing more to say except I wanted one phone call to call my lawyer. I had tried telling the troopers that I never had any intention of hurting them. I kept asking about my service dogs and reminding the troopers not to let them out of the house. The local wildlife near the pine barrens would've ensured they wouldn't survive long if they escaped. I knew they were shaken to their core and could only imagine the fear and dread they were experiencing.

Inside my cell there was a wooden bench roughly twenty inches up from the floor. It looked as if someone put a coat of varnish on it. It was just a matter of walking through the front double doors, past the lobby and turning left to get me to it. I stopped talking and asking about my pugs once we parked at Port Norris station. Now, I sat on that bench shivering and worrying about the pugs as I stared down at the floor. The station and cell had the typical tile floor with a coat of wax on it that is commonly used in hospitals or other government buildings. There was no graffiti on the wall of the holding cell. I had no intention of doing so and lacked the tools to do it unless I used the edges of the handcuffs to scrape something into the wood or walls. The walls were a pale blue and there was a four-inch rubber base where the wall met the tile floor. I was still bare-foot and I noticed that my feet were turning pale white with a tent of blue or purple to them. It was evidence to the cold I was feeling.

"Hey, yo! I want to call my lawyer!" I said when I heard the slot open. I couldn't see who it was, but it slid quickly back after making eye contact with me.

"Yo! I want to call my lawyer. I want my one phone call! I get a phone call! My lawyer knows I'm calling!" I yelled again as I stood up and took one step forward. That was essentially all it took until I was flush with the door. There was no response from the eyeballs that just looked at me. The NJSP would not document a check on me for more than 4 hours.

Trooper Guzman provided the most sworn testimony in federal court that could be refuted by the evidence. In other instances when he didn't want to lie, he answered evasively citing memory failure or uncertainty. Trooper Guzman testified that he went home shortly after five p.m. when the shift changed. Guzman also testified that he supervised the preliminary report written by his subordinate who rode to the scene with him. Trooper Galezniak confirmed he wrote the preliminary report which he submitted to Trooper Guzman who "changed what needed to be changed". Trooper Guzman testified that he did not know if -or when- a search warrant was obtained, but assumed as much claiming the detectives had taken his report and would proceed thereafter. Trooper Guzman also testified that because he went home shortly after five p.m. shift change, he did not participate in the search of my home. Interestingly, trooper Guzman is listed on the search warrant return with the itemized inventory of what was taken. Trooper Guzman did not go home as he helped execute the search warrant. Why would he lie about not being there?

When my defense attorneys, both state and federal, provided me with the NJSP crime scene photos from the execution of their warrant I reviewed them intensely. The first thing I noticed was the condition that my small game hunting rifle was in; the hunting license was attached to the trigger guard by a giant safety pin.

Another photo of the same rifle was taken at Port Norris station but this time it was laid out side by side with my other firearms and the hunting license was removed to make it less likely to be discerned as a small game hunting rifle, a .22 caliber. In a state where guns are hated more than republicans and conservatives, most residents do not own firearms and are committed to seeing the abolition of the Second Amendment. They are not firearm literate; the removal of the hunting license allowed it to be perceived NOT as it was found but with other firearms, assembled when previously disassembled, and the woodland camouflage made it appear to be some type of "sniper rifle". This was deliberate because, unbeknownst to me, the FBI and Capitol Police were already involved in this investigation. FBI Agent Joseph Furey is even listed on the NJSP preliminary report authored on the day of my arrest in the section listing "personnel involved". The preliminary report also listed a charge of threatening a congressman. If I invoke Miranda, the FBI can't come and interview me without my lawyer. This is the motive for denying I ever invoked. It was also the motive for my federal medical records being tampered with.

Most importantly, while reviewing that NJSP crime photos I would discover that the NJSP unplugged and tampered with my home security cameras. In one picture the power cable are attached and plugged in, while in later photos they are unplugged. It is indisputable and became the basis for another court-appointed lawyer filing a Motion for a new trial nearly 9 months after my trial. The Motion was filed in 20-12713 to remind the court that I was not the only person claiming prosecutorial misconduct. Copies of my fax records were attached as exhibits to the Motion to emphasize perjury by the NJSP.

The NJSP had coerced Dana into coming in and giving an exaggerated statement about me hoping that it would keep me out of prison. Dana and I had not lived together for 18 months at this time. Our communication was sporadic and, more times than not, it was unpleasant. Dana voluntarily agreed to give her phone over to have text messages extracted. The NJSP told her they were only interested in the SMS text messages with me. They lied. In fact, when the trooper returned her phone after the extract, he commented on her pictures of our pugs in her phone. Not only would our communications for the past 3 years be available to them, but our privacy including intimate photos and videos stored in her phone were now being reviewed by some pervert. Dana was clueless that the NJSP intended to use her recorded statement to put me in prison. It was the opposite of what they had claimed. Immediately after I left the station, I was taken to a local health system's hospital. I was assessed for nearly 11 hours, but part of the assessment involved her being interviewed by the attending physician / psychologist from the hospital's emergency room. Less than twelve hours after giving her recorded statement, knowing that I was in a hospital, she recanted her statement to NJSP saying I "MAY have made threats, but none that she was aware of" and she urged them to provide me with medication and help that the VA was failing to provide.

The clinical notes and interview of the conversation with Dana completely refuted her statement. After all, she was not present when I spoke to the chief of staff. Dana was 2 hours away from me when that occurred, I called her on the phone afterwards. She talked to me and, putting the text messages together, one could see that the only time I left my house was in the opposite direction of the congressional district office to get cannabis. The problem with using those texts is that the FBI and NJSP would use the text message I sent using voice to text in the rain (with raindrops hitting my screen and causing it to go completely wonky). This was what they claimed was an admission of "Threaten" versus what I really said in the voice to text. What I really said was "I am afraid they will SAY I threaten[ed] the chief of staff". This was something the NJSP and FBI immediately seized upon to build their case. From reading the syntax of the text (and knowing how well I can write), it was clear that something was wrong. Dana knew about my tremors' impact on my ability to text. Dana also knew I used voice to text, and she had received seemingly incoherent messages from me in the past but was able to understand what I was saying. I knew that text looked bad and that was why I immediately CALLED her to clarify after sending it. There was never any doubt in her mind if I would drive to that office when she got off of the phone with me. She knew that my intent was to expose corruption and I spent the evening doing so in my bed writing my op-ed.

I would see Dana briefly, one time at the station before her statement when they took me to use the bathroom. We briefly made eye contact and I could tell that she had been crying. I yelled to her to check on Geno and Isa, my pugs. She nodded her head back at me from the waiting room with tears now visibly streaming down her face. Doughboy rookie trooper Poeppel was escorting me and told me to turn around, not look at her, and shut my mouth. Poeppel was worse than just a rookie cop; he was a rookie who had an ego and disaffected sense of what criminal justice should mean. That walk to the bathroom was the only time I was allowed out, but on the way down, I repeated my yells down the hallway for my one phone call to call my lawyer. I could see the plain clothes officer and others through the glass windows. Trooper Poeppel continued to remind me to shut my mouth and go back to the holding cell. I stopped in the doorway of the holding cell to ask again about my one phone call. Trooper Poeppel negotiated with me that he would go directly down and ask the detective when I could call. The caveat was only IF I went back into the holding cell. I did and sat down on the wooden bench fastened to the wall. I felt stupid as time continued to pass without an answer, so I began screaming from the holding cell.

"I want my fucking phone call! I want to call my lawyer!" I yelled while hitting the handcuffs off of the door to my cell. They were still on incredibly tight so banging on the door was excruciatingly painful. The NJSP would later testify they had removed the handcuffs once I was in the cell, but that's a lie. Dana testified seeing me being led around the station with them on. They left them on for more than nine continuous hours and they were as tight as they could possibly be. It's a tactic that is deliberately done by cops to inflict pain on the prisoners. It shows which officers have a sadistic streak in their personality. There was no justification for doing what they had done with the handcuffs. I surrendered peacefully. I was not violent. I was not threatening violence or hurting myself. I only opened my mouth and raised my voice from the holding cell to ask for a phone call to call Vince.

"The detective wants to know the passcode to your phone" Poeppel said opening the slot in the door. I could recognize the doughboy round face and eyes through the slot. He was the rookie trooper and was getting the shit duties delegated to him while the other troopers were "investigating" and gathering evidence. It's the same reason that Guzman delegated the report writing to the other rookie, Galezniak.

"There's no fucking way I am giving that to you." Smith had tried to press me for it when he came to give me his Rocky Philadelphia t-shirt. There was no fucking way on earth I would give it up.

"Okay then, have it your way." Poeppel smugly replied and slid the slot closed.

"I want to call my lawyer!" I screamed and hollered from the cell. I didn't stop for a long period of time although I'm not sure how long I yelled for. Time was going incredibly slow as I suffered silently shivering in that holding cell.

The slot opened up and I heard voices laughing in the hallway.

"What's the pin to your cell phone?" Guzman laughed through the slot.

"I want to call my lawyer!" I responded angrily.

"You will get your phone call to call your lawyer or whoever you want but the detective said you need to give us something for us to give you something." The other set of eyes now chirped in.

"Not fucking happening." I defiantly growled.

"Then sit there." the other set of eyes said while slamming shut the slot in the door.

I didn't stop asking for "my one phone call" as I kept referring to it. I made it abundantly clear that I wanted to use that call to reach out to my lawyer. Eventually, I rolled my toes upward and backward and kicked the wood door with the ball of my right foot. I was kicking the door to make a knocking sound. I wasn't trying to break it down.

Guzman returned while I was standing at the door and opened the slot,

"Step back away from the door" Guzman sneered.

"I am entitled to one phone call, and I want to call my lawyer." I, yet again, defiantly replied not budging an inch back from the door.

"Step away from the door and sit down on the bench or we'll tase you." Guzman repeated, now adding a threat. Guzman is the type of corrupt cop who loves to humiliate people, utterly degrade them, and does not think that anyone he encounters has any rights. Guys like Guzman relish in the possibility that he could inflict pain on someone. I am a good judge of character. I knew that he wanted to inflict pain on me and that they would add a charge of resisting if they tased me. I finally stepped back and sat down with my hands on my lap. My feet were resting on the floor arched up. as The balls of my bare feet were making contact with the cold tile floor. I heard the key in the door and the door opened.

"Stop kicking the door." Galezniak said smugly from the hallway. I could see him and Guzman in the doorway. The door was open three-quarters of the way, and Galezniak held it while flexing his arm in case he needed to shut it quickly.

"Holy fuck! Look at those giant paws!" Guzman pointed at my feet laughing.

"Yeah, that explains the noise. Look at them." Galezniak added.

"Dude, you got some big-ass dogs there." Guzman said, referring to my feet now using the same term that infantrymen used. A common expression for grunts (infantrymen) when performing long road marches (hikes) is that their "dogs are barking." This is used to convey the feeling of "hotspots" and blisters that inevitably follow them.

"I want my phone call." I replied calmly not giving them a reason to follow through with their previous threat.

"Well, the detectives want the passcode to your phone…so what's it going to be?" Guzman smiled smugly, truly enjoying the leverage he believed he held over me. Suddenly, I remembered Dana was in the lobby earlier and might still be there. If I yelled loud enough now, while the door was open, she might be able to hear me and know to call for me.

"I want to call my lawyer!" I yelled loudly with the door opened. Dana, unbeknownst to me was no longer in the lobby, but my voice reached down the hallway.

"What's your attorneys name and number?" an unknown voice called out to me from down the hallway. I couldn't hear well, but well enough to discern this was not in the hallway right outside my holding cell. This voice was further down the hall and likely originating from the room where I saw the plain clothes officers gathering. I screamed out my attorney's name and phone number, slowly yet loud enough for him to hear.

"Well, I don't think your attorney is working right now. It's after eight o'clock at night and I don't know of any attorney who would be working this late" the voice now replied with echoes of laughter that were nearby the source of this unknown voice. I could hear uniformed laughter after he was finished saying this. This was clearly from the room that I saw earlier. My frustration was growing. These guys were fucking with me. I was in their custody, continuously handcuffed, for more than four hours now since he told me the time. I had not been read Miranda by this point in time or told what the charges were against me.

"Then let me call Dana and tell her to call my lawyer for me and to get my pugs!" I yelled down from the holding cell in response. Guzman truly enjoyed this back and forth and made a dramatic display of rolling his head toward me -when I spoke- and rolling it back in the direction to his right, down the hallway to where the unknown voice was calling from.

"Oh…she's busy with the detectives, she's not available but I can relay a message to her if you want" I could hear soft voices in the background and chuckling that reminded me of what teenage girls do on the playground during recess. Could this really be New Jersey's finest? Is this how they conducted themselves "professionally"?

Guzman rolled his head back to me with a smile on his face in the previous dramatic fashion. His sadistic enjoyment of watching someone be denied a basic civil right was something he relished in.

"Then let me call my lawyer and leave a message on his office's answering machine." I yelled again, reverting back to calling Vince directly.

"You don't get a phone call until you've been charged, and the detectives are still putting those together so you're gonna have to wait!" the voice replied.

"Tough shit, dickhead" Guzman clicked his tongue as he closed the door. That remark got a chuckle and smile from Galezniak. Galezniak no longer needed to flex his arm on the open door but needed to do some type of posturing among his peers. The smile and chuckle demonstrated he was all-in with what the senior troopers were doing. He was showing his solidarity with his superiors, even if it meant depriving a prisoner of a basic civil right.

I don't know who the voice down the hallway belonged to, but I knew that it wasn't doughboy Poeppel. Maybe he wasn't chubby? Maybe it was just that he wore a uniform two sizes too small? I soon realized that only love handles could push his utility belt out that far. He was a total fat ass and not in the typical shape of other troopers I had encountered. I stood up to go near the slot. It wasn't open but I knew they might still hear me if they were close enough. I stopped before the words could come out. There was no use in trying anymore. I was fucked. The NJSP were toying with me and the more I spoke the more they enjoyed it. I wasn't going to give them anymore pleasure than I already had. Fuck them.

It wasn't long after I heard the key jingle in the door. The slot didn't open this time, only the door. There standing in front of me was Dana, tears streaming down her face, and one of the plain clothes detectives behind her. I was handcuffed but lifted my arms to hug her and said "this is my girl!" I squeezed her close and whispered in her ear,

"Help me please, you have to call Vince!" I whispered, not sure if she heard me.

"You are going to get help? You will get your medicines" Dana replied through her tears.

"The pugs…" I said before Dana cut me off,

"I am going to check on them now," She said nodding at me to reassure me.

"I have been asking them about them, to make sure they didn't get out and run away, but they wouldn't answer me or tell me." I cried in frustration, tears now coming down my face.

"I am going there right now. I will take them home with me." Dana tried to reassure me.

"What if they got out? Then what!?" I frantically replied while fearing the worst.

"Don't worry just go with them. They are taking you to the hospital to get you checked out and you will get your medicine." Dana more insistently reassured me this time. At this point, I knew I was going to a hospital but not sure how soon. I hugged Dana again, we told each other we loved each other, and she disappeared down the hallway as the door closed. I could hear her crying as she walked down the hallway.

After more than an hour, I realized I wasn't going anywhere soon. I was overflowing with anxiety over the pugs. I was experiencing firsthand what these sadists would to do inflict physical and psychological torture. They toyed with me mentally using the possibility of getting a phone call. They physically tortured me knowing I was cold and shivering for hours. Had it not been for Smith, I'd still be shirtless. I knew that they HAD to have a blanket they could give me, but they never offered. The shivering and my suffering was a part of the physical torture they were using to break me down. So far, they hadn't attempted to interrogate me, but I attributed this to my incessant requests for my one phone call to call Vince. I thought a blanket might be offered with food when they DID decide to question me. So far, that wasn't happening, and I had to fight through the pain and discomfort. All of the treatment was designed to break my and give them the pin to open my phone.

The next time the door opened it was Doughboy sent to fingerprint me. He walked me out to the lobby where I had previously gone to the bathroom hours earlier. Dana wasn't there this time though. Hopefully, she found the pugs and took them home with her. They could find comfort with her and the other pugs. I had my fingerprints taken and Doughboy didn't seem like he knew what he was doing. Luckily, he knew how to operate a camera to take my mugshot. On the way back I yelled down the hallway asking to use the phone.

"At least let me call Dana and make sure my pugs are okay?" I yelled immediately after.

"What's her number?" a voice replied, to my utter shock and surprise.

"Nevermind. I have it." the voice called out again. I stood in the doorway of my holding cell waiting.

"There's no answer. It went to voicemail." the voice called out again. I walked in and sat back down on my bench. Did he really call her or was this another mind-fuck tactic. A minute passed and I heard a voice talking that was getting closer to my holding cell. I heard keys jingle and the door opened. There, standing with a cordless phone in hand, was the same plain clothes detective that allowed Dana to come hug me goodbye. Apparently, he was going to be playing the role of "good cop" in any future "good cop / bad cop" scenario.

"Here he is…she called back." He said into the phone before speaking to me while handing me the phone.

"Dana, are the pugs okay?" I asked her with the phone up to my left ear with both hands still being handcuffed. My right ear was essentially useless since serving in Iraq.

"Yeah, they're okay…but your house was trashed. There was broken glass all over the floors and the pugs peed and pooped…but they're okay." Dana said in an echo that happens sometimes when people talk on their blue tooth from inside their car.

"I was driving through an area with no service and when I looked at my phone next, I saw a missed call so I called right back." Dana continued, explaining why she didn't answer the first time they called. I think she was concerned that this was my one phone call and, since she missed it, that I wouldn't get another phone call.

"Yeah, they told me you called back. Dana, listen to me…get me a lawyer!" I said firmly and in a much clearer voice than earlier when I was overcome with emotion seeing her in my holding cell.

Immediately, the plain clothes detective grabbed the phone, and I heard the phone beep as he pushed the button to hang up. He looked at me with a flashing anger that led me to conclude my prospects of him being "good cop" were now long-gone. Dana later testified about this phone call in July 2018. Her Verizon cell phone records were presented to corroborate my claim of repeatedly asking to speak to my lawyer. They were also used to impeach detective Hanlin who testified before Dana on that same day.

Incredibly, in the face of hard evidence to the contrary, the judge ruled that Dana's "phone records were not credible" and that her testimony was nothing more than an 11th hour revelation i.e., an attempt to fabricate my Miranda invocation." The judge was looking at phone records that demonstrated the NJSP called Dana for 14 minutes prior to her interview and a call later again in the evening. In both instances, the phone records were devastating evidence of police coercion to get a statement. If the NJSP were lying about calling Dana, then a phone call expressly asking her to get me a lawyer should not have been inconceivable. If true, this could cause the case and charges to fall apart. The phone records SHOULD have put more than reasonable doubt into any fair and impartial jurist's mind that something wasn't right. The NJSP were evasive and had more memory failures than one of my TBI support group participants.. The jurist in my case was NOT fair and impartial, and he was not about to let any serious fuck-ups by the NJSP cause this case to unravel. Further proof of his bias, he the phone records and testimony that to grant an enhancement in sentencing the government sought for "obstruction of justice". At this point in time, I did not have visiting privileges with Dana. All of my phone calls were recorded. Surely, if I was trying to get her to testify a certain way to corroborate my testimony, the USAO would have evidence of it. There was no evidence because we were telling the truth. And the phone records were legit. It was impossible for us to "get our stories straight" as the judge claimed when we couldn't have visits to speak with each other. It was just nonsense and incredibly unjust. Even the Court of Appeals for the Third Circuit expressed concern over applying this "obstruction" enhancement for (supposedly) committing perjury and conspiring with Dana to concoct this story, yet there being no evidence of me [actually] committing perjury! The only way we could plan to do something would be through phone calls or letters. My letters were read and photocopies and my phone calls were recorded and listened to by the feds. The USAO knew that we weren't committing perjury but did not want to lose. It wasn't so much about seeking justice as it was for her to get a conviction.

Not only was there no evidence that I obstructed justice or committed perjury, but there was also hard evidence that the NJSP were committing perjury to conceal their civil rights violations. The only evidence that demonstrated perjury was presented against the NJSP. Later, that same judge would deny me an evidentiary hearing in my civil action to call back the NJSP and re-cross examine them since receiving [additional] evidence of perjury in the form of my [complete] VA medical records from my evaluation after leaving Port Norris station…NOT the version the USAO disclosed in discovery that removed the additional impeachment evidence that was contained in them.

My judge rejected Dana's cell phone record evidence in support of NJSP perjury allegations. Instead, according to my judge, we fabricated them and were enhanced for perjury despite no proof we lied. Then, again in the civil action I filed, the same judge was presented more voluminous evidence that the NJSP lied worse than previously thought…and that it was [actually] the government that obstructed justice, violating the Federal Records Act, in order to "concoct" their story as relayed through the perjury the USAO suborned. Again, this is not a baseless accusation; the evidence exists on the docket in the record.

The door to my holding cell didn't open again until 1:15 A.M on September 21, 2017. Trooper Poeppel was in the doorway when I looked up and he was holding a small, white card in his hard. It was the Miranda card the troopers used to ensure they recited Miranda verbatim. Trooper Poeppel needed this visual aid.

"I am going to read you your rights. You will have to sign this card showing that I read them to you, and then we are going transport you to the hospital in Bridgeton." I could hear radio chatter in the background calling a trooper to come in to perform the transport. Poeppel read me my Miranda rights, alone, in the holding cell; he signed his name under the advising officer. There was no witnessing officer present. He then handed the card to me with a pen.

"Can you take these off yet so I can sign this?" I asked holding the card in my right hand and his pen in my left hand.

"No. They need to stay on because we are getting ready to transport you to the hospital." Poeppel replied seeming unsure of himself and just reaching for an excuse to keep the cuffs on.

I place the card to my right side on the bench. I am left-handed and needed as much room as possible to sign. I signed my first name and stopped.

"If you are reading me my rights, then I have been charged with a crime. I should know what those charges are AND I should NOW get my phone call since the detective is OBVIOUSLY done preparing the charges. You guys said charges were needed before I got my phone call." I said this as arrogantly as I possibly could while slowly turning my head up to Poeppel. I could see he was not prepared how to answer this question. Poeppel was the kind of person who sat down to play checkers when the game was really chess. He could not circumvent my intelligence and convince me otherwise. These corrupt, vile cops kept telling me I had to wait for the detectives to charge me until they had to give me a call to my lawyer. Since they had no intention of interviewing me directly, they simply mirandized me and denied me a call to my lawyer anyway. Later, these same sadistic cops REPEATEDLY denied [and lied] under oath claiming that I had never asked for a phone call to call my lawyer. But they also denied I spoke to Dana at 10:11 P.M. on September 20, 2017. The phone call was for three minutes, evidenced by her Verizon records.

Regardless, Poeppel was now confused. He ripped the card away from the bench before I signed my last name. He held it against the wall and dated it as September 20, 2017. He clearly JUST wrote 1:15 A.M. as the time but was still (mentally) in the 20th. He never came back to the holding cell.

Trooper Torres did come to my holding cell. He opened the door and saw me sitting on the bench with my head in my cuffed hands.

"Stand up, let's go." Torres calmly spoke. Torres had come to my house once before because the VA called when I didn't answer my telephone. I explained then that I did not have cell service, and this was a deliberate overreaction by VA staff that was weaponizing the police to harass me. I had, after all, ruffled some serious feathers filing two separate OIG complaints for staff misconduct within four months of each other. Torress sympathized with me, or claimed to, telling me that his father was a veteran and had horrible experiences with the VA. Torres told me during that visit to my house that he was just doing his job but KNEW the VA was awful.

"Where are your shoes?" Torres asked, puzzled.

"I don't have any. I got this shirt from Smith." I replied shrugging and grabbing the bottom of the t-shirt directly in front of me with my cuffed hands. Torres stepped away and into another room not far from my holding cell. He returned with a pair of black flip flops,

"This is the best I can do." Torress said as he handed me the flip flops.

"Can I get a drink of water before we go? I haven't had shit to eat or drink the entire time I've been here...almost 10 hours!" I pleaded with Torres more calmly than the others. He wasn't being a dick and he appeared to be sympathetic

"What? You've had nothing?" Torres suspectedly inquired.

"Not a thing." I replied. Torres left shaking his head in disgust and came back with a generic 16 oz think water bottle like you could buy in bulk at your local bulk warehouse retailer. He also had a 6 pack of cookies in a yellow wrapper. I didn't know it at the time, but these would be a regular item in my prison diet everywhere I was detained. They were yellow and had banana crème in the middle. Just like Oreos only generic and banana crème on yellow cookies.

"This is the best I can do." the way that Torres said it convinced me that he was not shaking his head in disgust with me when he just left, but rather with my earlier captor's treatment of me.

Torres' CAD Abstract detailed our departure from Port Norris station -enroute to the Bridgeton hospital 30 minutes away; at 1:21 P.M. roughly five minutes after Poeppel left with the Miranda Card. Because Doughboy signed the card as the 20th, when Hanlin received it from Poeppel he signed as the witnessing officer. To correct the mistake, the time was altered to 11:25 but [STILL] read A.M. Another red flag for any impartial jurist. My judge was somehow convinced by Hanlin that it was a P.M. and attributed it to his "messy" and "sloppy" handwriting. What a fucking joke. Clown shoes. I knew that Torres' dad was a veteran so during the 30-minute trip to the hospital, I reminded him that his father and I served in defense of the constitution that ensured we had certain civil rights. I then laid into his coworkers describing how they had violated my civil rights in a manner that was much more serious than denying food and water. I kept emphasizing the irony of how I could fight to preserve those rights for other citizens, but that I couldn't exercise them myself when in custody of his fellow troopers.

I continued this diatribe during the transport with Torres. There was a repeated emphasis placed on being denied my phone calls to a lawyer. This transport, according to NJ state law, MUST BE recorded with the in-car camera in the exact same manner my transport from my house to the Port Norris station was recorded. The Torres' recording didn't exist and this absence of recording was in flagrant violation of NJ law. The USAO made a big display of how "talkative" I was in the transport after my arrest to the station. I was inquiring about my pugs and denying any intentions of hurting anyone. But where was the recording of Torres' transport? The USAO and NJSP didn't want that tape produced in evidence because it would be evidence that I was denied a call to my lawyer when requested. During the Torres' transport, I spoke about how badly I had been abused by the NJSP. Torres testified under oath summarizing the 30-minute diatribe as "he [Brodie] said he felt like we weren't treating him like a citizen." It was a bit more than that summarization, but "the [whole] truth and nothing but the truth" is NOT a priority for the NJSP. Torres' CAD Abstract detailing the times of the transport was disclosed by the government, but there is no recording of THAT transport because it would support my claims of Fifth Amendment invocation. Guzman's CAD Abstract from the scene of my arrest is ignored because it was impeachment evidence, yet the recording of my transport immediately after my arrest was used to show how "talkative" I was with law enforcement. The USAO said it was demonstrative that I never invoked my Fifth Amendment rights and couldn't wait to talk to police? That is not justice. That is fucking awful. That is tyrannical oppression that begins with the petty tyrants in the NJSP, to the lawfare tyrants in the USAO, to the biased and prejudiced tyrant presiding over my case.

There was one other issue; it was another elephant in the room in which a herd were already present. At the time of my arrest, NJSP were required to wear their body cameras in situations like mine i.e., when they claimed they were doing a wellness check. A law from 2016 ensured all NJSP would be equipped with body cameras. During the evidentiary hearings in July of 2018, the NJSP testified they were not wearing body cameras. Trooper Poeppel testified that Port Norris station did not receive body cameras until January of 2018. I requested information and receipts to ascertain when cameras were issued to Port Norris station through a Freedom of Information Act (FOIA), but it was denied and ignored. Most disturbing, was that Dana informed my counsel after the July 16th, 2018 evidentiary hearing that, not only were the troopers sharing testimony, but Dana ALSO informed my absentee lawyer that during their exchanges they discussed questions under cross examination. Specifically, they shared questions about being asked if they were wearing body cameras. Dana specifically heard one of the troopers say "I turned mine off." The FBI immediately identified Dana sitting across from them in the lobby and discreetly nudged them to be quiet while indicating and informing them who she was.

The NJ law from 2016 ALSO stated that until troopers received their body cameras, they were to record with their dashboard cameras in their place. My home had nearly 100 feet of driveway space. My own vehicle was not blocking their vehicles. My car was parked around the back of my house and concealed by those three flags that were hung vertically from the clothesline. The NJSP deliberately parked on the shoulders of NJ 718; at first, I thought it was an attempt to avoid detection of my cameras, but I also believe it was to face their dashboard cameras away from the encounter. Remember, this SAME NJ state law required them to record transports. We know that they utilized the camera during my transport from home to the Port Norris station. They did not use them for a medical transport when Torres transported me despite this being required by law. Essentially, the NJSP took deliberate actions to evade the intent and letter of the law passed to curtail any police abuses of citizens civil rights. Yet, the NJSP Port Norris troopers took calculated steps and measures to evade their obligations under that law and violated my right to have counsel present for any "questioning". A recording would have demonstrated that would only come after they had a warrant to compel me. Trooper Ciaurelli was asked WHY he turned on the dashboard camera when transporting me and he responded that "there was no particular reason". When ask what prompted him to do so during THAT transport, Ciaurelli replied "It seemed like a good thing to do."

No particular reason? A good thing to do? How about…it's the fucking law and the NJSP was required to do so. If trooper Ciaurelli said that in testimony, I would be able to demand the Torres video of his transport to the Bridgeton Hospital. There was no way they could or would do that because that recording would have been a half hour diatribe about how I wanted to call my lawyer and had been denied several dozens of times when I asked at their station.

Any person could see what had transpired here. In spite of these blatant violations in which I alleged countless civil rights violations, the judge in my case would not waver. No matter how many times the NJSP troopers contradicted themselves about who read me Miranda, when, where and what I said as well as their actions when I was in their custody…the judge still dismissed it. There was nothing that could convince this judge otherwise and that's why I consider him a tyrant. Remember, after I asked the plain clothes detective at my home for a warrant and lawyer (and that the two would be intertwined), I retreated back inside my home. I watched the troopers huddle on my surveillance cameras and even opened the device's camera and narrated what had just happened and who I invoked Miranda to. I repeatedly begged, pleaded, and implored my absentee lawyer to get the device since January 8th, 2018 during our first attorney client meeting. I informed him that he was appointed because the federal public defender before him had been asked since October of 2017 and failed to do so. My lawyer was sandbagging my case. I wrote six different letters to the phone company requesting official records. Between January 8, 2018 and my July evidentiary hearings, I wrote these letters pleading for my phone records. AT&T denied those requests stating that only a subpoena could compel them. They're my fucking records and I need them as evidence of police misconduct. Not only had AT&T stonewalled me, but when we did receive the records via subpoena, there were calls between myself and the VA liaison missing from my AT&T records, but they appeared on his records. This is evidence of tampering with my AT&T records. It helps explain why the FBI, NJSP, and USAO were so adamant about my not having access to my phone for comparison with the records. That would raise more questions than it would answer. Dana wrote the judge to inform him of my attempts to acquire the AT&T records. She also expressed concern of the failures of my absentee lawyer to request the records for months. A month before the first evidentiary hearing, the judge received her letter and blasted Dana in court telling her how inappropriate it was to write him directly to tell him about the inaction of my absentee lawyer. I was happy she did because any attempt I made exparte (privately in the courtroom without the USAO present) to have him removed for ineffective assistance of counsel, my judge REJECTED. Finally, and only on the first day of the evidentiary hearings, on July 16th, 2018 the judge signed an order filed as Document 52 on my criminal case's docket, ORDERING the USAO and FBI to turn the device over for an independent, third party digital forensic extraction. We had agreed to use an independent expert that could perform the extraction at the federal detention center with the FBI present. The order stated they must do so by July 24th, 2018 which would allow me to review it to present impeachment evidence against the NJSP that testified on

July 16th, 2018. It would also serve to prepare cross examination for the troopers who would testify two days later on July 26th, 2018.

The government didn't comply with the order and my attorney did waste a breath objecting to their contempt. The government claimed that there were jurisdictional issues and complaints that delayed the NJSP from handing over the device to the FBI. No shit, they were probably afraid a forensic examination would corroborate what the phone records later did…that they had illegally accessed the device without a warrant and at a time I was in solitary confinement. And when the FBI finally did accept possession of my cellular phone, they claimed that they were unable to "crack into it" and, subsequently, had sent it off to various other experts to attempt to do so. The FBI claimed that they had sent it to [so] many experts that they lost track of where it was and didn't know its exact location. I'm not joking…this is in the transcripts. The USAO did not turn over the device for extraction before the 24th of July. Instead, they brought it to Court on July 26th, 2018 and arranged for the forensic expert to meet us there for the extraction. This was deliberate gamesmanship and obstruction by the FBI and USAO. The extraction itself would take hours and I was supposed to be present with the FBI in an office while it occurred to ensure they did not do anything to coerce, alter or delete the independent expert. Instead, the U.S. Marshalls led me up to an office in the Mitchell Cohen Courthouse a floor above, took me inside and sat me down at a table in the office where the FBI was already seated and waiting with the forensic expert. Once I unlocked the device, I was escorted back downstairs in the elevator and into the courtroom to begin the July 26th 2018 evidentiary hearing. July 26th was the day detective Hanlin would commit countless instances of perjury and swear his "A" was really a "P". I would invite the reader to review that Miranda card in evidence in the record and decide for yourself. You can also compare the signing of my last name with another example. Remember, I never signed my full name but stopped after the first and reminded Poeppel that NOW I wanted my phone call. That dipshit thought I was done signing and ran out. I don't know who signed the last name of that Miranda card in evidence but thorough comparisons with other documents I submitted

-dating back twenty years earlier- consistently demonstrated that the signatures were not in any, shape, way or form alike. The FBI was alone in a room doing G-d knows what with the evidence I desperately needed from that phone. The terms of the agreement were violated without a word, objection or complaint from my absentee lawyer. In fact, despite my adamant objections to his agreement, while reminding him of his constitutional duties to represent me in my best interests, he signed off and made no objections to the governments "bait and switch". My absentee lawyer did not even receive the records for review until AFTER the judge made his rulings on the evidentiary hearings. My lawyer did not review the device content in its entirety with me. In fact, later records and communications with the forensic expert would show that my absentee lawyer never even [requested] a complete extract of the phone. When I did meet with him weeks before my trial began, he provided me with limited call and text extracts between myself and trooper Smith. When I asked him where the rest of the contents were, knowing what video evidence I had in my phone, he told me, "he did not have the time to meet with me and review the entire device because it would take at least 1,000 hours".

Court appointed lawyers receive the same stipend payment with limits to what else they can claim. This occurs whether a case is settled by a plea agreement or goes to trial. Court appointed attorney's interests are that they push their clients into plea agreements so as to do the least amount of work possible. Then, they can move on to the next client [payment]. Somehow, I think that this is NOT what the framers of the Constitution had in mind at its inception, nor do I think this defines competent counsel. The system is flawed and encourages lawyers to press their clients into agreeing to plead out, regardless of their guilt or innocence. Many times, they are forced to plead to crimes that the prosecutor adds for no purpose other than leverage. The prosecution knows they won't stick, but the leverage that exists as potential additional time is overwhelming to anyone who thinks twice about it. And if you go to trial, you better be prepared because you will likely encounter what Sydney Powell described as "an epidemic of prosecutorial misconduct that only good judges can prevent." I was out of luck in that regard because there was no way that my judge would deny a single motion filed by the government over the course of my prosecution. The judge certainly made a point to deny any Motion my defense attorney submitted. It might seem ridiculous or unbelievable that this happens in contemporary America, but public awareness is increasing. The everyday American is not as stupid as the government and deep state wish they were. It's not hard to fathom how the USAO has a 95% conviction rate when they receive everything that they want to present their case. If need be, they will then tamper with or destroy impeachment and exculpatory evidence, suborn perjury, and likely have a judge who will deny every motion submitted by the defense.

The worst part was that I was mocked, degraded and humiliated by my judge for not "presenting a scintilla of evidence" to corroborate my claims. This was also cited to enhance me for obstruction of justice. I merely testified to the contrary of the government and its witnesses. He criminally enhanced me for exercising that constitutional right. When I finally presented the impeachment and exculpatory evidence, the judge completely exonerated the government of [actual] tampering with my federal medical records. The judge then claimed -in hindsight- that it would not have affected his credibility determinations and findings regarding those evidentiary hearings. It was clear the government's case was flawed and could only obtain a conviction by suborning the perjury of the NJSP. When I finally produced MORE than "a scintilla of evidence", the same judge dismissed it all and exonerated the government of any wrongdoing… while at the same time denying me an evidentiary to present the evidence's relevance as impeachment and exculpatory materials. The judge also denied a certificate of appealability to prevent any judicial review of the evidentiary discrepancies he was presented with in my subsequent civil action. Yes, America, this is your criminal justice system and why all of those involved deserve the label "tyrants". For those enlightened with these details of my case (and likely you the reader), it's been -thus far- a unanimous assessment of the totality of evidence. This is tyranny is its most vile form. It is occurring under the sanction of the United States government and department of injustice.

I want to caution you (the reader) that it will only get worse in the next chapter. If that notion seems impossible after this far into my book, I will convince you to the contrary in the next chapter.

CHAPTER 12

POLICE, PROSECUTORIAL & JUDICIAL MISCONDUCT: LESSONS IN TYRANNY

I forewarned you that it will only get worse and more unbelievable in this chapter, so fasten your seatbelt. Not recording the legally mandated transport to the Bridgeton hospital (or deleting it because of my complaints about being denied a phone call to counsel -contrary to the government's argument) was just the beginning. Up until this point in time, I thought that trooper Torres was an honorable man who was sympathetic to the mistreatment of the VA. Trooper Torres' testimony on July 26th, 2018, eradicated any preconceived notion that I possessed regarding that position. I once read that the only people who hate dirty cops more than their victims are the good cops. But what about the cops who see things happen and don't do anything to report it or expose it? They will be ostracized by their coworkers, eternally, and will operate in an otherwise hostile work environment. Who wants to do that? Just "go along to get along" in law enforcement has been mostly aptly summarized as 'The Sacred Blue Wall of Silence". If you violate that in any shape, way, or form… your career in law enforcement will be a miserable one thereafter. What could possibly be worse than those cops that remain silent? The cops who cave under incredible pressure to -not only- remain silent, but also speak lies and vagaries that corroborate the corrupt cops version. That is where trooper Torres was on the spectrum. My medical records from the Bridgeton hospital are proof of that. Those records consisted of 59 pages total; twenty of those pages were the clinical interview conducted with me. It also contained the telephonic interview with Dana. The FBI was in Bridgeton on September 26th, 2017 to interview me at the Cumberland County Prison (dungeon). The USAO would have you believe that my hospital records from that Bridgeton hospital were requested by the VAMC in Wilmington, Delaware for billing and administrative records. The problem was that the VA version of my medical records was [now] only seventeen pages. More than two-thirds of my medical records from that night were removed. VA medical records constitute federal records; and "to alter, modify or delete any portion of a federal record" is criminally prohibited under 18 U.S.C. § 641 & § 2071(b). My evidentiary submissions in the civil action filed subsequent to my conviction demonstrated that portions of my VHA records were altered, modified AND deleted. They were supposed to be identical and complete; the remaining pages were provided a new heading in the top margin. The stupid, incompetent, and corrupt tyrants in the VA renumbered the remaining pages in the new header, but failed to remove the [original] page numbers at the bottom of the pages. Whether the VA did it or the government asked the VA to do it is irrelevant. I find it highly suspect that the records were requested on the same day that the FBI was in Bridgeton to interview me. Regardless, the USAO has a duty to disclose true, accurate, and complete records of evidence in discovery. They did not. The government has repeatedly denied there is any difference in their records versus the original. They have denied involvement in the federal record tampering. Any person that looks at the two sets of records knows that the government is gaslighting in their court filings about these records. When closely examined as I presented in my civil action, it is clear that all of the pages removed benefitted BOTH the VAMC in Wilmington AND the USAO.I broke it down "Sesame Street Style" for my judge who then preemptively exonerated the government with no chance of an evidentiary hearing to ascertain who did it and how it exists as

Brady materials. No judicial review granted to appeal to the Court of Appeals. The judge said it was irrelevant and wouldn't have changed his mind. Fine. But the constitution, existing case law and Supreme Court decisions contradict his position. The Supremacy Clause of the U.S. Constitution says that the constitution is "the supreme law of the land", but try and tell that to a tyrant in a black robe banging a little hammer against a man whom he had an axe to grind. In truth, I don't think anyone has any "rights". George Carlin said it best: We have "privileges" that the government can usurp or nullify whenever they want. To quote Sydney Powell, "anything the government says is fact, and any evidence or testimony the defendant presents is obstruction of justice, perjury, etc." I couldn't say it any better than the former assistant United States Attorney. Nor could I say it better than Justice Louis Brandeis who once opined, "The government cannot become a lawbreaker. When the government becomes a lawbreaker, it breeds contempt for the rule of law…it invites anarchy."

At the time that I am writing this, contemporary opinion in our criminal justice system is (likely) irreparably damaged. Depending on who you would ask, the causality would be different and likely attributed to politics as the motivating factor. But there is no disputing there is a "two-tier system of justice" in our contemporary society. Politics can certainly play a role, but as I argued in the beginning of this book it is more about class. With class comes the ultimate trump cards in any government institution or system. Class is equivocal with power and wealth; elitism is the [actual] supreme law of the land. Nothing, and I mean NOTHING, trumps elitism. The elites run the system and look out for each other regardless of any of the other differences they might have. It's a private club and the average American can never attain "membership" regardless of their virtues, education, or humble origins. It is elitism that perpetuates the system of injustice in our nation and manifests itself in the purest form of absolute tyranny.

The troop car pulled to a stop in a parking spot about twenty feet from a set of double doors with "EMERGENCY" written in big read neon letters. The letters were domineering and made me realize that this situation was an "emergency" in so many ways. Torres radioed that we arrived and step out of the car to walk around the front and come to my door. I was seated behind the passenger seat. He opened the door and my flip flops fell off when I swung my legs over the door jam. I tried to put my foot back in but hit gravel; the flip flops were black like the macadam the parking lot was paved with.

The hospital was (apparently) expecting my arrival. Torres escorted me in with his hand on my right bicep. The walk from the car to the emergency department was relatively short, but this was not a front door drop-off. I sat on a blue plastic chair whose back had a pear shape. The chair reminded me of a larger version I had sat on in elementary school when I was a kid. Torres spoke quietly with a nurse a few feet away. It was safe to assume that this was not the first time someone was brought in by the police.

"Okay, would you mind coming with me?" the nurse smiled as she stepped toward me. She had a smile that would make any person reciprocate and undoubtedly served her well in her profession. So many people who were seriously injured or ill would find comfort in having a nurse like her attending to them.

"Yes, Maam." I reciprocated a smile, despite the circumstances.

"Are you former military?" She asked with a suspicious smile on her face.

"Yes, Maam. What gave it away? My haircut or the 'maam'" I smiled again.

"It was both, actually." She smiled and led me toward a bed in an individual room. It was the first room on the left when you entered the double doors, but in far enough that it was directly across from the front counter nurse's station.

"Have a seat her." She patted on the bed and I hopped up.

"You can bring that chair in here and have a seat. We're going to be here awhile." The nurse nodded at the chair I had just been sitting in opposite the wall of my room.

"We need to take your vitals, so we have to take these off." She said as she looked toward Torres and then back down to my handcuffs (still) restraining me. Torres explained I had to remain cuffed but he uncuffed me and re-cuffed my right hand to the bed. I asked him to have my left hand free to sign the documents that I was sure were imminent. Immediately visible, my left wrist had a deep impression from the pressure placed on by hours of excessively tight pressure. I tried to rub my wrist on the affected area after the nurse looked down at it with the first flash of any sort of unpleasantness. I accomplished this by moving it over to my right hand and rubbing it as best as I could quickly before bringing my left arm back to the waiting Velcro arm cuff of the blood pressure monitor.

The nurse slipped the cuff on and reached up with a thermometer attached to the same machine.

"Open up for a moment please." The nurse asked politely.

"Thank you, maam." I mumbled with the thermometer under my tongue, clearly trying to keep it in my mouth with my tongue. The machine beeped quickly after, and she removed the thermometer from my mouth. She then took the arm cuff off my left arm. I couldn't see what the readings were and didn't ask.

"How are you feeling tonight?" this nurse was clearly the triage nurse. My oldest brother was an oncology nurse at a children's hospital before he passed away more than a decade earlier.

"I feel pretty good. I need my medication though." I calmly replied.

"What medications do you take?" she asked me while she brought her clip board up to her chest to take notes. I told her the medications I was taking and for what reasons.

"Why did you stop taking them?" she asked because the medications were for PTSD and seizures.

"It wasn't voluntary. The VA stopped sending me the refills. I had refills left, but they couldn't send them to the right address. I had recently moved, and they were incapable of getting an address right. So, I called my old doctor at the VA medical center in Lebanon Pennsylvania. He said he would mail me refills but that it would only be enough for a month. My doctor told me that my current VA should get things figured out by then. They didn't and so I didn't receive them." I explained as Torres' now sat down stone-faced on the blue chair.

"So… you didn't… voluntarily… stop taking them? On purpose?" the nurse asked for clarification.

"No" I replied.

"Okay, you just didn't have any available to you, that's what you're telling me?" she asked.

"Yes, maam. Otherwise, I always take my medication as prescribed." I added.

"When was the last time you had them?" she asked while raising an eyebrow.

"I haven't had the anti-seizure medication for more than a month and a half. The PTSD was two weeks longer than that but still more than a month for both." I explained to the nurse who was clearly trying to get a clearer picture. Unbeknownst to me was that the NJSP called in advance to inform them that they were bringing in a suicidal veteran who was off his meds and tried to commit suicide by cop.

"Have you had any seizures since then?" She asked

"Two. One was bad. I pissed and shit myself." I replied, adding an apology for the crudeness of piss and shit.

"Anything else?" She asked.

"The withdrawals from the med for my PTSD has been horrific." I added.

"Yeah, that's common for that medication…especially if you have been on it for a long time. How long were you taking it?" She asked.

"Since my return from Iraq in 2003." I replied immediately noticing her eyes dramatically open as she shrugged her head.

"Yeah, that would do it. I am going to go put these notes in and let the doctor know. I'm also going to get you some Ativan to help you out and calm you down a little." The nurse said standing in front of me. She turned in her sneakers and pivoted toward the door. I saw her typing at the front counter and then she disappeared. When she returned, she had a small, white paper cup holding the Ativan. I was a fraction of the size that you would normally use in a dispenser in your private bathroom at home. In her other hand was a bluish-gray water pitcher with ice in it.

"I'll work on getting you a bigger cup but just use this until I come back with one." She smiled again and took the empty paper cup and filled it with some water. She put the pitcher on the table next to my bed. It was the standard type of table that you would see in a hospital room in which patients are served their meals. It could raise or lower as needed, but at this point it just sat next to my bed.

"You can put your feet up and relax. Are you cold?" She asked as she seemed to be checking off some mental checklist that she had seared into her memory from repetition.

"I'm freezing." I replied, drawing at the 'ee' in freezing.

"Okay, I'll get you a blanket." She checked off her mental list and stepped out of the room. She returned a few minutes later and gave me the white hospital blanket and placed a plastic mug that matched the pitcher on the table. The mug reminded me of cafeteria dishware from school. She adjusted the back of my bed upright as far as could be so, while my feet were up on the bed, I was still upright.

The nurse repeated her checks on me every fifteen minutes. She would ask me how I felt and if I needed anything. Every so often in these visits, she would retake my vitals. At one point, she told me that Ativan must be helping because my pulse, respiration and blood pressure were all down. In between her visits, a phlebotomist came in to draw a couple vials of blood. I sat there staring around the room and watching the staff operate and move about the emergency department. I was not aware of any serious injuries brought in that night. It didn't look like a big hospital from the outside. Torres stepped outside the room and had a hushed phone call with someone after radioing them from the mic attached to his shoulder.

Hours had passed that were completely boring. After mentioning this to the nurse on one of her regular visits, she returned with a TV on a wheeled cart and handed me the remote. I thanked her and smiled.

"Here you go, you can watch this to help with your boredom, but I'm not sure what the channels are. Will you eat breakfast in a little if we put a meal request in for you?" she asked before leaving.

"Sure, I'm starving. I haven't eaten anything for more than twelve hours except a few cookies that he gave me." I said nodding at

Torres. It was clear from the radio chatter that his shift was coming to an end soon and his relief was enroute to replace him. He seemed eager to leave and finish his shift. I was beginning to wonder if his relief was late relieving him, but gave up caring about the shift times of the NJSP. The nurse smiled again and walked out.

Before Torres left, he spoke with a doctor. The doctor then came in and asked me a bunch of questions. Torres had already briefed him on what he had been told, but the information he was giving to the physician was second-hand. Torres wasn't present at the scene of my arrest and had no idea what really transpired other than what the other troopers told him.

The questioning ensued for some time. The physician asked him to leave so that he could interview me privately, but Torres refused to leave and stated he was not allowed to do so.

"Really? He's handcuffed to the bed I don't think he's going any-where" the physician nodded at the handcuff attached to the metal railing of the bed.

"I can't leave. I'm sorry." Torres stood firm and the doctor was unhappy with the response.

"So how are you feeling?" the doctor asked

"Good. Frustrated. I've been trying to call my lawyer since they arrested me, but they won't let me call. They told me I couldn't call until I had been charged. When they finally read me my Miranda rights, I realized that charges had been issued but they never told me. Can I use YOUR phone to call my lawyer?" I explained in a way to express a shared frustration with the police.

"So... you don't know what your charges are?" the doctor asked.

"Nope, no one told me and so far, Torres here is anything but a conversationalist." I replied wittingly at Torres' perceived expense. I wasn't angry or being hostile but witty and trying to find humor in this G-d-awful situation.

"You can't tell him his charges?" the doctor asked.

"Threatening a congressman and firearm violations." Torres said, visibly agitated that I put him on the spot.

"You also said suicide by cop, right?" the doctor asked Torres.

"Yeah, that too." Torres added on.

"What?! No! I did not attempt suicide by cop. I surrendered to them and voluntarily gave them my rifle. I did not try to commit suicide by cop! I explained what I was doing to them before and as I did that very slowly, so they would NOT shoot me!" I retorted angrily emphasizing that I did not do any such thing. This moment was the first time I was hearing my charges and it was only because of that doctor. I would've felt bad for Torres if he hadn't been such a dick once we got to the hospital. The irritation of the doctor was radiating off of him past me and right at Torres.

"So… you didn't try to commit suicide by cop?" the doctor asked his question again.

"No! and I did NOT threaten the congressman. I haven't spoken to him since May, and we had a pleasant phone call. He was awesome to talk to if we're being honest." I added making sure that I denied threatening the congressman.

"You called the congressional office and threatened the chief of staff two days ago, the FBI are also involved and investigating!" T6rres interjected now clarifying my objection.

"I did NOT threaten the congressman OR ANYONE at his office. And I did NOT try to commit suicide by cop. This is complete BULLSHIT!" emphasizing my denials and disdain. Dana had probably told them my fear of being deliberately misconstrued, or the worst-case scenario, was that he called in retaliation for me sending out that op-ed. I couldn't see the chief doing that because that would involve him having to turn over a recording of the call. It would raise more questions than it did answers…especially as the dick pic revelation went. I also thought that if he did so, he would've called the police right away if he wanted to lay a charge on me. The truth was that the chief of staff never called the police. No one in the office called the police. They didn't shelter in place or close the office early as one would expect three months after the congressional shooting attack in D.C. Quite to the contrary, they continued to email me throughout the night and into the next morning. At my trial, the district office manager testified she received and reviewed the email that was count 2 of my instant indictment. She testified under oath before the jury that she "saw it, read it, and thought nothing of it" and went back to business as usual. Somehow, this was lost on the jury by that point, as I'm sure they hated to see a large portrait of Donald Trump in my home. It was visible in a few of the NJSP crime scene photos. I thought this was inflammatory considering where my trial was being conducted. The USAO deliberately showed those photos. It was designed to evoke a negative reaction in the jury from a state that has been overwhelmingly voting democratic socialist for decades.

"I was asleep in my bed when these fuckers showed up, and I thought they were at my house to assassinate me." I added while nodding at Torres and placing an emphasis on the fact that I thought they were going to find a reason to shoot up my home or kill me. I realized that this would sound delusional, but I was not delusional, and the doctor later noted that in my records. He [literally] noted I was not delusional but that I "thought the NJSP were at my home to murder me."

"Why would they show up at your house to kill you? Do you really believe that?" The doctor asked to see if I was delusional.

"That's something I am only going to discuss with my lawyer. Can I use your fucking phone -PLEASE- to call my lawyer, since these fuckers wouldn't?" I asked the doctor for my phone call now specifically describing things that even this doctor knew were not supposed to happen when you're arrested. You are typically told your charges, why you're being arrested, and you get a phone call to call your family or your lawyer. He was beginning to suspect that things were not as they appeared at face value.

"No, I don't think I can do that." the doctor looked at Torres' who was nodding no in a disapproving fashion.

"Well, would you call him if I gave you his info and tell him that the police won't allow me to call him?" I quickly responded to his negative answer.

"No, I can't do that either." The doctor finished.

Unbeknownst to me, Dana's interview was quite the exaggeration. She was speaking personally about me and my habits, but Dana and I hadn't lived together for 18 months. We didn't see each other much and when we did communicate with each other it was more heated than not. Dana's statement, regardless of the coercion and her intent when giving it, should've been viewed with an air of skepticism that an ex-girlfriend could say. People typically don't speak highly of their exes, that's why they're exes. Especially if the police told her they had been in my phone and saw I was talking with other girls. Dana's interview was very adversarial toward me, but I saw the phone records and understood she was doing the best she could to help me. I knew that she was legitimately concerned about me having a seizure and dying in front of the pugs without anyone around to call an ambulance or take care of my pugs. Her intent became clear shortly after this interview with the emergency department doctor was over.

"Something is not right here. I am going to go make some calls. I have to page the psychiatrist on duty and update him." the doctor said with a clear tone of frustration in his voice. He threw his hands up to his waist and shrugged while shaking his hands. He seemed genuine and that he believed me. Later, I would reveal the notes that the government did not disclose; I was listed as "awake, alert, and cooperative." My denials and suspicions of the NJSP's intent was also documented.

By the time that doctor returned, Torres' had been relieved by Trooper Spadafora. He seemed like a young guy and his age and inexperience warranted him this type of duty. I am sure that he would've rather been anywhere else. When the doctor returned, he asked Spadafora to leave the room and he agreed that he could (and would) but that he would sit outside the room.

"I talked to Dana." the doctor said with his eyebrows raised.

"And…" I wanted the suspense to end.

"She said you've been having problems with the VA sending you collection notices and you're having a nervous breakdown." the doctor began telling me things only that he needed clarification on.

"No. I couldn't get appointments with the VA, so I went into the Choice Program to see a doctor in the community of my choice. The bills are supposed to be sent to them for payment. But they didn't pay the choice providers and I received several collection notices from the doctor's office since the beginning of the summer." I added, calmly explaining to clarify any questions.

"She said you contacted the congressman for help, and he didn't help." the doctor was probing.

"That's true. I did. And like I already told you… we had a good conversation. It was friendly. The VA was angry with me for getting him involved. AND, I filed two complaints with the inspector general in the past 6 months for staff misconduct!" I continued to explain, hoping that I could give some context to what brought me into the emergency room and that it was not because I was suicidal or homicidal.

"Is that why you threatened the staff, because things went badly once they got involved?" The doctor tried again but I wasn't having it.

"I did NOT threaten ANYONE…" I said as I sighed out a bit of frustration.

"Well, I talked to Dana, and she didn't know one way or the other if you did. Do you use any street drugs? Pot? Coke?" the doctor was prying now, likely to test my honesty.

"I had a pot prescription for PTSD and seizures. I drink rarely, and it is typically to mitigate withdrawal effects when the VA doesn't fill them in time." I continued to add.

"Well, we drug tested you and I saw the pot. And alcohol but there's nothing else. No hallucinogens. Nothing." The doctor responded reaffirming what I had just told him. He had to know I wasn't lying to him in that regard. I suspected he believed me about the other accusations. This doctor would have been an amazing defense witness if my absentee lawyer called him.

"I did not try to commit suicide. I am not homicidal nor suicidal…and I am compliant with my medications WHEN I get them. I am NOT hallucinating, and I am not delusional." I added, checking off the most important questions an interviewing professional asks to assess for imminent danger.

"So, this has happened before with the VA? Am I wrong from interpreting what you just said?" the doctor probed more.

"Yes, it has happened MANY times." I confirmed for the doctor. The truth is, I don't know what he was thinking, but I can tell you he repeatedly assessed me about suicidal or homicidal ideation and intent. I was negative on all of those every time he checked. I just remained calm while reflecting my frustration. The medical records notes reported that I was calm, alert, and cooperative. The visits were on every quarter of the hour. I had no reason to be angry with the emergency department staff. Hell, they brought me a TV and a great breakfast that was not stereotypical hospital food. The doctor and his staff recorded all of these except for the moment I was a smartass and asked to call my lawyer.

The real question is why would Torres get on the witness stand in Camden Federal Court and testify that "within 5 minutes of arriving in the emergency room" I "fell asleep and stayed asleep the entire time…until my shift ended and my relief arrived." Torres provided sworn testimony to that effect. I knew he didn't like me from the diatribe on the way over, but that wasn't the motivation for lying. He knew he told me my charges and if I invoked Miranda before then, it would be liberally construed to the FBI's duplicate charge.

On September 22, 2017, I appeared in New Jersey Superior Court to be arraigned on charges. I invoked my right to counsel, to remain silent, and proclaimed my innocence. It wasn't a plea hearing or arraignment, just a bail hearing. I still invoked Miranda and I was already told the feds were involved. The Supreme Court has ruled that people who are not formally trained in law should have their invocation construed liberally, even IF the interviewing party was not aware of the invocation. When the FBI arrived in Bridgeton to interview me at Cumberland County Prison, they conducted an interview in which I denied making threats, overt threats, and anything that could be remotely misconstrued as "veiled threats". It's in the transcripts, but that didn't matter. The judge went against the Supreme Court's opinion and allowed the interview into evidence. The interview was improper and should not have been admissible. Certainly not in an edited form.

The government proclaimed that it was a "confession" in press releases. Any jury pool would now be exposed to official statements from the USAO that I had already confessed. There was no way that I would ever get a fair trial. There's a cheesy cliché that says truth is sometimes stranger than fiction. No one would believe me and certainly not when the deck keeps getting stacked against me in the governments favor.

I told my absentee lawyer about what happened at the hospital. I signed releases for him to get those records. Instead, he relied on the records copy that the government disclosed in discovery. Had he utilized the releases I signed with him when I first met him on January 8, 2018, I could've exposed the alteration of these records to exclude impeachment evidence and much more. I asked my absentee lawyer to call that doctor as a witness, but he told me it was irrelevant and immaterial to the threat. I disagreed; that witness could provide impeachment evidence against Torres. I didn't have effective assistance of counsel, and I was assigned a lawyer who [admittedly] told me he didn't have time to prepare my defense. Just like the contents of my phone that contained the security camera recordings of the charged phone call and interaction with the NJSP at the time of my arrest, my court appointed lawyer did not even bother to request the records. Had he done so, he would have seen the government disclosed altered, modified, and deleted VA medical records from the night of my arrest for profit and gain. The altered records were intended to help secure inadmissible evidence into my trial. The records (coincidentally) excluded impeachment and exculpatory evidence. This is supposed to be a serious offense. It is a felony for a prosecutor to do so and they can lose their law license. Without an evidentiary hearing about these records, my judge completely exonerated the government that disclosed the records and said they were (essentially) immaterial to his credibility findings regarding my invocation to have my lawyer present for any and all questioning.

My judge not only rejected my claims of ineffective assistance of counsel. He added that I had excellent counsel... from what he observed. He then added insult to injury dismissing my claims as more "obstruction of justice" and lies. My judge opined in my civil action that I am a compulsive liar without any hard evidence. Meanwhile, he turned a blind eye against the government witnesses' perjury and exculpatory evidence. The judge excluded that evidence in every subsequent Motion but had no problem including the improper interview with the FBI. That is the epitome of a biased, prejudicial judge who is, not only, ignoring prosecutorial misconduct, but doing so while making prejudicial remarks toward me that, in and of itself, constitutes judicial misconduct with malice.

CHAPTER 13

EVERYBODY— EVENTUALLY—BREAKS

Torture. Everyone eventually breaks when tortured. It's not a question of "IF" but rather "WHEN". That's what was ingrained into my psyche during basic training in the summer of 1998 at Parris Island Marine Corps Recruit Depot. It was reinforced after 9/11 when I re-enlisted with the United States Army. I was a rifleman, and it carries a greater risk of capture than most military occupational specialties (MOS). It's a startling reality but you'd be hard pressed to find a grunt that is deterred by the risk. I was constantly reminded that, in the event I was captured, I would provide my name, rank and service number. That was it, nothing more. But we were also warned, if our captors used torture, we would break. Some guys would proclaim how "hard" they were and that they would not crack before other guys. This is true. But eventually…everyone breaks.

The attending physician in the emergency department had come into my room after noon on September 21, 2017. Trooper Spadafora was forewarned and, while the doctor came to inform me of these obvious changes in my status with the hospital, he radioed to his dispatch to notify them I was being discharged. The doctor stated that it was his opinion -and the psychiatrist- that I was not a threat or imminent danger to self, others or property. I was never a danger to self, others, or property. I was rated on the hospital's threat index as minimal to zero. In fact, he wrote that after speaking to Dana, there appeared to be an attempt to get me psychiatric treatment instead of going to prison. Dana swore this was to get me the medication she knew would come with an admission to the hospital. Once she knew I was in the hospital and could receive my medications, she immediately recanted the information in the coerced NJSP interview. They coerced her to say, "anything and everything she could so they could help me" and now that I was in the hospital, the goal had been reached.

Further evidence of the coercive interview she recanted less than 10 hours later is that she repudiated nearly all her remarks to the NJSP. And while the lead detective -Hanlin- claimed no such phone call occurred, he claimed ignorance when shown the phone records of that fourteen- minute call. Many of the things she told the doctor, as far as my behavioral habits for the previous eighteen months, were speculation just as she informed the doctor; she didn't know one way or the other if I had made any threats. She wasn't privy to my call with the chief. What she did know was from SMS text messages that were significantly impeded by voice to text technical malfunctions. Other text messages in which I was "filling sandbags" and other *Rambo* sarcastic examples were nothing more than satirical humor and hyperbole. SMS text messages are one dimensional and can be interpreted subjectively from one individual to another with varying implications.

As I stated earlier, no one at that office reported a threat to law enforcement or changed anything from normal operations. It was NOT reported immediately, and it wasn't reported the next day. In fact, the congressional staff NEVER reported a threat to anyone. To the contrary, the staff were silent on the issue and I ascribe that to the picture message I received. It was the FBI that was involved from the start of the NJSP investigation. The FBI was listed on the NJSP preliminary reports. The FBI notified Capitol Police who [then] reached out to the congressional staff. Realizing that I was in prison and the FBI had custody of my electronic devices containing the "evidence" I wanted to present to his boss, the chief went along with every request to help frame me. During the evidentiary hearings to decide the admissibility of my mere ownership of firearms, FBI Special Agent was simultaneously texting a staffer. That staffer specifically stated in a text that in no shape, way, or form did I ever threaten him with a firearm. He wasn't even sure how he learned that I owned firearms. In an FBI interview, he inaccurately claimed "maybe an AK" That statement goes back to what Smith stated when he came to my house to confiscate my weapons. Galezniak went as far as to say that when I was handcuffed at my house, I told him there was an AK in my home. No other troopers testified that they heard me say that to them. Just Galezniak. That AK mark kept coming out. And why would I tell a staffer or the NJSP that I owned or possessed a rifle that was never found. No purchase record for one ever existed. The "phantom AK-47" began with Smith. Galezniak claimed I said it to help get a search warrant. Then, somehow, the VA Liaison (a former police office of fourteen years) regurgitates this "phantom AK -47" If the FBI agent can use his cell phone in the courtroom and live-text a witness and [purported] as testimony is happening, something is seriously wrong with that. It exceeds the offense of merely using a cell phone in a courtroom. The FBI agent was trying to elicit statements through text message while I was testifying. I know this because he was forced to turn the text messages over. After the VA liaison denied I ever threatened him with a firearm, he said he wasn't sure how he heard I had an AK-47 and that it might have been the police that told him that piece of information. This is insanity that this is permissible. No wonder our criminal justice system is a joke.

The staffers later submitted emails that the FBI could misrepresent as "threatening" or "offensive". The FBI submitted a third count of threats until full disclosure by a Rule 17c subpoena produced an internal email -specifically about that email in the proposed third count- and literally said "it isn't a threat to go to capitol police with at this time." The USAO was operating like a Marxist Communist prosecutor presenting evidence that was "offensive" to criminalize free speech. In Marxist New Jersey, the odds of a jury pool being offended by that is substantial. Earlier I spoke about the FBI interview on September 26, 2017. Transcripts of that interview corroborate my statements denying threatening anyone, overtly or covertly, and denying any intent. The FBI conducted this interview six days after they first became involved. Why did they wait six days to attempt an interview? It wasn't a weekend or holiday, so why wait those six days? Because they knew that the warden of that decrepit dungeon would sit me in the worst conditions of one of the worst and oldest prisons in the state. In this chapter, I will discuss the 6 days preceding that interview. That prison is under video surveillance and my holding cell in SHU even had a camera in the corner of my cell. When my state lawyer would ask the Special Investigations Unit (SIU) to produce that video or it would be subpoenaed, they simply told him the video of my cell was "not preserved." How convenient. Since I couldn't show anyone, I am now going to tell you about 6 days in hell and the FBI's deliberate torture to "grease the gears" and induce an interview.

After the doctor informed me I was being discharged to prison, I signed for my personal belongings. That signature page made the seventeen-page cut of the government's discovery disclosure. The ride to the prison was uneventful and short. I did not even attempt to engage Spadafora in conversation on that ride. When I was finally released from SHU into general population, I learned that the prison went into a lockdown status prior to my arrival. Before I could be processed, the prison was in danger of a "white supremacist, racist, Trump-supporting terrorist". Once the prison was secured, Spadafora could sign over the custody transfer documents, and I was led out of the lobby to the receiving and discharge (R&D) department of CCP. Spadafora removed my cuffs, but only after one of their guards was there to place their own handcuffs on me. And this began the worst six days of my life.

I will simply refer to my escorting officer as Michael Clarke-Duncan, because I think he might have been bigger than "MCD". I first had to sign a document certifying that I had signed for an inmate handbook and was aware of the rules, rights, regulations, and expectations of the prison. This signature would hold me accountable if I failed to adhere to their rules. It could result in disciplinary action and additional charges. I never received an inmate handbook at CCP, but I was forced to sign that I did. I was not about to get into a pissing contest while MCD was standing next to me. I simply kept my mouth shut and addressed everyone as "sir" & "maam".

Next, I was taken to a room and strip-searched for any contraband. I was given an orange jumper to wear after my clothing items were confiscated and placed in storage. I would not see them again until I was moved out of CCP. I had never been to prison, so I had no idea what to expect. I was led through several, elongated hallways, and into [and out of] an elevator, and arrived in a room that was a makeshift medical department.

The medical department's staff instructed me to sit down. My handcuffs were in the front and not overly tight like the NJSP had deliberately done. Once I sat down, they took my blood pressure and temperature just as four more guards entered the room and filled the hallway outside. Apparently, MCD wasn't enough or (more likely) people were curious to meet this "domestic terrorist" that shut down the entire prison. I was an exhibit at the zoo that resembled Hannibal Lector at that moment. The medical staff did not impede my view of my blood pressure. It was 180/110 with a heartrate of 141 beats per minute. The medical staff were alarmed.

I was given an Ativan and led into and out of the elevator. It continued to go up and I eventually stepped out of the elevator. Notably, when you are a prisoner and use the elevator, you must face the wall at the back of the elevator. I was led to the front of the SHU and stopped outside again. I was stripped and searched again and handed the infamous green "turtle suit". I was given nothing else but a one inch thick "mattress". When I entered the unit, the guards instructed me to change in the closet. There was nothing in it except for a mop bucket and cleaning supplies. MCD squeezed in behind me and closed the door as far as he could. My heart literally stopped in that moment.

"Listen to me. Calm down. You need to relax or you're going to have a stroke or a heart attack." MCD shocked me because I could tell he was genuinely concerned after my visit to medical. I just nod-ded my head.

"Whatever you did or didn't do, it's not the end of the world and you will likely be out of here and back with your family in less than a week" MCD continued, clearly trying to calm me down. I knew what he was saying wasn't true, but I nodded my head in agree-ment. He patted my back with his gigantic hand as I struggled to strap the turtle suit on. The Velcro straps were beyond worn out and no longer held the garment together when warn. I had to hold it on my body while handcuffed and led to my cell. I dropped it many times in that short walk from entrance of the unit to my cell. I was naked for most of that walk. Once I went into my cell, I would stay there for six days in the cell from hell.

The cell was in decay; a silver toilet/sink combo was in the front of the cell opposite the front door. These cells do not have bars but the cell doors are steel with a 10 x 10-inch window. There is interlocking wire in the middle of the panes of glass. The glass is unbreakable, and the wiring resembles the pattern you would see on a chain link fence. The window in the cell was translucent but not transparent. There was a cloudy film on the window to prevent anyone from seeing out-side. It was translucent enough to let daylight in. The camera was in the corner opposite the entry of the door. Technically, I was given a turtle suit… but for all intents and purposes, I was naked. A camera was being monitored by a guard who could be male or female and I had no idea who was watching.

I was not allowed out of my cell one time during my stay in the hell-cell. I was not given a mandatory recreational period required by law. I did not receive a shower during my time there. I did not have toilet paper to wipe with, nor a cup to drink the water that sputtered out of my toilet-sink. I did not have hand-soap and had to eat with the my bare hands which I also wiped excrement from my anus. At night, the lights were turned ON in my cell "for my safety and security". The camera in the cell that was feeding the livestream on a monitor was not enough. The truth is that they use the lights to [deliberately] keep you awake. It is designed to induce sleep depri-vation and exhaust you. The food servings were minimal, and the nutritional content was suspect. I couldn't use a phone to call home like the other inmates in SHU. I had no contact with anyone except my guards when they opened the door and dropped my food tray on the floor. Thursday, September 21ˢᵗ, 2017, was eventful but only day one. Other inmates in the SHU deliberately kicked their cell doors My first contact with another person came in the form of the prison psychiatrist knocking on the door Friday morning after I was given my breakfast.

"Hello…" a voice barely called through the door and knuckles lightly knocked on it. I was sitting on the cold concrete naked with my knees bent facing the ceiling and my arms and head leaned forward into my thighs. I jumped at the sounds emanating a few feet away on the other side of the door.

"Yes…" I hoarsely responded while trying to hold up the broken turtle suit.

"Mr.Brodie?" I now placed a face to the voice. It was an old man with white hair, mid sixties and wearing thin framed eyeglasses.

"Yes" I replied for the second time.

"I'm the psychologist here at the prison. How are you doing?" the old man asked.

"How do I look like I'm doing" I softly replied still raspy because I've gone hours without speaking.

"Well, not good but that's why I am here. I want to place you under the least restrictive environment possible, but I need to know that you promise that you wont hurt yourself." the psychologist continued. Inside, I'm pissed. I was just released from the hospital after being deemed not a threat to self, others, or property, but the prison was now suggesting something contrary. There was no legitimate cause or event from the time of my hospital discharge until my reception at CCP to justify this. What could have possibly changed in that brief period of time? The truth was the government cited the bogus claim of suicide-by-cop [fabrication] that the prison used to put me in the SHU under these horrible conditions. The warden was informed I was being discharged and cleared for any potential threat, yet they claimed I was put back in SHU for my own safety. Thus, the green turtle suit.

"I don't understand. I told the doctor at the hospital I am not a threat to anyone or anything, INCLUDING myself. This is bullshit Why am I in here?" I spoke with less hoarseness as before.

"Well, you have a hearing for bail later this morning to see if you can be released. If you do not get bail, I will make sure that when you come back you will be given a jumper and allowed regular privileges appropriate for this unit. If you improve more, then we can put you in GP (general population).

"Please." I begged.

"I am making my rounds now but before I leave, I will notify the officer to give you a blanket, a book and regular jumper." The psychologist was now assuring me, if not promising me.

"What about toilet paper? What about a spork? I have no soap to wash the shit off of my hands?" I pleaded.

"You were not given anything? The blanket I could understand until I cleared you, but you should have toilet paper and soap. I will remind the officers about that.

"Thank you." I replied and watched as the face in the window moved on to the cell to my left where I heard him knocking on that cell door. Within an hour, a guard was opening my door and tossed and orange jumper inside onto the floor. I was grateful that the psychologist upheld his promise. I was then led off the unit to what I realized would be a bail hearing.

I previously told how the bail hearing went and won't revisit that event. September 22, 2017, was a Friday. It was a video court appearance from the prison so that I didn't have to move through a tunnel to await a judge. The courthouse was connected to the prison, but it was just easier for the lazy guards to move us up and down an elevator while never having to uncuff us whereas utilizing the tunnel would require that extra work. After being denied eligible for bail, I was returned to my cell. I had met with a public defender appointed to me. He was a young, awkward, Indian American. After my hearing, he told me he would be back Monday morning to go over my case, the charges, and a plan moving forward. He didn't show up on Monday.

I was escorted back through the prison to the SHU. When the main door to the unit was buzzed open, I was immediately handed the turtle suit again. I was strip searched again and put back in my cell. There was no blanket, and it became obvious that the psychologist did not uphold his assurances/promises. If he did, the guards didn't get the memo.

It turns out that the psychologist did, in fact, tell the unit officers. It was ignored by the SHU lieutenant and his officers. The intent was not to keep me safe but to make me break. The cell was damp and smelled musty. Water would drip on my head whenever someone used the shower directly above my cell. The water, lack of blanket, and cold cement floor made the night cold. I shivered every night on the green pad that was referred to as a "mattress". I cried because I feared for Geno and Isa. I cried because my current circumstances were a hellish reality that I did not deserve and could do nothing to improve. I cried from a migraine that resulted from the constant banging of inmates kicking on the door which was designed to "buck" the guards. Despite the recent warm daytime temperatures, the nights were quickly becoming colder and my cell window was drafty. It contributed to my shivering and the lights were constantly on at night. Even IF the other inmates weren't screaming obscenities at each other [and the guards], that four foot long light on the wall of my cell inhibited any attempt to get sleep.

I stared at the camera a lot and at the red dot beneath it. I counted the number of blocks in the cinderblock walls. I read the graffiti laden with poor grammar and obscenities. I began to smell. Monday I was taken back to court, but this time through the tunnel. It was another bail hearing that was denied but this time, when the judge asked me if I had any questions, I lashed out at her over my treatment and the conditions I was enduring. I complained about needing my medications. It did nothing to change my circumstances. My lawyer that day was different than Friday and while he told me to shut up, I told him to do his job or that HE should shut up. The same country I served in the Marines and Army now put me in the hell-cell for crimes and reasons that I was innocent of. I went through the same process again when I went back to the SHU. This trip took more time because I had gone through the tunnel to court and not to the first- floor video booth.

Time wasn't something I was able to keep track of in the dungeon. I had little to no sleep, no medication, and when I tried to eat I smelled fecal matter no matter how long I held my hands under water. I was beginning to dehydrate and having diarrhea twenty times per day. My migraine headaches were now exacerbated by a state of dehydration. I could not tell you how long I sat in my cell after my second bail hearing, but eventually an obese woman in nursing scrubs starting to bang on my door. At first, I thought it was the inmate next door kicking his door again, but it wasn't. He was sleeping during the day and kicking his door only at night.

"Hey! Hellooooo! You!" a face looked at me through the door pounding with what sounded like a closed fist. It sounded more like a thud than a knock from knuckles.

"Yeah" I mumbled as I stood up and stepped to the door. I was desperately holding my defective turtle suit over me. The face that stared at me reminded me of the mother of the villains in *Goonies* who was also in *Throw Mama From A Train*. For the life of me, I couldn't remember her name.

"You Brodie?" the voice was sharp and clearly unpleasant.

"Yes" I replied waiting for what was next. I was praying it wouldn't be anything loud or obnoxious that would further worsen my headache.

"I'm here because you went into court today and did a lot of complaining telling the judge we're abusing you! How are we abusing you?" the ogre-like face yelled through the cell door window.

"I didn't say that" I replied

"Yes...YOU DID!" she was yelling now.

"Were you there? No, I don't think so." It was obvious I wasn't getting a reprieve from my headache and this woman, despite her nurses clothing, would've likely enjoyed knowing she was bringing me pain through this encounter.

"So how are we abusing you?" the voice asked me.

"I need my medications, soap, a shower…the psychologist was here Friday morning and told me my restrictions would be lifted and I could get these." I replied angrily.

"I can't help you with any of that. That's not my responsibilities. As far as your medicine, you were told that we didn't have that here and would have to order out for it." This woman was really taking this personally and letting me have it.

"No…I wasn't told that." I replied with more hostility.

"Yes…YOU WERE!" the woman insisted.

"Were you there? Again? NO." I replied dismissing her hearsay claims.

"You will get your medications as soon as we get it in. Stop spreading lies. Your situation can get much worse." The woman was now threatening me through the door in a voice loud enough that I'm sure the camera in my cell caught all of this…if it had audio.

"Yeah, I'm sure I will" I replied walking away and sitting down on the floor. The medicine never came that day. It didn't come in the afternoon medication dispersals, nor in the evening. I wasn't suicidal before I got in there, but my overall condition was failing -physically and mentally- to a point where death would've been welcomed. I couldn't quit though; besides, I had an earful waiting for my lawyer who no-showed.

I didn't sleep Monday night and had now been in my cell for five days. Tuesday's breakfast was followed by the first dispersal of my PTSD medication. I was told they couldn't get my seizure medication. It was not allowed in the facility because the warden said it was abused by inmates. Lunch came hours later. The guard came back to my cell a few minutes after dropping my Styrofoam tray on the floor just inside my door. I wasn't eating but I figured it was not enough time to eat it if I could have done so.

"Go stand over there and face the wall. Put your hands on the wall." The guard barked while pointing at the wall in between the window on the left of my cell and the security camera hanging in the right, back corner. I followed the instructions without a reply. Long gone were the "sir's" and "maam's". They were replaced with a broken silence.

The guard entered my cell and patted me down. I didn't even bother with the turtle suit and still this rocket scientist needed to pat down my naked body. He told me to put my hands behind my back and handcuffed me. He instructed me NOT to turn around until he said so, which I quickly observed, was to allow him to back out of my cell.

"Turn around" the guard barked. I turned around and a middle-aged black man was standing there in a black suit.

"Where are his clothes?" the man asked the guard.

"He has a turtle suit, but the Velcro is shot." The guard replied pointing to my turtle suit laying on the center of my cell floor. It was right at the base of my sleeping mat which was wet from the morning showers on the floor above me. The cell smelled of mold and mildew and the paint and plaster on the ceiling was peeled downward. It was stained black and yellow.

"You! Come here." The man in the suit spoke with authority. I stepped forward and opened my mouth to speak an acknowledgement, but my attempt to speak failed.

"Have you had enough of this? Do you want it to stop?" the man asked me. I just nodded my head yes while staring at the ground and nodding my head. Today was going to be day 6 but I didn't think I could take anymore.

"I am the only person who can help you get out of here. Not my officers and certainly not the psychologist, do you understand what I am saying?" the suit sternly spoke to me to demonstrate that HE was the ultimate source of power in the prison. I imagined this was the warden even though he never introduced himself. In retrospect, I think it was deliberate because that camera would identify him as a person who is using intimidation to coerce an inmate. I also believe that he spoke softly to avoid any audio recording on the camera. Perhaps he was just trying to show me what a "badass" he was? I stopped caring.

"Now…here's your options. Option A, you put a jumper on, and you and I take a walk upstairs. There are some people here who want to talk to you. If you agree to do this, I will make sure that within an hour of you returning here, that you will be released and put into general population. Option B, you can continue to sit here without any idea of when you will go to GP" the suit's voice sliced through the air and cut my soul. This was it; after six days…I was broken. I simply nodded my head in agreement.

My cell door stayed open while the officer went and retrieved an orange jumper. They removed my handcuffs freely now and told me to put it on. I was then handcuffed again, but in the front this time. The warden said "shackles" and the guard returned with ankle cuffs that had longer chains. They locked them shut and I was shuffled out of my cell by the guard. When I arrived at the front door of the unit by the guards station, the suit took my arm, firmly grabbing my bicep to the extent that ensured bruising.

The warden (suit) escorted me down the hallway to an elevator. I had to stand with my face up against the wall opposite of the elevator while waiting for the door to open. I heard the doors shuffle open and received the command to step back and turn around. I was marched right into the elevator until my face was pressed up against the wall. The ride was short, likely one story up. I was taken down the hallway in the same direction I had departed from on the lower floor. I was led into a room where two more suits were waiting for me. A white guy whose face was flushed bright red. Clearly, this guy had high blood pressure and it was likely from drinking. Some of the worst alcoholics are bureaucrats and cops. The white guy was sitting on a chair at a table pressed up against the wall. There was a chair next to it which I was instructed to sit in. Unbeknownst to me, a hidden camera was opposite me where the wall met the ceiling and was secretly recording this. The man in the suit is visible in the video escorting me to this chair. Once I was in it, I observed the other man sitting five feet to my left. He was a large black man in a suit. I figured he was a cop who liked donuts because he had a pot belly that was doing a number on his dress shirt, tie, and belt. What came next was my FBI interview in which I denied making any overt, implicit, or intended threats. Regardless, the fact that I participated in this was enough for the USAO to characterize it as a "confession."

"Do you know who we are?" the white guy asked.

"Secret Service?" I replied. I knew they had to be feds and based on what trooper Torres said I knew the feds were investigating.

"No." the white guy replied tapping a blue binder with his fountain pen. He then flipped it over to show me the FBI logo. Maybe it was the DOJ, but I couldn't see for sure.

"I am special agent Furey. I'm with the FBI and this is Capitol police officer Garreth Stith." Furey continued. He then proceeded to give me his background and told me he was assigned to bank robberies but had picked this case up. Immediately, I was concerned. I love reading John Grisham and Harlan Coben, so I wasn't sure which author wrote it, but I remember the Northfield FBI office near Atlantic City being depicted as unbelievably corrupt. I googled it after reading that and, sure enough, there were pages of comments from various forums discussing how the federal agents there were worse than the mafia they had been trying to run out of Atlantic City casinos. I could understand the Capitol Police, but Furey creeped me out and his presence felt wrong. My gut told me this was a very, VERY corrupt guy.

"We want to ask you some questions, but we need you to read this and sign it in order for us to do so" Furey continued sliding a Miranda waiver to not have counsel present. At this point, my lawyer was unknown and absentee. I knew the feds were involved from the night at the hospital. Me invoking my rights on the 22nd in Superior Court SHOULD have been enough to make this interview improper and inadmissible in federal proceedings. I had no intention of lying or making a false confession. The warden told me all I had to do was meet and agree to talk to these guys to get out of my dungeon's cell. The warden didn't tell me that I needed to confess, and I had no intention of doing so. I don't think the warden would ever ask that on camera either.

I read the waiver, signed it, and slid it back across. I wanted to tell them what was really going on. I could tell them about the conversation I had with the VA liaison in which he told me, in not so many words, that he believed funds were being embezzled somewhere in the VA and that it was the source of 17,000 veterans -including myself- getting collection notices for unpaid Choice appointments. I also wanted to tell him about the text messages and conversation I had with trooper Smith…about the fliers on my property and Smith's response to that. I first wanted to tell him the real reason I thought I was arrested, and that was because I told the chief of staff about the picture I received from "Mike FR in Mays Landing". I described the picture as someone holding their erect penis. I wouldn't tell him that I knew for certain it was the VA liaison who had been hitting on me on the phone after I met him months earlier at the VA clinic. But, I would tell him that I told the chief of staff that before our call ended.

"You sent an email the other day. I want to show you it to verify that you sent this email" Furey said as he slid another piece of paper across the desk. I took the paper and looked at it. It was the email sent to the chief of staff forwarding an email from June where I supplied information and a news story link of the democrat operative in New Jersey instructing radicals how to #huntrepublicancongressmen. I took the paper and nodded.

"I need you to initial this right here as proof that I showed this to you." Furey added, tapping the bottom corner of the page. I took the paper back and signed my three initials in the bottom corner. That was a huge mistake because the government would now argue that I had signed it as a confession. I was only asked to sign it to acknowledge that Furey had shown it to me, not to "confess".

The questioning began about the phone call before and I could tell that these men were only interesting in talking about "threats". I had to quickly pull the stop on this and hit the brakes if I was going to tell them about everything.

"I need to know…if I say something here and tell you something here, will it stay here? It won't get shared with anyone out there? I stopped Furey's attempt to ask about "threats".

"We are not here to talk about any 'secrets' you might have or want to talk about, we are only here to talk about the threats you made." Furey immediately cut me off. I knew that they were going to control how this interview went and any attempt to discuss the truth from my perspective (which I could prove with evidence in my phone) would be immediately denied and shot down. I was fucked but I would not confess.

Both of the feds asked me about the phone call with the chief of staff five or six times. They presented the same questions about my intent or "threats" with different delivery, but it was the same question that I answered consistently. "No, I didn't threaten anyone. No, I did not intend to threaten anyone or carry out any threat, let alone leave my home and go to the congressional office." When I was asked about how the phone call ended, I recalled it in detail and said,

"and then I said what I said."

I meant what I said about the dick pic, going public with it, but nothing that I could (or would be allowed) to talk about openly in this interview. The FBI, Capitol Police and USAO would say that I confessed because of that statement. It was not a confession but, because the chief of staff was now lying saying that I ended the call as a threat, that was what they were going to go with. The interview ended with the same [specific] answers of denying "making any threat, intent to convey a threat, or carry out a threat". It didn't matter; the feds had enough to make a federal case of it, at least in their minds. They were right because I would not get a fair trial with the judge assigned to this case.

I left that interview with a greater sense of frustration than when I entered. After all I had endured, that spoke volumes. I was discouraged that no one would be open to listening to me and that the gears in the system were already moving in one direction, which was to convict me for a crime I didn't commit. The FBI would later claim that they were unable to "crack into" my cell phone, but I doubt that. In my phone, the remaining SMS text messages between me and trooper Smith included the names of the Chief of Police and Captain of a police department whom I relayed tips to regarding issues in the community. The messages gave the exact name and department for him to reach out to verify my credibility. Incredibly, these interactions and a high volume of emails between myself and these two individuals would be subject to tampering and an inexplicable failure to comply with a FOIA request. I never would have known this, but the FBI would submit documents from these 2015 reports to show that I was "uncooperative" and hostile to those police officers. They showed the report narratives to the judge who cited this as a "pattern of behavior" toward law enforcement. I had not seen these reports and desperately wanted to because in these reports I was either a victim of a hate or bias crime (wearing my kippah in public or Dana being threatened while walking our dog) or was listed as the reporting person. I was always sure to get copies of these reports and told my lawyer that we could demonstrate this was not true.

My absentee lawyer could care less about viewing what I had to counter these reports. When I finally received these reports from 2015 which were being cited in May of 2018, I noticed that the reports had a new section titled "New Narrative added" and it was dated 30 April of 2018. It further read to "See supplement" or "See addendum" but those were not provided. I had zero contact with those officers and moved to Dover, Delaware in early 2016 to prepare my work with the Trump Presidential Campaign. Why, in ALL instances 27-30 months later, would these reports need to be updated with "New Narratives"? Where were the voluminous emails directly between me and the chief? The captain? They were gone and never provided. But some of those emails I sent to them I had blind-copied -Bcc: - Dana on, so she would know that I had reported the harassment she had endured. She produced the emails to my lawyer who barely looked at them. Clearly, the FBI was not disclosing everything they received from that police department. The were only providing "updated reports" with "New Narratives" added years later…and, coincidentally, a month after the feds indicted me? So, at this point, I realized that the local police, state police, and federal law enforcement were all working in tandem to portray me as negative (and inaccurately) as possible. My lawyer would do nothing to question it.

Dana is the person who submitted a FOIA request to the local police department asking for all official records. She had copies of the emails that I sent to the Chief and Captain at their official pd.com email addresses. The request took longer than it should have, but the emails were never included. The emails would have undermined the "New Narratives" listing me and Dana as uncooperative & hostile when we were really the victims of hate/bias crimes of which we reached out to police. Those officers couldn't have cared less about the targeting of Jews. I realized that there is some element of neo-Nazi antisemitism in ALL levels of law enforcement in New Jersey. I would later submit an evidentiary exhibit in my civil action to overturn my conviction of the FOIA request, incomplete response, and the emails that revealed something much different than those "New Narratives." What could be the catalyst for updating reports two and half years old, without any contact, if it wasn't the FBI calling in a "cop favor". That police department has had its own issues relating to police misconduct, excessive force, and civil rights violations. I submitted an appeal to the state's attorney general citing a failure to disclose those official emails but never received a response. A recorded interview I gave after Dana and I were victims of an anti-Semitic attack also disappeared, but we had emails referencing it. I believe this HAD to disappear because the NJSP and feds were presenting me as a Trump-loving white supremacist in their press releases for months before my actual indictment. Simply stated, you can't report a guy as a neo-Nazi when there exists evidence of him being Jewish and a victim of antisemitic hate crimes in the same state two years earlier. That would nullify the bias the feds and USAO were publicly trying to create. It was designed to taint any jury pool. I just couldn't make this story up and, because it sounds so outrageous, it's why I am sharing it with you. If you ever doubt [anything] I am claiming, simply refer to the dozens of evidentiary supplements made after my conviction illuminating these instances of misconduct, perjury, and obstruction of justice by law enforcement.

After the interview, the Warden being true to his word, let me out of my dungeon in SHU. I didn't have to exchange my jumper for the turtle suit. I could stay in my jumper and within an hour I was "dropping" from SHU to general population. I would finally get to use the phones and call Dana. When I did, she told me what she had done and why. She was angry because the police made innuendo that I had been cheating on her the whole time we were together. The FBI and NJSP told Dana they found evidence in my phone that I was cheating on her throughout our entire relationship. She told me about her interactions with the NJSP and the feds. They told us different versions of their intent and lied [repeatedly] to us both. They knew from our text messages that Dana was a very jealous person. They played that against me via eluding to evidence that would be shown at trial. They visited Dana on Valentine's Day after my arrest and told her I was cheating on her. Furey told Dana that he had been in my phone and saw text messages going back years. The FBI told her to talk me out of going to trial or that the messages of me texting other girls while Dana and I were engaged would be presented in evidence and humiliate her.

This was impossible and I'll explain why. The phone they had seized was one that I had only had for 15 months prior to my arrest. We were broken up, living in separate states, and there could not possibly have been any evidence of such on that phone "dating years back" because the phones history [itself] didn't date back that far. This is a tried, tested, and effective technique the feds use to flip spouses, girlfriends, and significant others.

Legally speaking, the feds had claimed that the NJSP were withholding my cell phone from the feds in some type of jurisdictional pissing contest for [months] after my arrest. And according to the USAO, once the FBI had the phone, they were "unable to crack into" my phones. This was used as justification to explain why they were not complying with the July 2018 court order to turn it over for impeachment and exculpatory evidence. The USAO claimed that the FBI had sent it to "so many different experts" to try to get into it that "they had lost track of its actual location". I'm not joking, that is literally in the transcripts. So, either Furey was lying about being in my phone, or they were withholding it for as long as possible to prevent the independent expert we hired from detecting their unlawful access and obstruction of any evidence valuable for my defense. The NJSP never obtained (nor sought) a search warrant to go into my cell phone. The FBI did not receive their warrant to search it until after my indictment.

This is some dirty shit that our government does in the name of justice. My judge couldn't have cared less; he was not a defense attorney before being judge and a pattern of open hostility and anger for any attempt to testify or obtain evidence for my defense was met with chastisement in the courtroom. I can't tell you if everything done in my case was on the level, but I sincerely believe that there is enough evidence that illegal behaviors were done in numerous instances. I believe it was supported by hard, material evidence- my constitutional rights were denied [or nullified] by the judge. Was it some sense of "the ends justify the means"? Probably. I think a lot of it reflects the "win at any cost" attitude of the federal government. The USAO's job is to seek justice…NOT convictions.

Dana would later tell me that she watched my FBI interview in horror. She could tell I was broken and unmedicated. She would watch the DVD of that interview on her tv. Isa and Geno were living with her and the two other pugs (Axl Rose & Vin Diesel). Dana explained that whenever she watched it, the pugs would hear my voice and immediately run to the TV and bark. She watched it so many times, that there were more-than-a-few instances in which she watched the motion picture *Shooter* with Mark Wahlberg with "pug-fits". In the ending, when Mark Wahlberg's character is led into court wearing an orange jumper played, it would cause my pugs to go ape-shit at the television… barking and whining, Isa took it the worst. She was only 8 months old when the NJSP took me from her. Isa was the sweetest pug as a puppy, but she was certainly traumatized. To this day, any time Isa hears someone approaching my home, or sees them outside my home, she is incredibly aggressive in posturing her defense of me and our home. Isa thinks that anyone who comes near our house poses a threat to "take her daddy away from her". Isa is my emotional support dog for my combat PTSD, yet she has been traumatized by corrupt cops. Dana and I still talk about it to this day; Dana agrees with my assessment, but says that when she first arrived at my home after leaving the Port Norris station on the night of my arrest, that my house had been trashed by the NJSP. The house had been vandalized in an apparent search and there was broken glass and furniture everywhere. The NJSP left no stone unturned in executing their search. I can imagine my two small pugs shaking in fear as these tyrants took their father and then destroyed their home. What is most disturbing is that Dana encountered that scene at all. Let me explain.

When Dana left the Port Norris station to retrieve the pugs and take them home with her, it was after her NJSP [coerced] interview that ended around 8:30 p.m. on September 20, 2017. She left after seeing me and went straight to my house less than two miles away. The travel time between the station and my home was minimal. The NJSP did NOT have a search warrant signed until 9:05 P.M. The search warrant return shows it was not executed until 9:20 P.M. That was the first [and only] time detective Hanlin was ever at my home. The CAD Abstract demonstrates he was NOT at the scene during my arrest, yet he testified he was present. Hanlin also made outrageous claims of statements I [purportedly] made that no other trooper heard. Hanlin had demonstrably perjured himself in federal court. This was designed to conceal the presence of the off-duty detective of station A-90, who [was] present and who I invoked Miranda to. Quite simply, the NJSP testified to replace the off-duty detective with detective Hanlin as being at the scene, but the Guzman CAD Abstract refuted that claim. Regardless, It was clear to Dana that the police had destroyed my home. But…she was there before the search warrant was endorsed by the New Jersey judge. How does anyone reconcile that? Not only was the time of the search warrant inexplicably illegal, but Section 5.b-"Probable Cause" of the affidavit submitted by detective Hanlin was deliberately loaded with countless prevarications. Hanlin lied about who was present, what happened, how long they were at my home, what -if anything- I said to the NJSP.

The NJSP could not get their stories straight no matter how much the FBI tried to coach them in their testimony during pre-trial evidentiary hearings. Nothing could help them because their versions were still untrue. The truth is consistent and never changes, such as my subpoenaed phone, fax and federal medical records that are material, corroborating evidence. That same evidence (should have) nullified the NJSP' testimony individually AND collectively to such a vast, criminal extent that a referral for charges of perjury should've ensued. But not in my case. Not in my judge's courtroom. During my trial, I told the jury, while looking at each of them in their eyes, that I was being "railroaded" and repeated my denials of making any threats.

The trial jury DID see the inappropriate, unlawful, and constitutionally inadmissible FBI interview. The government submitted a pre-trial motion to "edit" the interview so as not to reveal anything about my interactions with the state police. The USAO claimed it would cause prejudice against me in my state prosecution. That was bullshit; the USAO [literally] wanted to edit-out anything that would raise questions about the events after my arrest. This is crucial for determining intent and any actions take to carry it out. In reality, I wasn't allowed to talk about anything related to the state case: I couldn't talk about how I fought for a call to my lawyer, how I was mirandized, how I was read my charges and questioned by a trooper in the emergency room of the hospital in the presence of the attending physician. I couldn't mention how the NJSP initially charged me with a duplicate crime to the federal government. If I did, then the jury might realize that my invocation for legal counsel would have applied to both cases, state and federal, and the interview would be seen for what it was…an unlawful, horrific crime of an interview obtained illegally in violation of multiple constitutional protections and that the interview was induced through psychological and physical torture. My judge was adamant about me not testifying about ANYTHING related to the state or NJSP and warned me several times about it.

The government submitted motions regarding 404(b) evidence stating their intent to release character assassination evidence if I violated any of their terms. 404(b) evidence is unrelated evidence that is designed to inflame a jury against a defendant. Whether or not it is relevant to the charged crimes is irrelevant. It is about making the jury hate the defendant to an extent that they will hate him. The government made many threats to introduce their "evidence"; including their threat to release op-ed editorials I had written in various newspapers. The USAO deemed they were "threatening" and existed as a history of making threats. No joke. I countered that when Dana acquired a copy of the "rules for submission" policy with those newspapers. The newspapers refused to print anything that mentioned a politician or public official by name or that included "threats". As such, it would NOT be printed in their newspapers. The fact that my op-eds were printed, meant it was understood by the editor that they were not threatening. Does that matter to the USAO? Will a federal judge check them on that? Essentially, they were trying to criminalize free speech and my First Amendment right as a citizen journalist, of which I was acting as a freelance, contributing member.

As I write this, I am watching indictment after indictment be handed down against President Trump. Just recently, I saw the prosecutor file a Motion to silence our former president's speech which he deemed "threatening". In my situation, the Supreme Court decided the parameters establishing what constitutes a "true threat" in Watts v. United States (1965). If the same constitutional standard was applied to my case, I never would have spent years in prison for a crime that I didn't commit. The problem is our federal judges serve for life and become corrupted by the swamp in Washington D.C. Judges today couldn't care less about precedent or what the Supreme Court rules. They all suffer from enormous egos and "G-d Complexes". Our founding fathers warned us of the type of people who wanted to serve endlessly in public service without term limits. Public service meant to them that they would sacrifice time otherwise spend earning a more profitable living than what they would make serving the public. Their biggest mistake was never including term limits on government employees.

In contemporary society we see politicians who serve for decades in office and become unjustifiably wealthy. Their power is absolute and the corruption that buys them perpetuates it. Don't think that judges are not political or influenced by material wealth. They all value their status in society with the other "elitists" in Washington, D.C. To this point, Supreme Court Justice Ruth Bader-Ginsburg opined "judges can be tyrants too". And if there is one lesson I want you to take out of my story its that the elites always look out for AND protect their own...regardless of their political affiliation or ideologies. Our contemporary American society is in danger. We are being subjugated by term-limitless tyrants in every aspect of government and in our daily lives. Our constitutional freedoms are being undermined by these term-limitless tyrants. I fear that this will not end well. If history has taught us anything, it's that all empires of tyranny end badly. They collapse from within, and from a state of decadence and moral decay. As an observant Jew, I firmly believe that the Creator is, first and foremost, a G-d of Justice. Adonai Elohim Tzva'ot. Nothing is eviler in His eyes than deliberately subverting justice. And nothing angers the Creator more than those who do so. It is not my place to take vigilante revenge, nor was it ever my "intent" to do so for crimes perceived or real. My "revenge" is exposing these events in this book. Vengeance is His, not mine and I accept that completely. What happens in this life echoes throughout eternity. I believe that these things will be made right, if not here, then on another plane of existence. I believe that no senses of "justice" I could ever exact would come close to the Divine Justice that awaits them… in this life or the next. I find comfort in telling my story and knowing that their fate still awaits them. Divine Justice, unlike our own, will always prevail.

AFTERTHOUGHT

As I am writing this, Isa is sitting next to me on my sectional sofa and Geno is on the cushion behind me, sitting on my right shoulder. Last month, Geno -who is now 10 and a half- had a kidney and his spleen removed. Geno developed a rare kidney cancer that metastasized and spread to his spleen. Two days ago, I went to meet his oncologist near Philadelphia. Dana met me there with Vin Diesel -our brindle pug- who's been with Geno since he was 8 weeks old. He's now eight and a half years old himself. Dana and I have since separated, and I moved to northeast Pennsylvania where I finally bought a home with my VA home loan. Geno's sister, Isa, also went with us to his oncology appointment for "moral support". The prognosis was not what we expected.

Geno started Palladia yesterday; it's a chemo drug that blocks cells from receiving cancer cell messages since the spread has already begun. We thought that because it was all removed it was gone, but that is not the case. Palladia is more of an attempt to slow down the cancer from reappearing. We were told it will likely go to his liver or lungs, although a biopsy of his liver obtained during his surgery was negative. This appointment was a month after his surgery. He wasn't given pain medication except for his post-surgery fentanyl patch which fell off after 5 days. Geno was enduring this with no symptoms except some weight gain which I thought was just old age. I was wrong.

The First Step Act, and my programming in the FBOP, resulted in me getting a release date in January of 2022. Because the DOJ dragged their feet implementing the final rule, I sued the FBOP in the Southern District of New York (SDNY). My case was 22-cv-3821-

LGS. The judge ruled in my favor that the FBOP needed to give me full time credits and that the final rule was implemented so every person that came after my lawsuit who was awaiting credits would now receive them. The judge gave the government 2 weeks to update credits and implement a real-time system for calculating FSA time credits. The USAO in SDNY asked for a week extension, but the end result was the same. The case was decided in my favor in November 2022. Forbes Magazine did a story in mid-November about my case. Forbes reached out to Dana because I listed her name as a plaintiff. By doing so, I had the documents sent to her home in New Jersey with her home phone listed as the number to call. Forbes contacted Dana after the article was printed trying to ascertain if she was my lawyer. Dana informed them that I had represented myself and filed my motions all by myself. I took on the FBOP and DOJ and spanked them in a Manhattan courtroom before the senior judge. Walter Pavlo wrote the story for Forbes on November 14th, 2022.

After years of being fucked over and fucked with by the DOJ, I got the last laugh. In my final "fuck you", I helped ensure tens of thousands of eligible inmates received their real-time FSA time credits. These inmates were low recidivism, low security individuals who probably should never have been in federal prison to begin with. They weren't chomos or murderers. The FSA was long overdue; it was (nearly) unanimously supported by both parties in congress and signed into law by President Trump in December of 2018.

I had been placed in an RRC beginning June 1st 2022. I didn't begin house arrest July 11th, 2022. This was because the FBOP and DOJ were stonewalling the will of the people through their efforts to reject the FSA. My civil suit ensured that eligible inmates would receive more time in RRC's and home confinement than what the DOJ would otherwise give them. I was on house arrest for only a few weeks after I received Judge Lorna G Schneider's decision. I was discharged completely on December 20th 2022. I bought my home and moved to Pennsylvania with Geno and Isa in mid-March of 2023. Dana and I remain very close, and she pushed me to tell my story as she lived it with me. She was always supportive and there for me throughout this entire ordeal. She has witnessed what I've written and more; I plan to write -at least- two more books about my experience in the FBOP and what I've seen. Change is needed in this system and the people cannot push for reform and change if they don't know about the issues. I will share my experience in great detail in my upcoming books. I meticulously journaled, wrote letters, and saved reports, administrative complaints I filed of the abuse that I endured and witnessed from the correctional officers (CO). As I said with this book, I will be able to prove what I allege and will -more than happily- sit down for a polygraph. I don't need to lie or exaggerate my experiences…they are bad enough told as they truly happened.

I have not received justice and my judge has done everything to stop me from elevating what happened in his courtroom to the higher courts. I will never get justice if he presides over the case. Am I bitter? Sure. Am I angry? Not so much anymore. My eight year relationship with Dana was completely destroyed. Our family split up and we live hours away from each other now. We still have pug visits and spend days together binge watching our favorite television programs. Prison was especially hard for me during COVID with combat PTSD. When I came back home, I was ever more damaged than before. I was not a good person to be in a relationship with because I couldn't be comfortable in my own skin. I go to therapy regularly and when I tell people my story, they don't believe me until I pull up a few choice exhibits that I submitted in federal court showing the misconduct of the tyrants who were involved in my case. And make no mistake, that's what they are…tyrants.

I lost 4 + years (sentenced originally to 87 months) of my life. Sitting here seeing Geno try to reposition himself and get comfortable because of the pain he is in makes me really angry. Isa does not trust strangers and barks at anyone who passes the large bow window in the front of my house. Isa was traumatized by the NJSP and the whole ordeal. I cannot begin to explain the bond that is shared between a veteran and their service dog. I know that, with good luck, Geno and I have about 6-12 months left together. Those tyrants took 4 years from me with him. For pugs, that's a lot. Isa is 6, almost 7, and I have repaired the bond we had before I was taken from her.

Geno has been like a father to her more than her brother, but its safe to say that he is her protector. She senses something is wrong with him and is fiercely protective of him with any human or when the other pugs visit. Dana rescued a pug puppy from China (the meat markets) and he's a joyous bundle of pug-puppy energy. She named him Bronx. Bronx loves "Grandpa Geno" and knows that Auntie Isa does NOT like to play pug-puppy games.

Also, at the time of this writing, the United States Army has finally corrected my discharge from 2003. Twenty years later. The United States Army unlawfully, and in violation of multiple army regulations, denied me a medical evaluation board for PTSD and traumatic brain injury to discharge me without any benefits. I am waiting for the check in the mail. I guess later is better than never. I only became interested in it when the USAO attacked my military service because of that discharge. That woman (the AUSA) is one of the most evil, vicious liars I have ever met. Her interactions with the judge in front of courtroom observers caused whispers outside the courtroom. I made a point to correct my retirement status with the Army after what she did and how she misrepresented my service. She even used the cover of *Soldiers* magazine against me. The war in Iraq began March 20, 2003; the magazine was a monthly periodical of which I appeared on the cover for the April 2003 Iraq War issue. The AUSA was allowed to use it, and show it to the jury, where she described me as" Rambo" and "a highly trained combat killer trained to kill with his own hands". That woman has no respect for veterans and knows nothing about what it truly means to serve and protect the constitution of The United States of America. She has never shed blood, sweat, or tears in defense of it. Instead, she extorts people into plea agreements in a heavily flawed system that favors her extortions. She destroys people's lives, families, and has no moral compass. That is not the type of person we want representing the interests of "*We The People*" in federal court. The AUSA and her partner should be disbarred and imprisoned. They are truly sick, evil people.

As previously mentioned, I plan on writing at least two more books. I started a book on my time in Iraq in 2003 as a machine gunner in the infantry and Arabic interpreter. I have to write the book about what goes on in the FBOP. *In The Belly of The Beast* should be released within six months to a year. Writing is therapeutic for me, and I truly enjoy it. I once had a photographic memory that I inherited from my father but now know that the cognitive impairments from my brain injury have forced me to keep meticulous notes of everything…and I do. I regret not completing my dissertation for my doctorate but was honored to receive the honorary Ph.D. in Ukraine before the war started. I truly loved Ukraine and treasure my memories from there. I have reconnected with my daughter, now eighteen, who wants to go into the military. I am horrified at it and in my sentencing allocution in 2019, I begged and pleaded for parents not to let their children serve, "Learn from my case" I said. Listen to my story and send them to technical schools.

Although I started writing my book on Iraq two decades ago, this will be my first book to be published. Writing is a learning process in which we evolve so I hope that you enjoyed what I have written and will continue to read what I write about. By doing so, it's my hope that you will see my evolution, growth and development as a writer. I have already mentioned people who mattered and supported me through my ordeal. Many of my "friends" [and family] never wrote me a letter to ask how I was, or what happened to me. They are "fair weather friends" whom I hope read this book and learn the story it tells. It can happen to you, the reader. We have a serious problem with our department of injustice. Currently, I see former president Trump being indicted relentlessly and I recognize this for what it is: Lawfare. When Trump says that this can happen to anyone and he is standing in the way, there is some truth to that. While I am a completely apolitical person now, I know that you either love or hate Trump. The haters who support these political prosecutions and persecutions against the leading opposition candidate in our next presidential election should take a lesson from history. Know that if they do it to him now, they can do it to you later. The party in charge today might not be the party in charge next year. It sets a dangerous precedent and America is going into unchartered waters.

I think it would be fair for me to be a mean, angry, and bitter war veteran (I recently turned 44) who hates the United States of

America. My time in prison has turned my hair white and grey. My beard, if grown in, is completely white. I look 10-12 years older than I really am because of the toll this has had on me. I have nothing but contempt, disgust, distrust for, and despise the federal government of the United States of America. BUT…I love my country and I love the diverse groups and segments in America. I have traveled across our beautiful country in a car with my pugs and have seen much of it. I say that literally and metaphorically. 'We the people' need to heed the warnings. I have been writing about term limits for nearly two decades now. Executives have term limits but not the people who write the laws? Are you kidding me? The true power lies with those who control what laws are written and passed. They [literally] decide what is legal and illegal. We can't depend on the higher court's justices to overturn unconstitutional laws. If needed, they can overturn a presidential veto, don't forget that. That's where the power is, and you should also heed the warning of our founding fathers who warned of those who make careers out of public service in elected offices and others. Term limits are something I hear more frequently since being released from prison. I don't see two parties bickering with each other. I see [only] one group of entrenched elites that use the media to turn the American people against one another. Its all misdirection to keep our attention away from the real issues. I started out as a democrat, then became a libertarian, followed that as a republican and now… I am nothing. I've learned a lot but have no desire to be involved in politics. I don't have to deal with the VA anymore. The current administration struck a deal with the federal employee union that represents former VA employees who were fired for misconduct. The administration has brought them back to work in the VA. The choice program has been gutted and destroyed by it also.

I want nothing from the government other than to be left alone. But until it changes, I will keep exposing injustice while suggesting ideas how to correct the root causes. But otherwise, my plan is to fade away into nothingness.

PETITIONER'S EXHIBIT A

REFUTATION OF GOVERNMENT's RESPONSE IN OPPOSITION TO THE PETITIONER's MOTION TO VACATE, SET ASIDE, OR AMEND UNDER SECTION2255

**PROSECUTORIAL MISCONDUCT
&
OBSTRUCTION OF JUSTICE BY THE NJSP**

- **SUBORNATION OF PERJURY OF NJSP BY THE USAO**
- **EVIDENTIARY TAMPERING BY THE USAO, NJSP**
- **PERJURY, NJSP**
- **OBSTRUCTION OF JUSTICE BY THE NJSP, FALSIFYING AN AFFIDAVIT UNDER PROBABLE CAUSE SECTION 5.b FOR A SEARCH WARRANT**

New Jersey State Police

September 20, 2017
IR: A100-2017-00694
7188 Ackley Road, Millville, NJ

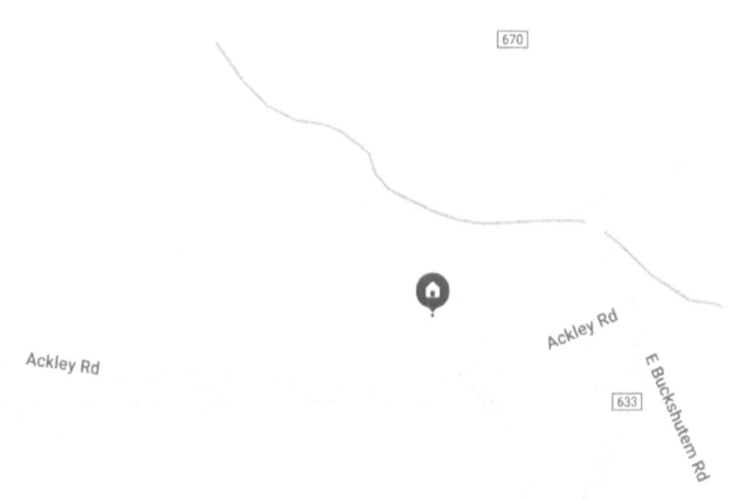

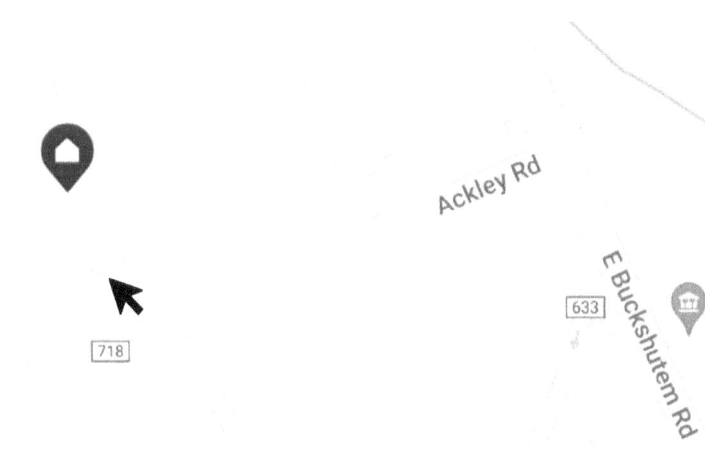

Ackley Rd
E Buckshutem Rd
718
633

NJSP TESTIFIED THERE IS AN ESTIMATED 500 FT OF DRIVEWAY
NOT 1 MARKED NJSP CAR PARKED IN 7188 ACKLEY's DRIVEWAY
DASHCAM RECORDING WAS IMPOSSIBLE
NJSP CARS ARE DELIBERATELY PARKED PERPENDICULAR i.e.,
-"ON SHOULDERS"- OF NJ 718/ACKLEY ROAD

Case 1:20-cv-12713-NLH Document 48-1 Filed 08/21/22 Page 8 of 118 PageID: 776
NJSP PARK ON SHOULDERS FACING AWAY FROM THE RESIDENCE TO PREVENT
RECORDING THE ENCOUNTER WITH THEIR DASHCAMS IN THE ABSENCE OF BODY
CAMERAS AS MANDATED BY A 2014 NJ STATE LAW

THIS WAS <u>NOT</u> A CRITICISM REGARDING THE "PARKING HABITS" OF THE NJSP...

...BUT RATHER THEIR DELIBERATE ATTEMPT TO AVOID ACCOUNTABILITY

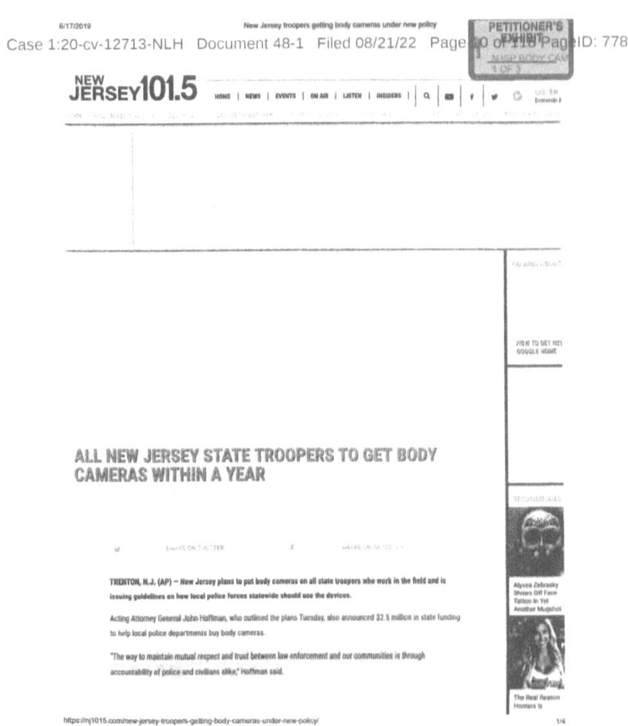

New Jersey troopers getting body cameras under new policy

Case 1:20-cv-12713-NLH   Document 48-1   Filed 08/21/22   Page 10 of 110   PageID: 778

JOSEPH BRODIE

ALL NEW JERSEY STATE TROOPERS TO GET BODY CAMERAS WITHIN A YEAR

TRENTON, N.J. (AP) — New Jersey plans to put body cameras on all state troopers who work in the field and is issuing guidelines on how local police forces statewide should use the devices.

Acting Attorney General John Hoffman, who outlined the plans Tuesday, also announced $2.5 million in state funding to help local police departments buy body cameras.

"The way to maintain mutual respect and trust between law enforcement and our communities is through accountability of police and civilians alike," Hoffman said.

https://nj1015.com/new-jersey-troopers-getting-body-cameras-under-new-policy/

New Jersey is among the first states with plans to put body cameras on all state troopers. Their use already was brewing as a hot topic in law enforcement before a spate of high-profile shootings by police nationally during the past year, including the death last August of Michael Brown in Ferguson, Missouri.

Civil rights groups and police officials generally support using them, though there's not universal agreement on what rules should be in place to balance the sometimes disparate interests of accountability and privacy.

"Whether body cameras are a good thing or a bad thing depends entirely on the policies behind them," Chad Marlow, the American Civil Liberties Union's advocacy and policy counsel, said in an interview Tuesday. He said it's important that all footage neither be required to be made public in open records requests nor exempted wholesale from state records laws.

Hoffman said New Jersey's rules strike the appropriate balance dealing with privacy, video retention and other issues. The NAACP and several other civil rights groups appeared with him as he unveiled the initiatives, though the ACLU was not among the groups.

The directive from Hoffman's office generally requires officers with cameras to have them on during certain types of interactions with the public but limits their use in homes, schools, hospitals and places of worship.

Hoffman said the state would buy 1,000 cameras for troopers during the next year or so at a cost of $1.5 million. The money also would cover computer upgrades needed to use the cameras.

The $2.5 million to help pay for local departments' cameras is to come from forfeiture funds.

About 30 law enforcement agencies in New Jersey are using cameras to some degree already. That number is expected to rise as a result of a 2014 law that requires that police cars have dashboard cameras or officers to have

https://nj1015.com/new-jersey-troopers-getting-body-cameras-under-new-policy/

New Jersey is among the first states with plans to put body cameras on all state troopers. Their use already was brewing as a hot topic in law enforcement before a spate of high-profile shootings by police nationally during the past year, including the death last August of Michael Brown in Ferguson, Missouri.

Civil rights groups and police officials generally support using them, though there's not universal agreement on what rules should be in place to balance the sometimes disparate interests of accountability and privacy.

"Whether body cameras are a good thing or a bad thing depends entirely on the policies behind them," Chad Marlow, the American Civil Liberties Union's advocacy and policy counsel, said in an interview Tuesday. He said it's important that all footage neither be required to be made public in open records requests nor exempted wholesale from state records laws.

Hoffman said New Jersey's rules strike the appropriate balance dealing with privacy, video retention and other issues. The NAACP and several other civil rights groups appeared with him as he unveiled the initiatives, though the ACLU was not among the groups.

The directive from Hoffman's office generally requires officers with cameras to have them on during certain types of interactions with the public but limits their use in homes, schools, hospitals and places of worship.

Hoffman said the state would buy 1,000 cameras for troopers during the next year or so at a cost of $1.5 million. The money also would cover computer upgrades needed to use the cameras.

The $2.5 million to help pay for local departments' cameras is to come from forfeiture funds.

Acting Attorney General John Hoffman holds a press conference announcing a new body cam plan for NJ State Police. (David Matthau, Townsquare Media NJ)

About 30 law enforcement agencies in New Jersey are using cameras to some degree already. That number is expected to rise as a result of a 2014 law that requires that police cars have dashboard cameras or officers to have

About 30 law enforcement agencies in New Jersey are using cameras to some degree already. That number is expected to rise as a result of a 2014 law that requires that police cars have dashboard cameras or officers to have body-mounted cameras. Body cameras cost less and have more versatility.

JOSEPH BRODIE

6/17/2019   New Jersey troopers getting body cameras under new policy

body-mounted cameras. Body cameras cost less and have more versatility.

Lawmakers in several states have been passing policies dealing with camera use.

A new South Carolina law requires all police officers to have them. Pending legislation in Connecticut and a policy in Alabama would put cameras on all troopers there.

Christopher Burgos, president of the State Troopers Fraternal Association of NJ Inc. issued a statement Tuesday regarding the initiative, saying the STFA was never asked for input on the implementation of the body cams. His statement reads:

"Our Association (STFA) was never asked for input or anything on this body cam matter. It was conceived behind closed doors, and don't get us wrong, we knew body cams were coming, but once again we were left out of the process purposely, and had to go to court...again, to attempt to get some clarity as to what was coming. We view this as a negotiable issue that affects terms and conditions of employment for our trooper members.

All of a sudden millions of dollars are available for this initiative, meanwhile, we are 500 Troopers below adequate staffing statewide, we had to file many complaints over the past several years against the State for not purchasing new hand guns in a timely manner, as the old ones wore out and malfunctioned often, and our transportation needs have been neglected due to budget balancing tricks called 'sweeping the accounts' every fiscal year that take the buying power away from us to get new patrol vehicles. Meanwhile we have cars with over 200,000 miles on patrol and emergent repairs often go between $5000 -$7500 per car to keep them running.

The funding gimmicks for body cams are troubling, as data storage, band width and Administrative costs will be significant...long term, as in the NJSP we have to keep all recordings on file forever. We foresee more funding battles down the road for our basic law enforcement mission and daily law enforcement needs statewide, as whenever new initiatives are created without dedicated funding, other areas usually suffer. We will continue doing our duty professionally and without fail, as we were the first agency in the state to have dash cams in all our patrol vehicles over a decade and a half ago, while other agencies shockingly still have none today. What I see here as of now is a policy that has more to do with "gotcha's" than truly having the best tools to serve the public. We would want to have a dialog with the state as this goes forward to implementation, and we will also be in the courts as well, to make sure we, as a major stakeholder have a seat at the table."

Kevin McArdle contributed to this report.

(Copyright 2015 The Associated Press. All rights reserved. This material may not be published, broadcast, rewritten or redistributed)

Categories: New Jersey News

Comments

https://nj1015.com/new-jersey-troopers-getting-body-cameras-under-new-policy/

3/4

---

body-mounted cameras. Body cameras cost less and have more versatility.

Lawmakers in several states have been passing policies dealing with camera use.

A new South Carolina law requires all police officers to have them. Pending legislation in Connecticut and a policy in Alabama would put cameras on all troopers there.

Christopher Burgos, president of the State Troopers Fraternal Association of NJ Inc. issued a statement Tuesday regarding the initiative, saying the STFA was never asked for input on the implementation of the body cams. His statement reads:

"Our Association (STFA) was never asked for input or anything on this body cam matter. It was conceived behind closed doors, and don't get us wrong, we knew body cams were coming, but once again we were left out of the process purposely, and had to go to court...again, to attempt to get some clarity as to what was coming. We view this as a negotiable issue that affects terms and conditions of employment for our trooper members.

All of a sudden millions of dollars are available for this initiative, meanwhile, we are 500 Troopers below adequate staffing statewide, we had to file many complaints over the past several years against the State for not purchasing new hand guns in a timely manner, as the old ones wore out and malfunctioned often, and our transportation needs have been neglected due to budget balancing tricks called 'sweeping the accounts' every fiscal year that take the buying power away from us to get new patrol vehicles. Meanwhile we have cars with over 200,000 miles on patrol and emergent repairs often go between $5000 -$7500 per car to keep them running.

All of a sudden millions of dollars are available for this initiative, meanwhile, we are 500 Troopers below adequate staffing statewide, we had to file many complaints over the past several years against the State for not purchasing new hand guns in a timely manner, as the old ones wore out and malfunctioned often, and our transportation needs have been neglected due to budget balancing tricks called 'sweeping the accounts' every fiscal year that take the buying power away from us to get new patrol vehicles. Meanwhile we have cars with over 200,000 miles on patrol and emergent repairs often go between $5000 -$7500 per car to keep them running.

The funding gimmicks for body cams are troubling, as data storage, band width and Administrative costs will be significant..long term, as in the NJSP we have to keep all recordings on file forever. We foresee more funding battles down the road for our basic law enforcement mission and daily law enforcement needs statewide, as whenever new initiatives are created without dedicated funding, other areas usually suffer. We will continue doing our duty professionally and without fail, as we were the first agency in the state to have dash cams in all our patrol vehicles over a decade and a half ago, while other agencies shockingly still have none today. What I see here as of now is a policy that has more to do with "gotcha's" than truly having the best tools to serve the public. We would want to have a dialog with the state as this goes forward to implementation, and we will also be in the courts as well, to make sure we, as a major stakeholder have a seat at the table."

Kevin McArdle contributed to this report.

Discovery Disk #2

- <u>**Trooper Luis Rivera-Guzman**</u>, 7534 Station A100 **(Port Norris)**
  - Author or **Report A-100-2017-00694**
  - **CAD Abstract**: Dispatched to 7188 Ackley at 4:09:25, Arrived 4:09:28
  -       AFTER 7555 (Townsend), BEFORE 7179 (Ciaurelli & Poeppel)
  - <u>Testified he **DID NOT** help **EXECUTE** any **SEARCH WARRANT** &</u>
  - <u>Testified he went home after his shift ended at 5 p.m. &</u>
  - <u>His report "was true & correct to the best of his knowledge"</u>

Dana Mednick Calls PNSP A-100 at 3:21 p.m. on 09-20-2017.
She asks for Trooper Phill Smith but is told his shift doesn't start until 5pm that day
Mednick requests Smith go out and see Brodie & ensure he was ok. Smith regularly
visited Brodie's home. They texted frequently. Both are Iraq war veterans.

Transaction Date/Time	Duration	Terminating Number	Originating Number	Original Dialed Number
9/20/2017 15:21:11	101	856██████0035	████9158	18567850035

At 10:12 am ON 09/19/2017, Smith spoke to Brodie warning of his imminent arrest for conversations with the congressional staff which would be deemed "threatening"

4	Inbox	From ████16471 Direction: Incoming	9/19/2017 10:12:49 AM(UTC-4)		+124044921 66	Read	Ok Source Extraction: Logical
5	Sent	To ████16471 Direction: Outgoing	9/19/2017 10:12:29 AM(UTC-4)			Sent	Jumping in shower call you right back Source Extraction: Logical
6	Sent	To ████16471 Direction: Outgoing	9/19/2017 9:37:46 AM(UTC-4)			Sent	This is why Dana called you guys out to check on me when I had 2seizures in early July. I gotta fix this. It sucks Source Extraction: Logical
7	Sent	To ████16471 Direction: Outgoing	9/19/2017 9:34:35 AM(UTC-4)			Sent	Dude, this cell service sucks. I got cricket for 25$ a month. The fact you didn't get my texts from the weekend or I got your call shows I either need a cellular signal booster here OR a new carrier. Source Extraction: Logical
8	Inbox	From ████16471 Direction: Incoming	9/19/2017 8:43:39 AM(UTC-4)		+124044921 66	Read	U need to call me .ogical

09/20/2017 16:08:28	7555	DISPATCHED	PAVLAK,SCOTT T / buena2
09/20/2017 16:08:30	7555	ARRIVED	PAVLAK,SCOTT T / buena2
09/21/2017 01:18:45	7555	COMPLETE	WHARTON,ROBERT A / portnorris1

(THIS IS GUZMAN'S CAD Abstract)
46 MINUTES AFTER DM's CALL TO PNSP A100....
[NOT 911]

7555 –TOWNSEND [ACTUALLY] arrived FIRST...
Nearly 1 MINUTE BEFORE
7179-CIAURELLI & POEPPEL
7534-GUZMAN & GALEZNIAK

INCREDIBLY,
Unit 7555 is NOT depicted accurately in Guzman's report or,
in Detective Hanlin's Search Warrant Affidavit
Under 5 b. "PROBABLE CAUSE"...

WHY?

09/20/2017 16:08:28	7555	DISPATCHED	PAVLAK,SCOTT T / buena2
09/20/2017 16:08:30	7555	ARRIVED	PAVLAK,SCOTT T / buena2
09/21/2017 01:18:45	7555	COMPLETE	WHARTON,ROBERT A / portnorris1

(THIS IS A SECTION OF GUZMAN's CAD ABSTRACT)
7555 –TOWNSEND- ARRIVES FIRST AT 4:08:30 PM

7555 IS EXCLUDED FROM GUZMAN'S REPORT

7555 IS EXCLUDED FROM HANLIN'S
AFFIDAVIT FOR A SEARCH WARRANT

ALL OTHER RESPONDING TROOPERS TESTIFIED THAT
TOWNSEND ARRIVED LAST

WHY?

Case 1:20-cv-12713-NLH Document 48-1 Filed 08/21/22 Page 25 of 118 PageID: 793

09/20/2017 16:09:28	7534	ARRIVED	SILIPENA,CARA-JENE V / buena1
09/20/2017 16:50:35	7534	CONTINUING INVESTIGATION	PAVLAK,SCOTT T / buena2
09/20/2017 21:23:25	7534	ARRIVED	DELUCIA,JOHN F / buena1

(GUZMAN's CAD Abstract)
Guzman & Galezniak, 7534, arrive 2nd

Case 1:20-cv-12713-NLH Document 48-1 Filed 08/21/22 Page 26 of 118 PageID: 794

Unit Statuses

Date/Time	Unit ID	Status	Dispatcher / Position
09/20/2017 21:20:53	6261	DISPATCHED	VAUGHN,KERIN M / buena2
09/20/2017 21:20:59	6261	ARRIVED	VAUGHN,KERIN M / buena2
09/20/2017 22:13:38	6261	CONTINUING INVESTIGATION	VAUGHN,KERIN M / buena2
09/21/2017 01:19:09	6261	COMPLETE	WHARTON,ROBERT A / portnorris1
09/20/2017 16:09:20	7179	DISPATCHED	SILIPENA,CARA-JENE V / buena1
09/20/2017 16:09:30	7179	ARRIVED	SILIPENA,CARA-JENE V / buena1
09/20/2017 16:45:16	7179	TRANSPORT/RELAY	PAVLAK,SCOTT T / buena2
09/20/2017 17:04:54	7179	COMPLETE	PAVLAK,SCOTT T / buena2

Page1 of 2   Generated on :09/25/2017 14:26:40

(GUZMAN'S CAD ABSTRACT, UNIT STATUS SECTION)

FINALLY...

7179 –Poeppel & Ciaurelli Arrive LAST at 4:09:30 pm

JOSEPH BRODIE

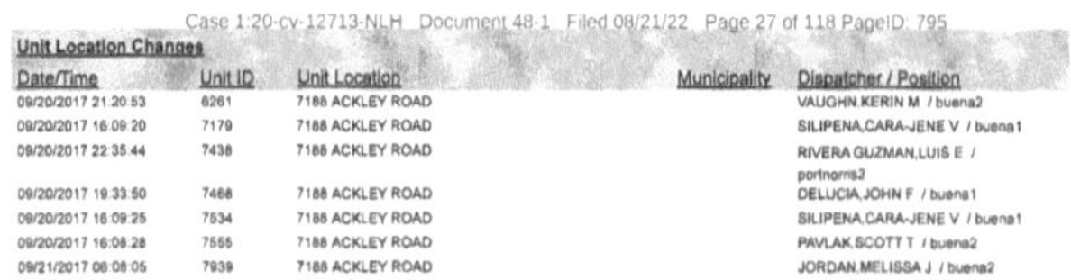

Unit Location Changes

Date/Time	Unit ID	Unit Location	Municipality	Dispatcher / Position
09/20/2017 21:20:53	6261	7188 ACKLEY ROAD		VAUGHN,KERIN M / buena2
09/20/2017 16:09:20	7179	7188 ACKLEY ROAD		SILIPENA,CARA-JENE V / buena1
09/20/2017 22:35:44	7438	7188 ACKLEY ROAD		RIVERA GUZMAN,LUIS E / portnorris2
09/20/2017 19:33:50	7468	7188 ACKLEY ROAD		DELUCIA,JOHN F / buena1
09/20/2017 16:09:25	7534	7188 ACKLEY ROAD		SILIPENA,CARA-JENE V / buena1
09/20/2017 16:08:28	7555	7188 ACKLEY ROAD		PAVLAK,SCOTT T / buena2
09/21/2017 08:08:05	7939	7188 ACKLEY ROAD		JORDAN,MELISSA J / buena2

THIS IS THE "UNIT LOCATION CHANGES" SECTION OF THE GUZMAN CAD ABSTRACT

THE USAO (DISINGENUOUSLY) ARGUES THAT THE PETITIONER IS MISREPRESENTING DISPATCHES & ARRIVALS AS BEING ON SCENE WHEN THESE OFFICERS WERE NOT REALLY ON SCENE
HOWEVER....
HERE THE CLAIMS OF THE PETITIONER ARE CORROBORATED
[SEE UNIT LOCATION, 7188 ACKLEY ROAD]

THE GOVERNMENT ATTACKS FACTS CLEARLY EVIDENT IN THE CAD ABSTRACT AND INSINUATES TO THE COURT THAT THE PETITIONER IS MISTAKEN.

THE USAO's CLAIM IS AS OBTUSE AS IT IS DISINGENUOUS

NO LESS THAN 5 NJSP TROOPERS ARE ON SCENE AT 409PM

BRODIE TESTIFIED A PLAIN CLOTHES DETECTIVE
[NOW IDENTIFIED AS] -STEVEN HILLESHEIM 7486-
IS THE PLAIN CLOTHES DETECTIVE BRODIE INVOKED HIS MIRANDA RIGHTS TO OUTSIDE HIS FRONT DOOR
-HILLESHEIM IS OFF DUTY-
TROOPER SMITH VISITED BRODIE IN HIS HOLDING CELL AFTER HIS ARREST AND INFORMED HIM HILLESHEIM WAS "OFF DUTY AND JUST HAPPENED TO BE IN THE AREA" TO RESPOND ON SCENE

**THIS WAS NOT AN "ARMED STANDOFF"
NO MATTER HOW MANY TIMES THE USAO SAYS IT
OR HOW DESPERATELY THE USAO WANTS YOU TO BELIEVE THAT**

**"OK ON SCENE"
NO CRISIS NEGOTIATOR FOR AN "ARMED STANDOFF"
& NO SWAT TEAM**

Response Notes :

Date/Time	Note	Dispatcher / Position
09/20/2017 16:06:57	CALLER STATED THAT JOSEPH BRODY ADVISED THAT HE WANTS TO SHOOT HIMSELF IN THE CHEST WITH A PISTOL	NOCON,ERIC S / portnorris1
09/20/2017 16:07:01	- - RESPONSE CREATED - -	NOCON,ERIC S / portnorris1
09/20/2017 16:08:41	Response Acknowledgment received from 7555	TOWNSEND,KEVEN L / NJNSPM229
09/20/2017 16:09:26	Response Acknowledgment received from 7179	CIAURELLI,CHARLES J / NJNSPM714
09/20/2017 16:11:30	CALLER DANA MEDNICK 732-742-4791	NOCON,ERIC S / portnorris1
09/20/2017 16:12:07	OK ON SCENE	PAVLAK,SCOTT T / buena2
09/20/2017 16:13:41	Response Acknowledgment received from 7534	RIVERA GUZMAN,LUIS E / NJNSPM127
09/20/2017 16:55:49	JOSEPH BRODY IN CELL 1 SECURE AND OK	NOCON,ERIC S / portnorris1
09/20/2017 21:33:07	JOSEPH BRODY LYING ON BENCH IN CELL	WHARTON,ROBERT A / portnorris1
09/20/2017 22:15:20	Response Acknowledgment received from 7468	D'AUGUSTINE,MATTHEW R / NJNSPM003
09/20/2017 22:35:48	Response Acknowledgment received from 7438	TORRES,RUBEN H / NJNSPM127
09/21/2017 01:28:20	Response Acknowledgment received from 7438	TORRES,RUBEN H / NJNSPM127
09/21/2017 05:09:30	mvr check ok. divr check okay.	RIVERA GUZMAN,LUIS E / NJNSPM714
09/21/2017 06:08:10	Response Acknowledgment received from 7939	SPADAFORA,TRAVIS W / NJNSPM900

**GUZMAN testified he
did NOT help execute
any search warrant**

131

————GUZMAN - DIRECT - ALIABADI————

```
 1  information from us and they pretty much took over the

 2  investigation.

 3  Q.   Do you know what sort of information they were gathering?

 4  A.   As far as the particulars about what happened.

 5  Q.   Do you know why they were gathering information?

 6  A.   No.

 7  Q.   Do you know whether a search warrant was ever sought or

 8  obtained for Mr. Brodie?

 9  A.   Not that I recall from my end.  I did an initial report

10  and the detectives took over the investigation.  Our

11  investigation was basically the community caretaking aspect of

12  it, to make sure that it correlates with the wellbeing check,

13  making sure he was okay, but as far as anything else, the

14  detectives would have taken over at that point and that's

15  usually what happens in that sort of situation.
```

JOSEPH BRODIE

YET...

List of Officers Executing Search Warrant

The attached search warrant was executed by the following personnel:

Detective Sergeant J. Del Sordo #6261   Port Norris Station – CIO

Detective S. Hillesheim #7486   Port Norris Station – CIO

Trooper J. McKay #7662   Port Norris Station – CIO

Trooper M. D'Augustine #7468   Port Norris Station

Trooper L. Guzman-Rivera #7534   Port Norris Station

Trooper B. Galezniak #8000   Port Norris Station

Trooper J. Poeppel #8069   Port Norris Station

Trooper K. Minnes #8045   Port Norris Station

Date and Time of Execution

On September 20th, 2016 at 09:20 PM, the warrant was executed upon:

The residence of 7188 Ackley Road located in Commercial Township, Cumberland County, New Jersey, 08322.

AND

Case 1:20-cv-12713-NLH   Document 48-1   Filed 08/21/22   Page 34 of 118 PageID: 802

09/20/2017 16:09:25	7534	DISPATCHED	SILIPENA,CARA-JENE V / buena1
09/20/2017 16:09:28	7534	ARRIVED	SILIPENA,CARA-JENE V / buena1
09/20/2017 16:50:35	7534	CONTINUING INVESTIGATION	PAVLAK,SCOTT T / buena2
09/20/2017 21:23:25	7534	ARRIVED	DELUCIA,JOHN F / buena1
09/20/2017 22:16:30	7534	CONTINUING INVESTIGATION	VAUGHN,KERIN M / buena2
09/21/2017 01:19:32	7534	COMPLETE	WHARTON,ROBERT A / portnorris1

Unit 7534 (Guzman, ARRIVES at 9:23 pm to help execute the SEARCH warrant

HERE IS GUZMAN AGAIN

**...yet Guzman testified that he went
home after his shift ended at 5 p.m.???**

```
16 | Q.   Did you stay at the station after you initially went back

17 | there and handed the investigation over to the detectives?

18 | A.   We stayed there for -- I don't recall how long we stayed

19 | there just giving our statements to the detectives and then we

20 | went home for the day.

21 | Q.   Was your shift over by then?

22 | A.   That day we were working dayshift, so we were working

23 | from 5:00 a.m. to 5:00 p.m., so we stayed over a little longer

24 | after 5:00 p.m.  I don't recall what time the incident

25 | occurred.  I just remember it was in the afternoon.  It was
```

United States District Court
Camden, New Jersey

**EVIDENCE OF GUZMAN's PERJURY
i.e.,DELIBERATELY LYING UNDER OATH
IN CAMDEN FEDERAL COURT**

**1. GUZMAN'S [own] CAD ABSTRACT
2. HANLIN's SEARCH WARRANT RETURN**

GUZMAN IS NOT CREDIBLE

Case 1:20-cv-12713-NLH Document 48-1 Filed 08/21/22 Page 37 of 118 PageID: 805

09/20/2017 22:35:44	7438		DISPATCHED	RIVERA GUZMAN,LUIS E / portnorris2
09/20/2017 22:35:52	7438		ARRIVED	RIVERA GUZMAN,LUIS E / portnorris2
09/21/2017 01:24:22	7438		TRANSPORT/RELAY	VAUGHN,KERIN M / buena2
09/21/2017 01:48:28	7438		CONTINUING INVESTIGATION	VAUGHN,KERIN M / buena2
09/21/2017 07:33:27	7438		COMPLETE	NOCON,ERIC S / portnorris1
09/20/2017 19:33:50	7468		DISPATCHED	DELUCIA,JOHN F / buena1
09/20/2017 19:33:54	7468		ARRIVED	DELUCIA,JOHN F / buena1
09/20/2017 22:22:14	7468		COMPLETE	D'AUGUSTINE,MATTHEW R / NJNSPM003
09/20/2017 16:09:25	7534	3 seconds between	DISPATCHED	SILIPENA,CARA-JENE V / buena1
09/20/2017 16:09:28	7534		ARRIVED	SILIPENA,CARA-JENE V / buena1
09/20/2017 16:50:36	7534		CONTINUING INVESTIGATION	PAVLAK,SCOTT T / buena2
09/20/2017 21:23:25	7534	Search Warrant Executed	ARRIVED	DELUCIA,JOHN F / buena1
09/20/2017 22:16:30	7534		CONTINUING INVESTIGATION	VAUGHN,KERIN M / buena2
09/21/2017 01:19:32	7534	Investigation Ends	COMPLETE	WHARTON,ROBERT A / portnorris1
09/20/2017 16:08:28	7555		DISPATCHED	PAVLAK,SCOTT T / buena2
09/20/2017 16:08:30	7555		ARRIVED	PAVLAK,SCOTT T / buena2
09/21/2017 01:18:45	7555		COMPLETE	WHARTON,ROBERT A / portnorris1
09/21/2017 06:08:05	7939		DISPATCHED	JORDAN,MELISSA J / buena2
09/21/2017 06:08:08	7939		ENROUTE	JORDAN,MELISSA J / buena2
09/21/2017 06:38:16	7939		ARRIVED	SPADAFORA,TRAVIS W / NJNSPM900
09/21/2017 14:06:22	7939		TRANSPORT/RELAY	SMITHOUSER,DAVID J / buena1
09/21/2017 14:12:38	7939		ARRIVED	SMITHOUSER,DAVID J / buena1
09/21/2017 14:36:15	7939		COMPLETE	SMITHOUSER,DAVID J / buena1

ONE MORE TIME

Case 1:20-cv-12713-NLH   Document 48-1   Filed 08/21/22   Page 39 of 118 PageID: 807

```
22   Q.   If you had heard that -- well, I'll back up.  You
23   mentioned that you wrote a report in connection with this,
24   right?
25   A.   Yes, an initial report, basically myself and Trooper
```

United States District Court
Camden, New Jersey

**Trooper Guzman writes an initial report that alters events
TO EXCLUDE Townsend 7555 & Hillesheim 7486
Despite being 1st on scene, Townsend was INSTEAD listed as an
assisting trooper**

**Hillesheim omitted altogether
TO CONCEAL THE IDENTITY OF
The NJSP plain clothes trooper BRODIE INVOKED MIRANDA TO...
It makes sense he was in PLAIN CLOTHES,
HE WAS OFF DUTY!!!**

Case 1:20-cv-12713-NLH   Document 48-1   Filed 08/21/22   Page 40 of 118 PageID: 808

**HILLESHEIM was at 7188 Ackley
At the time of Brodie's arrest.
NOT
HANLIN**

**IF HANLIN RODE "WITH HIS BOSS" TO 7188
ACKLEY, IT WAS NOT UNTIL 9:20 PM**

DELSORDO IS 6261,

Unit Statuses

Date/Time	Unit ID	Status	Dispatcher / Position
09/20/2017 21:20:53	6261	DISPATCHED	VAUGHN,KERIN M / buena2
09/20/2017 21:20:59	6261	ARRIVED	VAUGHN,KERIN M / buena2
09/20/2017 22:13:38	6261	CONTINUING INVESTIGATION	VAUGHN,KERIN M / buena2
09/21/2017 01:19:09	6261	COMPLETE	WHARTON,ROBERT A / portnorris1

LOOK AGAIN
HANLIN WAS NOT ON SCENE...EVER
TOWNSEND ARRIVED FIRST

Unit Statuses

Date/Time	Unit ID	Status	Dispatcher / Position
09/20/2017 21:20:53	6261	DISPATCHED	VAUGHN,KERIN M / buena2
09/20/2017 21:20:59	6261	ARRIVED	VAUGHN,KERIN M / buena2
09/20/2017 22:13:38	6261	CONTINUING INVESTIGATION	VAUGHN,KERIN M / buena2
09/21/2017 01:19:09	6261	COMPLETE	WHARTON,ROBERT A / portnorris1
09/20/2017 16:09:20	7179	DISPATCHED	SILIPENA,CARA-JENE V / buena1
09/20/2017 16:09:30	7179	ARRIVED	SILIPENA,CARA-JENE V / buena1
09/20/2017 16:45:16	7179	TRANSPORT/RELAY	PAVLAK,SCOTT T / buena2
09/20/2017 17:04:54	7179	COMPLETE	PAVLAK,SCOTT T / buena2

		Page1 of 2	Generated on :09/25/2017 14:26:40
09/20/2017 22:35:44	7438	DISPATCHED	RIVERA GUZMAN,LUIS E / portnorris2
09/20/2017 22:35:52	7438	ARRIVED	RIVERA GUZMAN,LUIS E / portnorris2
09/21/2017 01:24:22	7438	TRANSPORT/RELAY	VAUGHN,KERIN M / buena2
09/21/2017 01:48:28	7438	CONTINUING INVESTIGATION	VAUGHN,KERIN M / buena2
09/21/2017 07:33:27	7438	COMPLETE	NOCON,ERIC S / portnorris1
09/20/2017 19:33:50	7468	DISPATCHED	DELUCIA,JOHN F / buena1
09/20/2017 19:33:54	7468	ARRIVED	DELUCIA,JOHN F / buena1
09/20/2017 22:22:14	7468	COMPLETE	D'AUGUSTINE,MATTHEW R / NJNSPM003
09/20/2017 16:09:25	7534	DISPATCHED	SILIPENA,CARA-JENE V / buena1
09/20/2017 16:09:28	7534	ARRIVED	SILIPENA,CARA-JENE V / buena1
09/20/2017 16:50:35	7534	CONTINUING INVESTIGATION	PAVLAK,SCOTT T / buena2
09/20/2017 21:23:25	7534	ARRIVED	DELUCIA,JOHN F / buena1
09/20/2017 22:16:30	7534	CONTINUING INVESTIGATION	VAUGHN,KERIN M / buena2
09/21/2017 01:19:32	7534	COMPLETE	WHARTON,ROBERT A / portnorris1
09/20/2017 16:08:28	7555	DISPATCHED	PAVLAK,SCOTT T / buena2
09/20/2017 16:08:30	7555	ARRIVED	PAVLAK,SCOTT T / buena2
09/21/2017 01:18:46	7555	COMPLETE	WHARTON,ROBERT A / portnorris1
09/21/2017 06:08:05	7939	DISPATCHED	JORDAN,MELISSA J / buena2
09/21/2017 06:08:08	7939	ENROUTE	JORDAN,MELISSA J / buena2
09/21/2017 06:38:16	7939	ARRIVED	SPADAFORA,TRAVIS W / NJNSPM900
09/21/2017 14:06:22	7939	TRANSPORT/RELAY	SMITHOUSER,DAVID J / buena1
09/21/2017 14:12:38	7939	ARRIVED	SMITHOUSER,DAVID J / buena1
09/21/2017 14:36:15	7939	COMPLETE	SMITHOUSER,DAVID J / buena1

ONE MORE TIME IN REPLY TO THE USAO's DISINGENUOUS RESPONSE

Unit Location Changes

Date/Time	Unit ID	Unit Location	Municipality	Dispatcher / Position
09/20/2017 21:20:53	6261	7188 ACKLEY ROAD		VAUGHN,KERIN M / buena2
09/20/2017 16:09:20	7179	7188 ACKLEY ROAD		SILIPENA,CARA-JENE V / buena1
09/20/2017 22:35:44	7438	7188 ACKLEY ROAD		RIVERA GUZMAN,LUIS E / portnorris2
09/20/2017 19:33:50	7466	7188 ACKLEY ROAD		DELUCIA,JOHN F / buena1
09/20/2017 16:09:25	7534	7188 ACKLEY ROAD		SILIPENA,CARA-JENE V / buena1
09/20/2017 16:08:28	7555	7188 ACKLEY ROAD		PAVLAK,SCOTT T / buena2
09/21/2017 06:08:05	7939	7188 ACKLEY ROAD		JORDAN,MELISSA J / buena2

Actions Taken

Date/Time	Trooper	Action	Number	Statute
09/21/2017 06:11:05	RIVERA GUZMAN,LUIS E	REPORT	A100-2017-00694	N/A

GUZMAN

FALSIFIED HIS REPORT

LIED UNDER OATH
ON JULY 16TH 2018
IN CAMDEN FEDERAL COURT

PARTICIPATED IN A SEARCH WARRANT
IN WHICH THE CRIME SCENE WAS
TAMPERED WITH

HANLIN

FALSIFIED [VIA OMISSION] HIS AFFIDAVIT
FOR A SEARCH WARRANT

THE EVIDENCE SECURED WAS USED IN BRODIE'S
CRIMINAL PROSECUTION AND
SHOWN TO THE JURY AT TRIAL

HANLIN COMMITTED PERJURY
IN CAMDEN FEDERAL COURT
ON JULY 26TH 2018

**THE OMISSION OF 7555 –TOWNSEND-
AND 7486 –HILLESHEIM-**

**WAS DELIBERATELY DONE TO CONCEAL
BRODIE's INVOCATION &
WANTING HIS LAWYER PRESENT**

**SUBPOENAED AT&T RECORDS
DEMONSTRATE
BRODIE**

**CALLED HIS LAWYER AFTER SPEAKING
WITH TROOPER SMITH
&
PRIOR TO THE NJSP's ARRIVAL**

SEE FOR YOURSELF…

18:18:28 UTC-4

=

14:18:28 PM EASTERN TIME

…

2:18:28 PM
FOR 15 MINUTES 36 SECONDS
IT'S NOT INCONCEIVABLE THAT BRODIE
INVOKED MIRANDA AFTER HAVING
SPOKEN TO HIS ATTORNEY
OR WHILE AT STATION A100

AND

GUZMAN

DOUBLED

DOWN

13 | Q.   Okay.   At the time that you reviewed the report, was

14 | everything in there when it was finalized true and correct to

15 | the best of your knowledge?

16 | A.   To the best of my knowledge, yes.

TRUE AND CORRECT TO THE BEST OF HIS KNOWLEDGE ? ? ? SHARED WITH THE USCP & FBI AND WHAT THE USAO RECOMMENDED CHARGES FOR...

Case 1:20-cv-12713-NLH   Document 48-1   Filed 08/21/22   Page 53 of 118 PageID: 821

```
21   Q.   How long was it from when you first arrived until Mr.
22   Brodie was put in handcuffs?
23   A.   How long?
24   Q.   Yes.
25   A.   I don't recall.
```

United States District Court
Camden, New Jersey

YET….Trooper Guzman cannot recall how long it was from his arrival until Brodie is handcuffed?

Case 1:20-cv-12713-NLH   Document 48-1   Filed 08/21/22   Page 54 of 118 PageID: 822   *135*

```
------------------GUZMAN - CROSS - JACOBS------------------
1   Q.   Give me your best estimate.  Five minutes, 10 minutes, an
2   hour?
3   A.   I don't recall.  I couldn't tell you.  It happened,
4   everything happened so fast, I don't know.
```

Unit Statuses

Date/Time	Unit ID	Status	Dispatcher / Position
09/20/2017 21:20:53	6261	DISPATCHED	VAUGHN,KERIN M / buena2
09/20/2017 21:20:59	6261	ARRIVED	VAUGHN,KERIN M / buena2
09/20/2017 22:13:38	6261	CONTINUING INVESTIGATION	VAUGHN,KERIN M / buena2
09/21/2017 01:19:09	6261	COMPLETE	WHARTON,ROBERT A / portnorris1
09/20/2017 16:09:20	7179	DISPATCHED	SILIPENA,CARA-JENE V / buena1
09/20/2017 16:09:30	7179	ARRIVED	SILIPENA,CARA-JENE V / buena1
09/20/2017 16:45:16	7179	TRANSPORT/RELAY	PAVLAK,SCOTT T / buena2
09/20/2017 17:04:54	7179	COMPLETE	PAVLAK,SCOTT T / buena2

36 minutes +++
At 7188 Ackley

Page1 of 2   Generated on :09/25/2017 14:26:40

NJSP were on scene from 4:08 pm and did NOT transport Brodie until 4:45 p.m.

Trooper Guzman "Could not recall" because everything was "happening so fast"

NJSP were on scene for no less than 36 minutes

All NJSP testimony is INCONSISTENT with the CAD regarding these details

NO DETECTIVES-<u>EXCEPT AN OFF-DUTY HILLESHEIM</u>- WERE ON SCENE AT THE TIME OF ARREST

If Hanlin traveled with Delsordo (6261) to 7188 Ackley, it was NOT until 9:20 PM to execute the search warrant

Unit Statuses

Date/Time	Unit ID	Status	Dispatcher / Position
09/20/2017 21:20:53	6261	DISPATCHED	VAUGHN,KERIN M / buena2
09/20/2017 21:20:59	6261	ARRIVED	VAUGHN,KERIN M / buena2
09/20/2017 22:13:38	6261	CONTINUING INVESTIGATION	VAUGHN,KERIN M / buena2
09/21/2017 01:19:09	6261	COMPLETE	WHARTON,ROBERT A / portnorris1
09/20/2017 16:09:20	7179	DISPATCHED	SILIPENA,CARA-JENE V / buena1
09/20/2017 16:09:30	7179	ARRIVED	SILIPENA,CARA-JENE V / buena1
09/20/2017 16:45:16	7179	TRANSPORT/RELAY	PAVLAK,SCOTT T / buena2
09/20/2017 17:04:54	7179	COMPLETE	PAVLAK,SCOTT T / buena2

Page1 of 2   Generated on :09/25/2017 14:26:40

GUZMAN & HANLIN WERE NOT THE ONLY MEMBERS OF LAW ENFORCEMENT TO FALSIFY A REPORT...

THE USCP DID ALSO.
[SEE NEXT SLIDE]

316
(8-01)
(WIN) PAD

UNITED STATES CAPITOL POLICE
WASHINGTON, D.C. 20510-7218

REPORT OF INVESTIGATION

Victim/Complainant/Subject: Congressman ███████	Date of Occurrence: 09/20/17		Date First Reported: 09/20/17	
Type of Case THREAT	CFN N/A	CCN N/A	CIS #	TAS # ███ 375
NARRATIVE			IS Case #	

On 09/20/17, U.S. Capitol Police, Threat Assessment (USCP-TAS) was advised by USCP/FBI-TFO that New Jersey State Police (NJSP) had responded to the residence of Joseph BRODIE for a potential suicide by cop call.

FBI NJ advised USCP TAS that BRODIE's brother had called Ms. Dana Mednick, BRODIE's ex-girlfriend and stated that BRODIE had shot himself. Ms. Mednick then called NJSP for a welfare check of BRODIE. NJSP responded to BRODIE's residence, where BRODIE exited his residence holding a SKS rifle and told the officers to kill him. BRODIE knelt down, put the barrel of the rifle in his mouth and pulled the trigger. BRODIE cycled the action of the rifle and pulled the trigger a total of three times. After the third time, BRODIE surrendered.

NJSP responded for a Well Being Check, not a "suicide by cop call" Even ACCORDING TO GUZMAN, Brodie NEVER "told the officers to kill him"

Shortly after, Mr. Brodie exited the front door while holding a black rifle, later identified as a Russian SKS 7.62x39 rifle (Serial# KO2121). Mr. Brodie stated, "I do not want to shoot you guys" as he walked towards the front yard. Mr. Brodie was given numerous verbal commands to drop his weapon to which he refused. Mr. Brodie was advised that we could provide him with the help that he needed. After approximately two minutes of this behavior, Mr. Brodie rotated the rifle and pointed the muzzle towards his head while kneeling on the ground and facing uniformed Troopers. Mr. Brodie proceeded to place the rifle's muzzle in his mouth and pull the trigger with his thumb, however, the rifle did not fire. From my position, I was unable to tell if the rifle was loaded or if a magazine was inserted. Mr. Brodie continued to disregard Troopers verbal commands. Mr. Brodie then racked the action several times and proceeded to place the muzzle back in his mouth and attempt to pull the trigger.

Eventually, Mr. Brodie stood to his feet and again rotated the rifle to a horizontal position. Mr. Brodie then laid the rifle on the ground and proceeded to put his hands in the air. At this point, Mr. Brodie began to follow commands to raise his shirt and show his waistband for any possible weapons. Mr. Brodie was then ordered to the ground, face down, with his legs spread and arms out. Mr. Brodie was handcuffed (double locked), searched for

Guzman's Report never mentions Brodie threatened the police or told them to shoot him
Brodie was barefoot & Shirtless so why is he asked to raise his shirt?

Trooper Smith provided Brodie with a "Rocky Philadelphia" T-Shirt. Guzman & Torres provided him with sandals while ALL troopers were visiting him in the holding cell, ridiculing his shivering half-naked body and questioning him for his cellular passcode.

**BRODIE TESTIFIED HE WAS
SHIRTLESS AND BAREFOOT
[07-06-2018]**

**THIS T-SHIRT WAS GIVEN TO
BRODIE BY SMITH AS
BRODIE SHIVERED SHIRTLESS
IN THE HOLDING CELL**

**NUMEROUS TROOPERS VISITED
BRODIE IN THE HOLDING CELL**

**EVEN TORRES TESTIFIED HE
GAVE HIM FOOD AND SANDALS
FOR HIS BARE FEET**

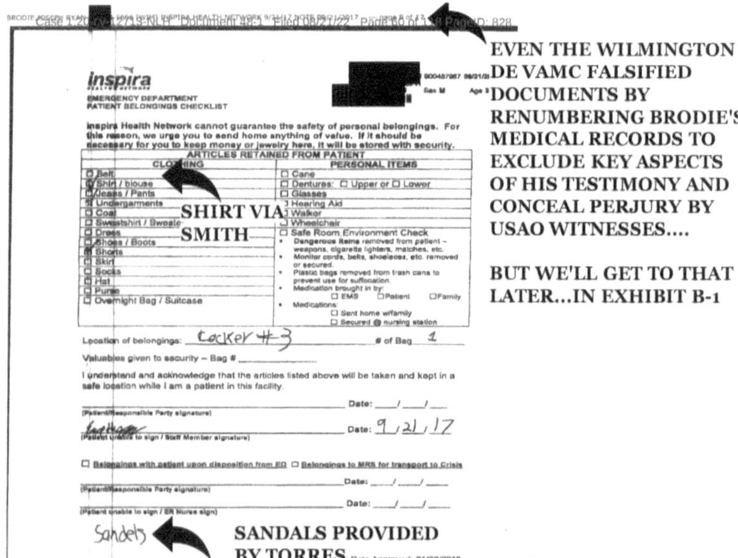

**EVEN THE WILMINGTON
DE VAMC FALSIFIED
DOCUMENTS BY
RENUMBERING BRODIE'S
MEDICAL RECORDS TO
EXCLUDE KEY ASPECTS
OF HIS TESTIMONY AND
CONCEAL PERJURY BY
USAO WITNESSES....**

**BUT WE'LL GET TO THAT
LATER...IN EXHIBIT B-1**

SHIRT VIA SMITH

**SANDALS PROVIDED
BY TORRES**

ADDITIONALLY,
DETECTIVE HANLIN TESTIFIED IT WAS BECAUSE OF PURPORTED COMMUNCIATIONS WITH THE CONGRESSIONAL STAFF THAT THE NJSP WENT TO 7188 ACKLEY

THIS CORROBORATES BRODIE'S TESTIMONY OF BEING ASKED TO ACCOMMPANY THE NJSP TO THEIR STATION TO ANSWER QUESTIONS ABOUT "INTERACTIONS WITH PUBLIC OFFICIALS"

BUT IT CONTRADICTS HANLINS's TESTIMONY
IN CAMDEN FEDERAL COURT ON JULY 26TH 2018

```
                    Detective. M. Hanlin - Direct              4

 1          Q.    And, was the nature of your call, is it fair
 2    to say, would be a welfare check, so to speak?
 3          A.    Yes.
 4          Q.    Okay.  And, were there concerns that Mr.
 5    Brodie had had some interactions with public officials
 6    that were concerning to the public official and/or the
 7    State Police?
 8          A.    Correct; yes.
 9          Q.    Okay.  And, based upon that, did you and other
10    personnel respond out to that residence and encounter
11    Mr. Brodie?
12          A.    We did.
```

HANLIN'S NJ STATE GRAND JURY TESTIMONY 10/24/2018

IT'S EVEN MORE LIKELY BRODIE INVOKED HIS RIGHTS
AFTER SPEAKING TO TROOPER SMITH ON 09/19/2017
AND LATER TO HIS LAWYER ON 09/20/2017

THIS [SMITH'S WARNING] IS WHY BRODIE REPEATED –3 TIMES- TO THE CHIEF OF STAFF
ON 09/19/2017 THAT HIS WORDS WERE NOT A "THREAT"...
IT ALSO EXPLAINS WHY THE USCP CALLED THE CONGRESSIONAL OFFICE
TO REPORT A "THREAT" 1-DAY LATER (09-20-2017),
AND NOT THE CONGRESSIONAL STAFF CALLING USCP
IMMEDIATELY AFTER THE "THREATENING" CALL & EMAIL ON (09-19-2017)
BRODIE WAS FOREWARNED BY SMITH
&
EMAILS AMONGST THE CONGRESSIONAL STAFF ACQUIRED VIA RULE 17(c) SUBPOENA
DEMONSTRATE SUCH ATTEMPTS TO CHARACTERIZE BRODIE'S STATEMENTS AS "THREATS"
&
WHAT WERE THE NJSP DOING FOR 36 MINUTES?
BETWEEN THEIR ARRIVAL AND TRANSPORTING A HANDCUFFED BRODIE
OTHER THAN ATTEMPTING TO GET HIM TO SPEAK ABOUT
WHAT HAD TRANSPIRED BETWEEN HE AND THE CONGRESSMAN

Unit Statuses

Date/Time	Unit ID		Status	Dispatcher / Position
09/20/2017 21:20:53	6261		DISPATCHED	VAUGHN,KERIN M / buena2
09/20/2017 21:20:59	6261		ARRIVED	VAUGHN,KERIN M / buena2
09/20/2017 22:13:38	6261		CONTINUING INVESTIGATION	VAUGHN,KERIN M / buena2
09/21/2017 01:19:09	6261	**Poeppel & Ciaurelli**	COMPLETE	WHARTON,ROBERT A / portnorris1
09/20/2017 16:09:20	7179	**Transport Brodie**	DISPATCHED	SILIPENA,CARA-JENE V / buena1
09/20/2017 16:09:30	7179		ARRIVED	SILIPENA,CARA-JENE V / buena1
09/20/2017 16:45:16	7179	**36 min**	TRANSPORT/RELAY	PAVLAK,SCOTT T / buena2
09/20/2017 17:04:54	7179	**After initial arrival**	COMPLETE	PAVLAK,SCOTT T / buena2

Why would Guzman lie about NOT BEING present for the search warrant's execution???

7188 Ackley Road was surrounded by ZMODO security cameras & the NJSP were well aware of them…SMS text messages with Trooper Phillip Smith Port Norris Station A100

342	Sent	To [redacted]6471 Direction: Outgoing	8/25/2017 6:15:19 PM(UTC-4)			Sent	I could tell he's a young guy, but his eyes kept drifting to my camera, so I knew you guys knew about it. Source Extraction: Logical
343	Sent	To [redacted]6471 Direction: Outgoing	8/25/2017 6:15:00 PM(UTC-4)			Sent	He said his first name is bill correct? Source Extraction: Logical
344	Sent	To [redacted]6471 Direction: Outgoing	8/25/2017 6:14:45 PM(UTC-4)			Sent	Yeah, I noticed trooper coming notice. Source Extraction: Logical
345	Inbox	From [redacted]6471 Direction: Incoming	8/25/2017 6:06:39 PM(UTC-4)		+124044921 66	Read	We were looking right at them Source Extraction: Logical
346	Sent	To [redacted]6471 Direction: Outgoing	8/25/2017 6:06:00 PM(UTC-4)			Sent	Lol it's all good, I'm glad you guys came because I never would have got to meet you if you guys didn't come. Source Extraction: Logical
347	Sent	To [redacted]6471 Direction: Outgoing	8/25/2017 6:05:41 PM(UTC-4)			Sent	To be honest, I know you guys knew I had secured a cameras before you came, that's why you parked down the way, but you didn't realize that my camera had that much of a view. Source Extraction: Logical

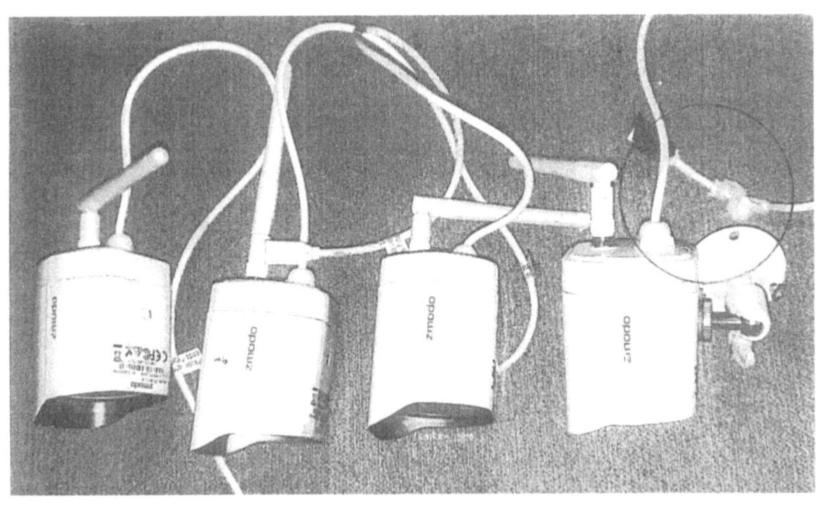

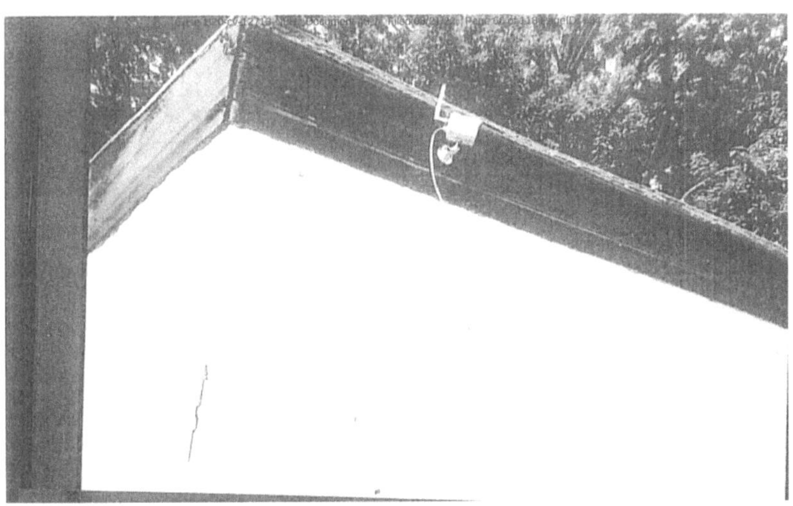

THAT'S BRODIE THERE

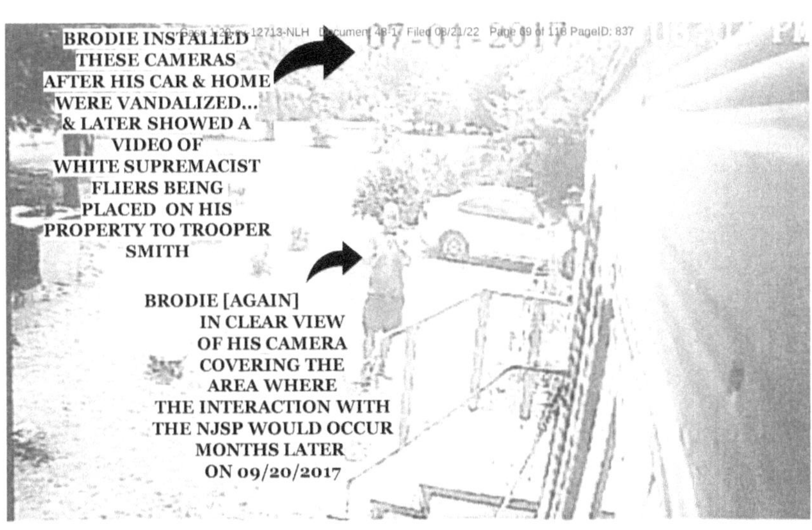

THE USAO MOCKED & RIDICULED BRODIE FOR CLAIMING TO HAVE CAMERAS AT THE RESIDENCE.

YET, THEY KNEW ALL ALONG BECAUSE THEY POSSESSED THESE TEXT MESSAGES FROM DANA MEDNICK's CELL PHONE. THIS WAS DELIBERATELY DONE TO DISCREDIT BRODIE's TESTIMONY & IT (APPARENTLY) WORKED.

ALSO, THE USAO STILL POSSESSED BRODIE's PHONE CONTAINING THE FOOTAGE WHILE BLAMING BRODIE FOR BEING THE CAUSE OF THE DELAY IN PRESENTING VIDEO & PICTURES... WHY WOULD BRODIE TRUST LAW ENFORCEMENT AFTER ALL THAT HAD HAPPENED?

96 degrees, here's a picture of the camera I got one out of 4 up a

nd running. It's actually online and running.

I made sure that the first1 covers my front door so if I don't get

all of them installed today, then I'll wait, but this is a pain in

the motherfucking ass.

These cameras were unplugged during the NJSP search

Plugged in, no magazine **Unplugged, magazine planted**

THIS CAMERA IS UNPLUGGED BECAUSE IT COVERS THE FRONT LAWN...
WHERE BRODIE ENCOUNTERED THE NJSP

.22 caliber hunting rifle

With a hunting license attached

Without a hunting license attached

**TAMPERING WITH EVIDENCE SEIZED WITH THE
FALSIFIED SEARCH WARRANT**

**THIS IS A TROOPER WITH A VERY DISTINCT TATTOO ON HIS LEFT FOREARM
&
HE IS STANDING EXACTLY WHERE THE .22. cal RIFLE IS STANDING UPRIGHT
-WITHOUT THE HUNTING TAG ATTACHED-
FROM THE PREVIOUS SLIDE**

**PERHAPS THIS TROOPER
KNOWS WHO REMOVED THE
HUNTING LICENSE FROM THE RIFLE
WHERE HE IS SHOWN STANDING???**

Look again...CLOSELY

.22 cal with hunting tag as seized

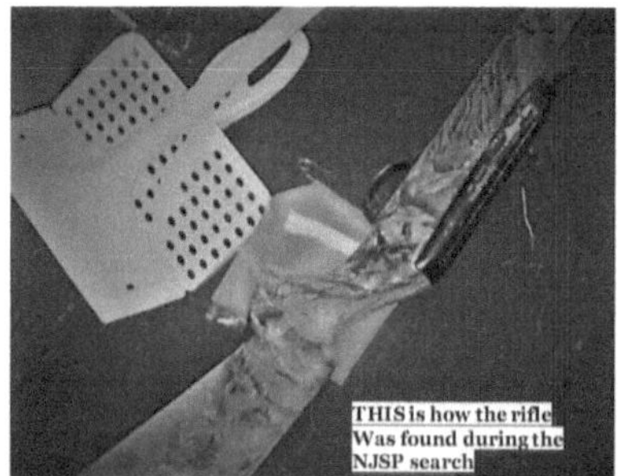

LOOKS LIKE A HUNTING RIFLE

.22 cal WITHOUT hunting tag

...NOW MORE LIKE A SNIPER RIFLE

CLOSER

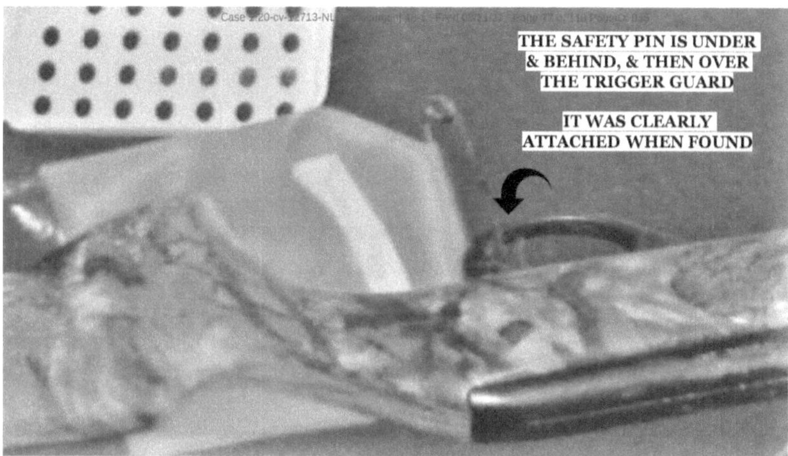

It's quite common for hunters to loop the LARGE safety pin through the trigger guard
when it's not being worn on their backs

The safety pin is large enough to pin through thick hunting garments.
It's length well-exceeds the size of the trigger guard of the .22 cal small game
hunting rifle.

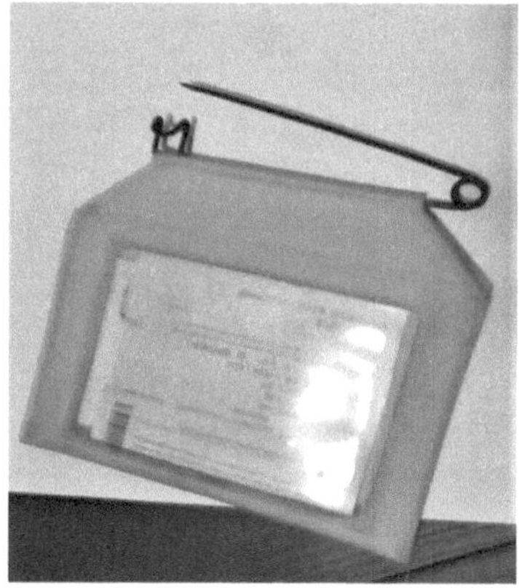

ALSO NOTEWORTHY...

Fax machine used to send documents to Trooper Phill Smith WAS subject to the search warrant but not seized because it would be physical evidence i.e. impeachment evidence

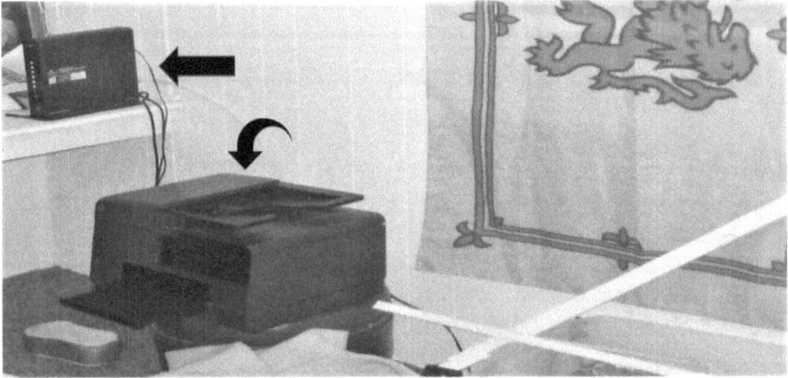

TYRANTS

AND...

CUMBERLAND COUNTY PROSECUTOR'S OFFICE
115 Vine St.
Cumberland, Bridgeton 08302
Property Inventory

Control #:	17-09-0904	Case Number: CASE_NO ● 2188
Crime Type	POSS OF WEAPON FOR UNLW PURP	
Victim:		
Defendant:	JOSEPH R. BRODIE	

Item Number	Evidence Item Category	Storage Location	Description	Contact / Recovered by
17-09-0904-2-13	OTHER	[Shelf 100 - 124] -Shelf-105	ONE (1) BLACK APPLE IPAD SERIAL NUMBER "DYTLX5TTDFHW" WITH CHARGING CORD. MARKED SH11	PORTNORRIS , TROOPER
17-09-0904-2-14	OTHER	[Shelf 100 - 124] -Shelf-105	ONE (1) BLACK "LG" CELL PHONE. MARKED SH12	PORTNORRIS , TROOPER
17-09-0904-2-15	OTHER	[Shelf 100 - 124] -Shelf-105	ONE (1) BLACK "SAMSUNG" CELL PHONE. MARKED SH13	PORTNORRIS , TROOPER
17-09-0904-2-16	OTHER	[Shelf 100 - 124] -Shelf-105	ONE (1) BLACK "CRICKET SAMSUNG" CELL PHONE WITH BLACK AND GRAY CHARGING CORD. MARKED SH14	PORTNORRIS , TROOPER

System Entries Completed	*[signature]*	PHIFER, WALT	Date	03/26/2018 12:28
	Signature	Print Name		
Property Delivered by	*[signature]*	PHIFER, WALT	Date	03/26/2018 12:25
	Signature	Print Name		
Property Received by	*[signature]*	S/A Patrick Mutotoke	Date	03/26/2018 12:25
	Signature	Print Name		

Page 1 of 1

SEE [ALSO]
HANLIN's FALSIFIED
SEARCH WARRANT
AFFIDAVIT

In case you forgot...

4.   Specific Description of What is to be Seized:

The evidence to be seized is a follows:

Any and all weapons that could cause harm to the subject, law enforcement or political figures, including but not limited to rifles, shotguns, automatic weapons, handguns; any chemicals, fuels, substances, materials, containers, equipment, edged weapons, or items associated with possession of a weapon, and/or any other items associated with possession of a Weapon, to include any and all records, papers, documents, manuals, books, scanners, cellular phones or any other evidence pertaining to the possession of a weapon for unlawful purpose, distribution, or use of controlled dangerous substances, and any other evidence reasonably related to this investigation that a thorough diligent search would tend to reveal.

TYRANTS

Again, with emphasis on...

4.   <u>**Specific Description of What is to be Seized:**</u>

The evidence to be seized is a follows:

Any and all weapons that could cause harm to the subject, law enforcement or political figures, including but not limited to rifles, shotguns, automatic weapons, handguns; any chemicals, fuels, substances, materials, containers, equipment, edged weapons, or items associated with possession of a weapon, and/or any other items associated with possession of a Weapon, to include any and all records, papers, documents, manuals, books, scanners, cellular phones or any other evidence pertaining to the possession of a weapon for unlawful purpose, distribution, or use of controlled dangerous substances, and any other evidence reasonably related to this investigation that a thorough diligent search would tend to reveal.

Faxes, scanners that could transmit evidence of criminal activities to the NJSP Station A100

I, Kimberly A. Schultz, of full age, making affirmation according to law, do hereby certify that:

1. I am an Assistant Deputy Public Defender in Cumberland County, and I am assigned to represent the above captioned defendant, and I am familiar with the circumstances of the case.

2. This matter involves an illegal firearm recovered allegedly recovered from my client during a warrant search.

3. I have been provided with credible information that Trooper Phil Smith, was assigned to the Port Norris New Jersey State Police Barracks in 2017, at the time of this alleged incident.

4. I have Comcast phone records that show that Mr. Brodie sent faxes to the Port Norris Barracks in late August 2017. (Exhibit A). I likewise have text messages between Trooper

27	8/25/2017 7:32		3438	NJSP 1281 O	0:03:02
28	8/25/2017 7:53		3438	302 5329 O	0:02:04
29	8/25/2017 7:56		3438	PN NJ 1281 O	0:02:21
30	8/25/2017 9:30		3438	856 5405 O	0:01:45
31	8/25/2017 10:43		3438	PN 1281 O	0:00:59
32	8/25/2017 10:46		3438	NJSP 1281 O	0:03:24

223

Case 1:**And evidence of what is below...** PageID: 855

Smith and Mr. Brodie detailing that Trooper Smith would routinely come by Mr. Brodie's house as they were both veterans and was aware that Mr. Brodie possessed the charged firearms. Mr. Brodie also contends that the State Police assured him that they were in compliance with New Jersey law. (Exhibit B).

5. Testimony from Mr. Brodie's federal trial also indicates that New Jersey State Police were at Mr. Brodie's house on many occasions and were aware that he possessed firearms. (Exhibit C).

6. I believe that there were internal investigations that arose from the relationship Trooper Smith and Mr. Brodie shared that was conducted by the New Jersey State Police and that those investigations would be contained in Trooper Smith's personnel file and/or the New Jersey State Police's disciplinary department.

7. The State Police fax retention policy is also relevant and could potentially contain exculpatory evidence. The policy regarding fax retentions and any/all faxes related to Mr. Brodie should be made available for review.

8. The above-referenced information and files would likely contain exculpatory evidence, pursuant to R. 3:13 and therefore should be made available to the Defense.

9. For all the above reasons, the State should be compelled to disclose the requested personnel files, the fax retention policy and any potential exculpatory information as outlined above.

/s Kimberly A. Schultz, Esq.

Case 1:20-cv-12713-NLH Document 48-1 Filed 08/21/22 Page 88 of 118 PageID: 856 **AND...**

35	8/25/2017 12:06	3438	PN NJSP 1281 O	0:03:44
36	8/25/2017 13:57	3438	PN NJSP 1281 O	0:02:17
37	8/25/2017 23:13	3438	302 5329 O	0:07:38
38	8/25/2017 23:22	3438	PN NJSP 1281 O	0:07:57
39	8/28/2017 13:29	3438	609 5071 O	0:00:50
40	8/28/2017 14:42	3438	PN NJSP 1281 O	0:00:06
41	8/28/2017 14:43	3438	PN NJSP 1281 O	0:00:00
42	8/28/2017 14:44	3438	1281 O	0:02:14
43	8/28/2017 14:48	3438	609 5071 O	0:01:22

CUM-17-002188   10/09/2019 3:37:55 PM   Pg 8 of 34   Trans ID: CRM2019917036

9/17/2019 1:17 PM FROM: Fax Office of the Public Defender 1407   PAGE: 005 OF 005

379	Inbox	From 6471 Direction: Incoming	8/25/2017 1:04:23 PM(UTC-4)		+124044921 66	Read	the VA Source Extraction: Logical
380	Inbox	From 6471 Direction: Incoming	8/25/2017 1:04:21 PM(UTC-4)		+124044921 66	Read	know if I'm going to make it (single dad life) but I definitely want to see the steps you are taking with your claims. Maybe it will help me with my issues with Source Extraction: Logical
381	Inbox	From 6471 Direction: Incoming	8/25/2017 1:04:19 PM(UTC-4)		+124044921 66	Read	You can just call me Phill, due to the fact you're older than me. Haha. I will be back in Monday morning. I'm going to try to get to the DMV today but I don't Source Extraction: Logical
382	Inbox	From 6471 Direction: Incoming	8/25/2017 12:58:36 PM(UTC-4)		+124044921 66	Read	Just try to be nicer to my troopers. Hahaha Source Extraction: Logical
383	Inbox	From 6471 Direction: Incoming	8/25/2017 12:56:23 PM(UTC-4)		+124044921 66	Read	Excellent. The more information I have the better I can document your situation. Source Extraction: Logical

FAXES THAT TROOPER SMITH RECEIVED AT STATION A100...

272	Inbox	From [redacted]6471 Direction: Incoming	8/28/2017 4:10:19 PM(UTC-4)				...didn't get anything yet I don't think. But I have a bad back at the station in a while. Source Extraction: Logical
273	Sent	To [redacted]6471 Direction: Outgoing	8/28/2017 3:44:11 PM(UTC-4)			Sent	I'm out and about atm. Source Extraction: Logical
274	Sent	To [redacted]6471 Direction: Outgoing	8/28/2017 3:44:10 PM(UTC-4)			Sent	I faxed a lot of it to you. Not much more to give. Did you get my fax from today? Source Extraction: Logical
275	Inbox	From [redacted]6471 Direction: Incoming	8/28/2017 3:22:14 PM(UTC-4)		+124044921 66	Read	You want me to swing by and grab that stuff. Source Extraction: Logical
276	Sent	To [redacted]6471 Direction: Outgoing	8/28/2017 9:26:06 AM(UTC-4)			Sent	Inspria's letter contradicts everything that she says a day earlier in a voicemail. Its comical. They obviously don't know I'm anal about saving evidence. Source Extraction: Logical
277	Sent	To [redacted]6471 Direction: Outgoing	8/28/2017 9:24:51 AM(UTC-4)			Sent	"Inspira Source Extraction: Logical
278	Sent	To [redacted]6471 Direction: Outgoing	8/28/2017 9:24:03 AM(UTC-4)			Sent	Yeah, I'll be sending you the apology letter from Inspiration AND a transcript of the voicemail Mary Rowinskie, billing chief of inspira left me, for you to read and compare. That's even more interesting. Source Extraction: Logical
279	Inbox	From [redacted]6471 Direction: Incoming	8/28/2017 9:22:20 AM(UTC-4)		+124044921 66	Read	Got all your paperwork. Some interesting reading haha. Source Extraction: Logical

208	Sent	To [redacted]6471 Direction: Outgoing	8/31/2017 8:56:08 PM(UTC-4)			Sent	We Need To Talk Of Record Source Extraction: Logical

And more texts like these...

| 90 | Sent | To ▮▮▮▮6471
Direction:
Outgoing | 9/5/2017
3:47:36 PM(UTC-4) | | | Sent | I understand that my text messages have put you in a very precarious position.

For what it's worth, get a detective at a upper level to review this, and you'll see that my messages are sincere.
Source Extraction: Logical |
| 91 | Sent | To ▮▮▮▮6471
Direction:
Outgoing | 9/5/2017
3:08:44 PM(UTC-4) | | | Sent | You know that I have a security camera and basically what it does, it covers 13 seconds worth of footage, but the cars are flying by my house sooooo fast that I cant even take a picture to show you. That's how bad they're speeding.
Source Extraction: Logical |

WHERE BRODIE ASKED SMITH TO SHARE HIS FAXES WITH AN "UPPER LEVEL DETECTIVE"

LOOK AGAIN

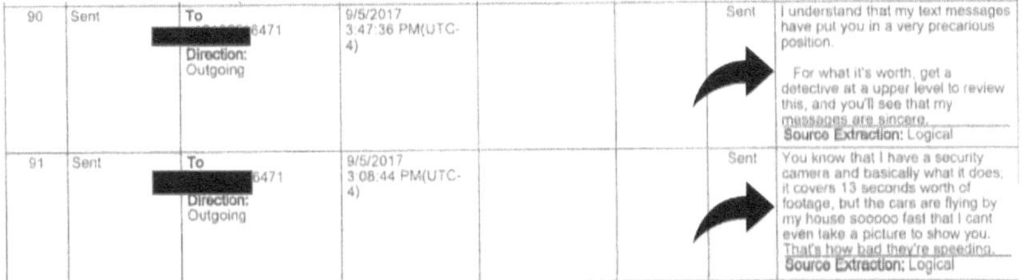

| 90 | Sent | To [redacted]6471
Direction:
Outgoing | 9/5/2017
3:47:36 PM(UTC-4) | | | Sent | I understand that my text messages have put you in a very precarious position.

For what it's worth, get a detective at a upper level to review this, and you'll see that my messages are sincere.
Source Extraction: Logical |
| 91 | Sent | To [redacted]6471
Direction:
Outgoing | 9/5/2017
3:08:44 PM(UTC-4) | | | Sent | You know that I have a security camera and basically what it does; it covers 13 seconds worth of footage, but the cars are flying by my house sooooo fast that I cant even take a picture to show you. That's how bad they're speeding.
Source Extraction: Logical |

TROOPER SMITH SHARED THIS INFORMATION WITH OTHER TROOPERS AT STATION A100

"THIS IS STUFF I POST AROUND THE STATION.

| 244 | Inbox | From ████6471 Direction: Incoming | 8/31/2017 1:36:22 PM(UTC-4) | | +124044921 66 | Read | Yeah keep me updated. This is stuff I I post around the station. So these guys know what's going on Source Extraction: Logical |

SO THESE GUYS KNOW WHAT'S GOING ON"

DESPITE THAT SMS
&
THE FAX TRANSMISSIONS TO A100...

THE NJSP DENIED HAVING VERY LITTLE
IF ANY
PRIOR KNOWLEDGE OF BRODIE

ALL NJSP TESTIFIED UNDER OATH IN CAMDEN FEDERAL COURT THAT THEY KNEW NOTHING ABOUT BRODIE OTHER THAN HE WAS A VETERAN WHO POSSESSED FIREARMS...
YET 1059 SMS MESSAGES WERE EXCHANGED BETWEEN BRODIE & SMITH BETWEEN 08/25/2017 & 09/20/2017

YET ONLY 383 WERE LEFT ON BRODIE'S CELL PHONE WHEN A FORENSIC EXPERT PERFORMED AN EXTRACTION A YEAR LATER...

656 SMS MESSAGES WERE DELETED...

**WHILE BRODIE WAS IN A JAIL CELL
& HIS CELLULAR PHONE WAS IN
THE CUSTODY OF THE NJSP...
SOMEONE WAS USING IT,
CALLING THE DEVICE SO TO
ANSWER CALLS AND BY-PASS THE
LOCKSCREEN TO GET TO THE
HOMESCREEN....
FROM THERE, THE SMS
WERE DELETED**

SEE FOR YOURSELF...

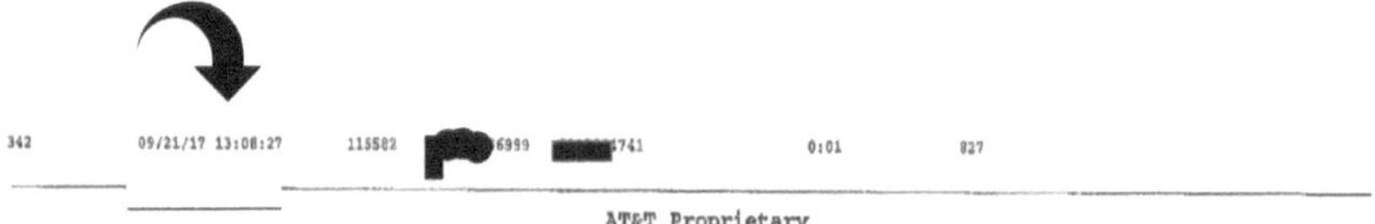

AND HERE AGAIN...
WHILE BRODIE IS STILL BEING
HELD IN SOLITARY CONFINEMENT

WHILE THE NJSP POSSESS HIS
CELLPHONE
&
THE NJSP DID NOT SEEK NOR
HAVE A SEARCH WARRANT
TO SEARCH THE PHONE

BRODIE's 4TH AMENDMENT
RIGHTS WERE VIOLATED TO
DESTROY IMPEACHMENT &
EXCULPATORY EVIDENCE

WIRELINE

2518536
07/22/2018

AT&T has queried for records from 01/01/2017 12:00:00am to 09/21/2017 11:59:59pm
AT&T has queried for records using Eastern Time Zone. AT&T's records are stored and provided in UTC.

```
Run Date:        07/22/2018
Run Time:        16:53:23
Voice Usage For:   ████████4741

Item       ConnDateTime      Originating   Sec. Orig.   Terminating   Dialed    Elapsed   CIC   Call Code   Orig.
           (UTC)             Number                     Number        Number    Time                        Acc.
343        09/21/17 16:43:45   1████        ██████281    █████4741               0:01            827
```

NOT ONLY ARE THE FRUITS OF HANLIN's WARRANT INADMISSIBLE, BUT THEY CONTAINED EVIDENCE OF CRIMES BY NJSP AND MEMBERS OF THE CONGRESSIONAL STAFF...

STILL, THE NJSP WERE DEEMED MORE CREDIBLE AND BRODIE WAS SENTENCED TO 87 MONTHS IN FEDERAL PRISON

These NJSP troopers were capable of observing details as minute as a Combat Infantryman Badge New Jersey State Issued License Plate

Details MATTER.
ESPECIALLY, when their testimony contains otherwise inexplicable memory lapses

| 310 | Inbox | From [redacted] 6471 Direction: Incoming | 8/25/2017 10:11:05 PM(UTC-4) | | +124044921 66 | Read | I noticed the CIB when I came Source Extraction: Logical |

206	Sent	To █████6471 Direction: Outgoing	8/31/2017 9:27:47 PM(UTC-4)			Sent	I want to have a personal, friendship relationship with you while respecting your profession. I will ALWAYS inform you of any potentially dangerous situations. I'm not asking you for anything. I don't want anything from you but your friendship. Source Extraction: Logical
207	Sent	To █████6471 Direction: Outgoing	8/31/2017 8:56:09 PM(UTC-4)			Sent	WNTTOR Source Extraction: Logical
208	Sent	To █████6471 Direction: Outgoing	8/31/2017 8:56:08 PM(UTC-4)			Sent	We Need To Talk Of Record Source Extraction: Logical
209	Sent	To █████6471 Direction: Outgoing	8/31/2017 8:50:50 PM(UTC-4)			Sent	NJSP won't be able to contain this. WNTTOR Source Extraction: Logical

TROOPER SMITH WAS AWARE THAT BRODIE WAS ACTING IN THE CAPACITY OF AN INVESTIGATIVE JOURNALIST & SMITH BENEFITED (PROFESSIONALLY) FROM INFORMATION GLEANED FROM BRODIE's SOURCES

SMITH DOESN'T WANT ANYONE AT THE BARRACKS TO KNOW SO SMITH ADVISES BRODIE NOT TO CALL THE BARRACKS FOR HIM REGARDING ANYTHING

MS.MEDNICK UNKNOWINGLY MADE THAT MISTAKE @3:21 PM ON SEPTEMBER 20TH 2017

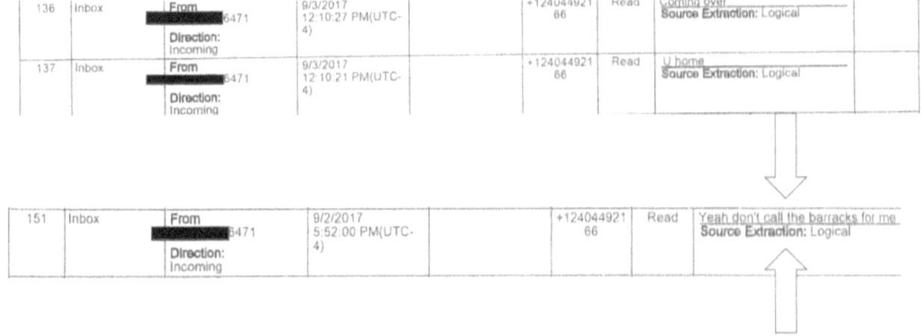

136	Inbox	From █████6471 Direction: Incoming	9/3/2017 12:10:27 PM(UTC-4)		+124044921 66	Read	Coming over Source Extraction: Logical
137	Inbox	From █████6471 Direction: Incoming	9/3/2017 12:10:21 PM(UTC-4)		+124044921 66	Read	U home Source Extraction: Logical

151	Inbox	From █████6471 Direction: Incoming	9/2/2017 5:52:00 PM(UTC-4)		+124044921 66	Read	Yeah don't call the barracks for me Source Extraction: Logical

**IN THIS PARTICULAR INSTANCE,
BRODIE IS ASKING A FOLLOW-UP QUESTION
REGARDING SURRENDERING AND/OR
REGISTERING HIS FIREARMS LEGALLY
THIS OCCURRED AFTER ONE OF SMITH's VISITS TO
BRODIE's HOME TO INSPECT THE WEAPONS
ONE WEAPON HE MISTOOK FOR AN "AK-47"
WHICH WAS REPORTEDLY HEARD BY GALEZNIAK AT THE
SCENE YET MORE LIKELY IT WAS RELAYED FROM
SMITH AFTER ONE OF HIS VISITS.
THIS IS WHY NO AK-47 WAS FOUND ON SCENE.
THIS (PURPORTED) STATEMENT IS USED AS A PRETEXT
FOR ACQUIRING A SEARCH WARRANT IF BRODIE
DIDN'T COOPERATE WITH NJSP REQUESTS**

| 70 | Inbox | From [redacted]6471
Direction:
Incoming | 9/7/2017
3:16:26 PM(UTC-4) | | +124044921
66 | Read | Sorry about that I'll give you a call when I get home
Source Extraction: Logical |
| 71 | Sent | To [redacted]6471
Direction:
Outgoing | 9/7/2017
2:50:51 PM(UTC-4) | | | Sent | Hey are you busy? Can I call you and ask you someting?
Source Extraction: Logical |

**SMITH USES IDENTICAL LANGUAGE ABOUT
THE VA HEALTHCARE SYSTEM
IN SMS MESSAGE AS BRODIE DID...
BRODIE WENT TO FEDERAL PRISON FOR IT**

63	Sent	To [redacted]6471 Direction: Outgoing	9/9/2017 3:02:39 PM(UTC-4)			Sent	Hey Buddy, how are you? I went to PA. Truck wasn't big enough for my four Wheeler have to go back in three weeks. Phillips game tonight? **Source Extraction:** Logical
64	Inbox	From [redacted]6471 Direction: Incoming	9/8/2017 8:48:29 AM(UTC-4)		+124044921 66	Read	Answer your phone **Source Extraction:** Logical
65	Sent	To [redacted]6471 Direction: Outgoing	9/8/2017 8:43:40 AM(UTC-4)			Sent	What's up dude? What happened? **Source Extraction:** Logical
66	Inbox	From [redacted]6471 Direction: Incoming	9/8/2017 8:41:38 AM(UTC-4)		+124044921 66	Read	Livid **Source Extraction:** Logical
67	Inbox	From [redacted]6471 Direction: Incoming	9/8/2017 8:41:26 AM(UTC-4)		+124044921 66	Read	I am fucking licit right now **Source Extraction:** Logical

**BRODIE REPORTED THE MMS
MESSAGE (D**K PIC) RECEIVED FROM MF
TO TROOPER SMITH, OFFERING TO SHOW HIM,
IN THE EVENT SMITH HAD TO CONTACT
HIS OFFICE FOR "ASSISTANCE" WITH THE VA,
& WHAT TO EXPECT**

**TROOPER SMITH, ASSUMING BRODIE WAS
REFERRING TO OFFICIAL 1 (HIMSELF)
AS THE SENDER OFF THAT MMS,
TOLD BRODIE
HE [SMITH] "HEARD HE WAS A 'F*G' "
& "IT WOULDN'T SURPRISE HIM"
OBVIOUSLY, THE NJSP WANTED THOSE SMS DELETED**

THE NJSP MIRANDA CARD

TROOPER POEPPEL SAID MIRANDA WAS READ AT 6PM.

HANLIN SAID AROUND 1130 PM.

BOTH TESTIFIED THAT THEY (PURPORTEDLY) MISTAKENLY SIGNED IN THE WRONG SPOT...

HANLIN READ (WHILE HE WAS AT 7188 ACKLEY-PER THE GUZMAN CAD ABSTRACT) AND POEPPEL WITNESSED...THEY JUST HAPPENED "TO SIGN IN THE WRONG PLACES".

:-)

I acknowledge that I have been advised of the constitutional rights found on the reverse side of this card.

Yo reconozco que he sido aconsejado de los derechos constitucionales encontrados en el lado contrario de esta tarjeta.

____
Accused or Suspect

Tpr. J. Rand #8069 _______ Det. M. Hanlin 7807
Advising Officer   Witnessing Officer

Date   9/20/17   Time   11:25pm

S.P. 429 (Rev 11-73)

A100-2017-00664

EXAMINE BRODIE's SIGNATURE
VS
THE CONTENTIOUS NJSP MIRANDA CARD

HANLIN CLAIMS THIS IS "PM"...&
DON'T LET YOUR EYES DECEIVE YOU &
THINK IT'S "AM" HANLIN EVEN APOLOGIZED FOR HIS "SLOPPY HANDWRITING"

Time _______ 11:25 _______

I acknowledge that I have been advised of the constitutional rights found on the reverse side of this card.

Yo reconozco que he sido advertido de mis derechos constitucionales encontrados en el lado contrario de esta tarjeta.

Accused or Suspect

TPR J Rand #9069
Advising Officer

Det M. Hanlin 7807
Witnessing Officer

Date 9/20/17   Time 11:25

SP 429 (Rev 11-73)

A10C-2017-00064

BRODIE TESTIFIED IT WAS A UNIFORMED TROOPER (POEPPEL) WHO READ HIM MIRANDA @ 1:15 AM IMMEDIATELY BEFORE HIS TRANSPORT TO IHCB EST TRAVEL TIME WAS 30-40 MINUTES. BRODIE ARRIVED AT IHCB AT 1:50 AM PER THE IHCB 09/21/2017 MEDICAL RECORDS. AND 1:24 DEPARTURE FROM A100PER TORRES CAD ... 1:15 AM MAKES SENSE.

BRODIE PAUSED AFTER SIGNING HIS FIRST NAME, ASKING FOR ASSURANCE THAT HE WOULD BE AFFORDED HIS "ONE-PHONE CALL" TO HIS LAWYER AS PROMISED THE UNIFORMED ADVISING OFFICER SNATCHED THE CARD AWAY THE REMAINDER OF THAT SIGNATURE IS NOT BRODIE's BRODIE PRESENTS CONSISTENT EXAMPLES OF HIS SIGNATURE DATING BACK 24 YEARS! NEARLY A ¼ CENTURY AND IT HAS RETAINED CERTAIN QUALITIES. BRODIE CONTENDS THIS IS WHY MANY SIGNATURE PAGES WERE REMOVED FROM BRODIE'S 09/21/2017 INSPIRA RECORDS

Case 1:20-cv-12713-NLH   Document 48-1   Filed 08/21/22   Page 113 of 118 PageID: 881

I acknowledge that I have been advised of the constitutional rights found on the reverse side of this card.

Yo reconozco que he sido acusado de los derechos encontrados en el lado contrario de esta tarjeta.

_____________________________ Accused or Suspect

TPR J Ronald #8069   Det M. Hardin 7807
Advising Officer   Witnessing Officer

Date   9/20/17   Time   11:25pm

S.P. 429 (Rev. 11-73)

A10C-2017-00664

BRODIE's SIGNATURE FROM HIS USMC RECORDS, DATED 03/31/1999
NOTICE HE INCLUDES "RYAN" IN HIS SIGNATURE
THE "J" IS DISTINCT AS IS THE EXAGERRATED LOOPING D IN HIS LAST NAME

Case 1:20-cv-12713-NLH   Document 48-1   Filed 08/21/22   Page 114 of 118 PageID: 882

17. DO YOU HAVE ANY OTHER QUESTIONS OR CONCERN ABOUT YOUR HEALTH? (If "YES" Explain.)
NO / **X** YES   KIDNEY FUNCTION.

18. AT THE PRESENT TIME, DO YOU INTEND TO SEEK DEPARTMENT OF VETERANS AFFAIRS (VA) DISABILITY?
(X one. If "YES" list conditions for which you will ask for VA Disability)

NO
X YES
UNCERTAIN

19. CERTIFICATION. I certify that the information provided above is true and complete to the best of my knowledge.

SIGNATURE OF SERVICE MEMBER	DATE SIGNED
Joseph Ryan Brodie	990331

JOSEPH BRODIE

17. DO YOU HAVE ANY OTHER QUESTIONS OR CONCERNS ABOUT YOUR HEALTH? (If "YES" explain)

| | NO | KIDNEY function. |
| X | YES | |

18. AT THE PRESENT TIME, DO YOU INTEND TO SEEK DEPARTMENT OF VETERANS AFFAIRS (VA) DISABILITY?
(X one. If "YES" list conditions for which you will ask for VA Disability)

	NO	
X	YES	
	UNCERTAIN	

19. CERTIFICATION. I certify that the information provided above is true and complete to the best of my knowledge.

SIGNATURE OF SERVICE MEMBER	DATE SIGNED

BRODIE's LAST NAME IS SIGNED IN LONG STROKES SIMILAR TO THE STROKES IN POEPPEL's LAST NAME

I acknowledge that I have been advised of the constitutional rights found on the reverse side of this card.

Yo reconozco que he sido aconsejado de los derechos constitucionales encontrados en el lado contrario de esta tarjeta.

Accused or Suspect

Advising Officer   Witnessing Officer

Date ___9/20/17___   Time ___11:25 am___

SP 429 (Rev. 11-73)

BRODIE's USMC ENLISTMENT FROM APRIL 11, 1998
THE DISTINCT "J" & EXAGERRATED LOOPING "D"
BRODIE HISTORICALLY HAS SIGNED
"JOSEPH RYAN BRODIE"
AS HE IS KNOWN BY HIS PARENTS
OR
SHORTENED IT TO JOSEPH R. BRODIE

PART C - STATEMENT OF UNDERSTANDING BY THE INDIVIDUAL

I have read and understand this statement, I understand that I may have the opportunity systems notices and current Marine Corps directives which pertain to forms which I am asked

___9 80411___

Date   Signature of the Individual

PRIVACY ACT STATEMENT FOR MARINE CORPS PERSONNEL AND PAY RECORDS
NAVMC 11000 (REV. 5-90) SN: 0000-00-006-6542 U/I: PAD (50 sheets per pad)

(File Original in OQR or SRB; Provide Copy to Individual)

FINALLY...TO ADD INSULT TO INJURY THE USAO AUTHORS PRESS RELEASES THAT "WHITE SUPREMACIST MATERIALS" WERE IN BRODIE'S RESIDENCE

INSINUATING THAT BRODIE, HIMSELF, IS A WHITE SUPREMACIST

Chanukah, 2015, Brodie & his dogs...
ALL wearing Kippahs after lighting their Menorah

Brodie speaks Hebrew, practices/observes Kashrut, and had previously shown the fliers to trooper Smith after finding them on his lawn and in his driveway.

Brodie's "demonstration" of his ZMODO system was a video of the fliers being placed there at night

JOSEPH BRODIE

THE MEDICAL RECORDS COMPARISON
BEGINS ON THE NEXT SLIDE

IN THE GOVERNMENT's RESPONSE
IT DENIES THAT THERE IS ANY DIFFERENCE
BETWEEN THESE RECORDS
OR THAT IT WOULD HAVE MADE AN IMPACT

THE USAO HAD A LICENSE TO LIE,
TO WIN AT ANY COST
&
IS ONLY PART OF
AN EPIDEMIC OF PROSECUTORIAL MISCONDUCT
IN THE CRIMINAL JUSTICE SYSTEM

THE POLITICAL WEAPONIZATION OF THE DOJ

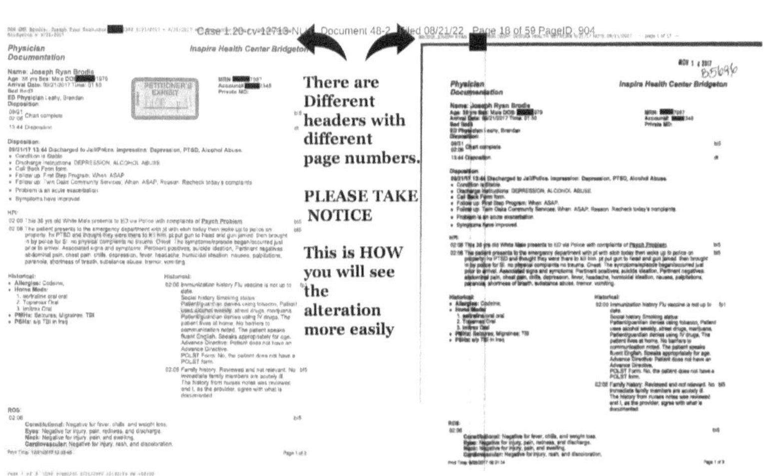

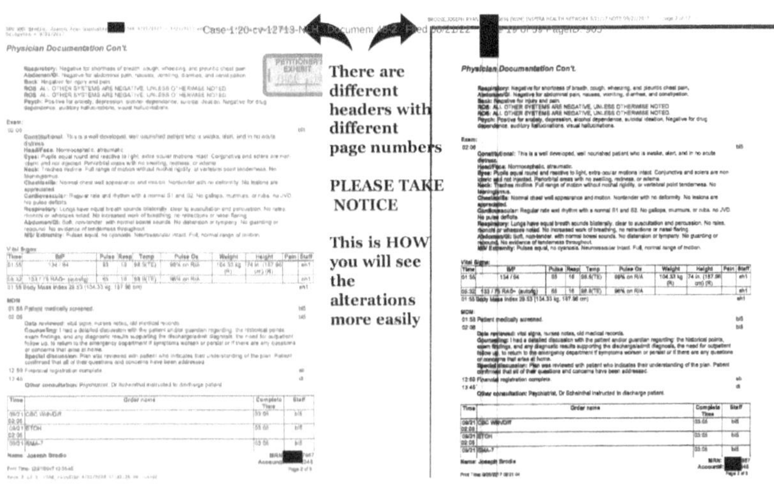
There are
different
headers with
different
page numbers

PLEASE TAKE
 NOTICE

This is HOW
you will see
the
alterations
more easily

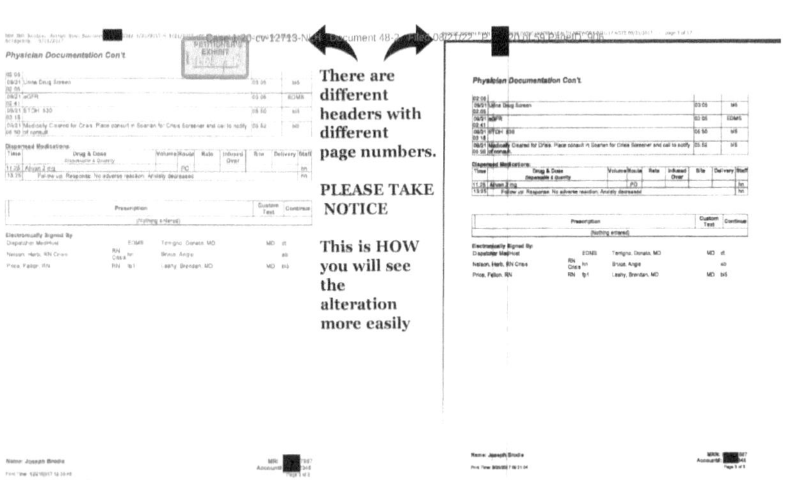
There are
different
headers with
different
page numbers.

PLEASE TAKE
 NOTICE

This is HOW
you will see
the
alteration
more easily

JOSEPH BRODIE

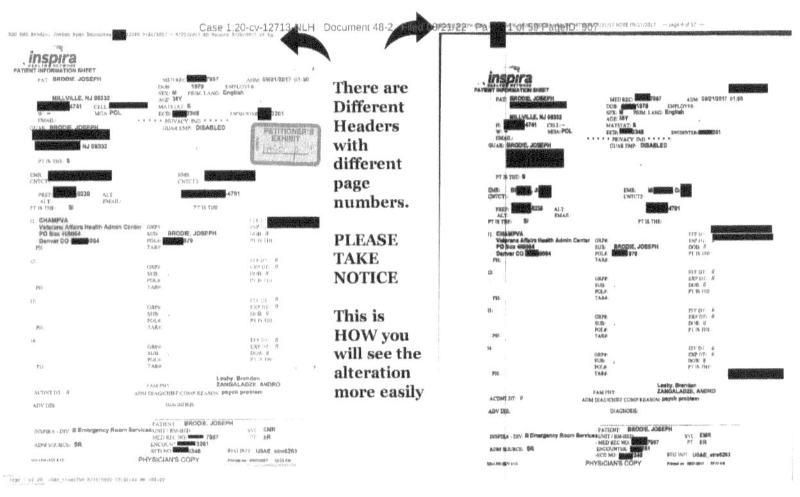

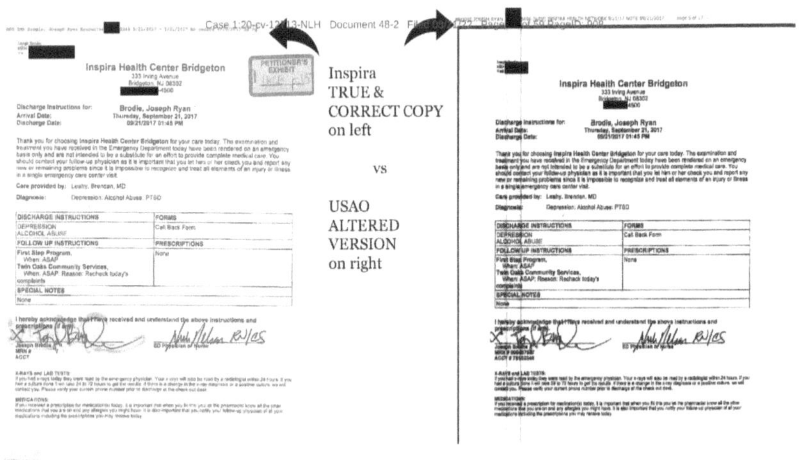

TYRANTS

Inspira 28 page on
LEFT

vs

USAO 17 page records
RIGHT

SAME pages but different
page numbers
in the top margin because
they have been **ALTERED
TO CONCEAL SPECIFIC
INFORMATION
DETRIMENTAL TO THE
GOVERNMENT'S
NARRATIVE**

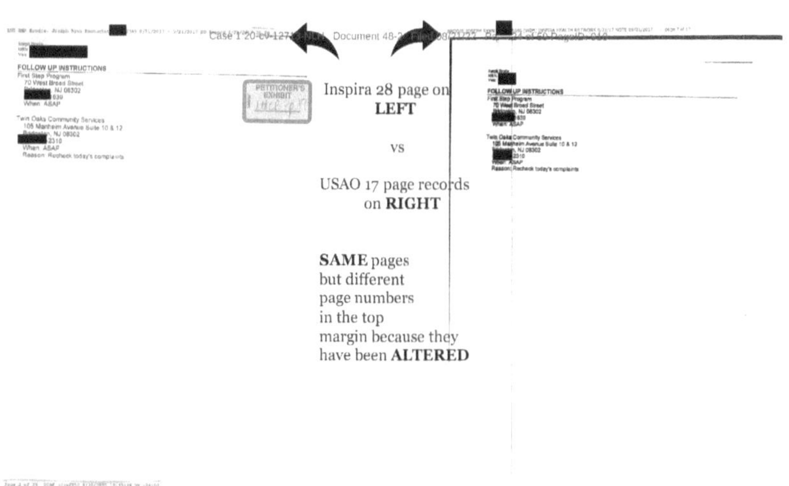

Inspira 28 page on
LEFT

vs

USAO 17 page records
on **RIGHT**

SAME pages
but different
page numbers
in the top
margin because they
have been **ALTERED**

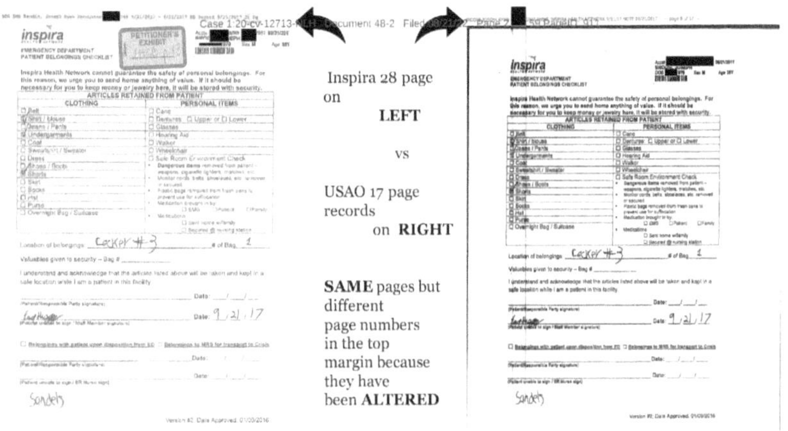

Inspira 28 page on

LEFT

vs

USAO 17 page records

on **RIGHT**

SAME pages but different page numbers in the top margin because they have been **ALTERED**

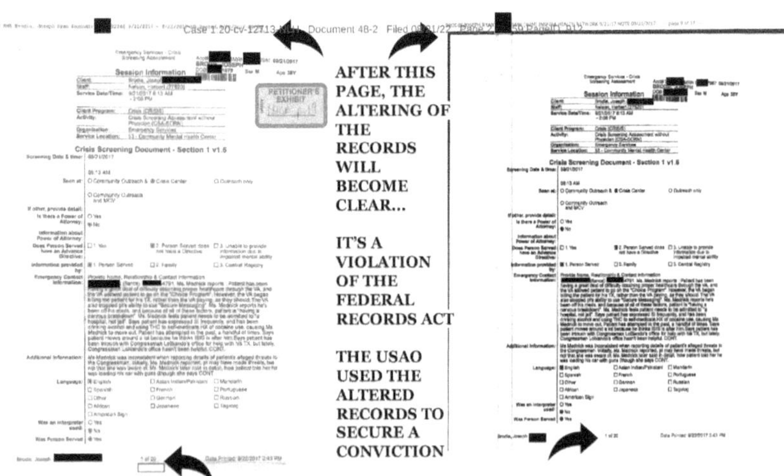

AFTER THIS PAGE, THE ALTERING OF THE RECORDS WILL BECOME CLEAR...

IT'S A VIOLATION OF THE FEDERAL RECORDS ACT

THE USAO USED THE ALTERED RECORDS TO SECURE A CONVICTION

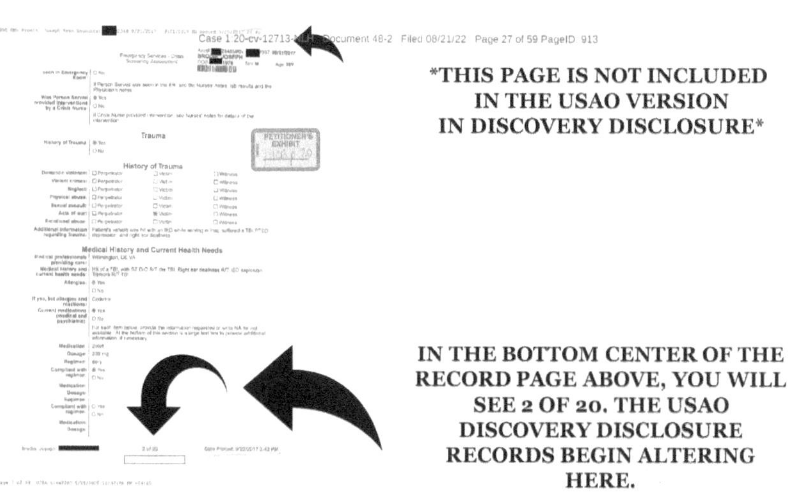

***THIS PAGE IS NOT INCLUDED
IN THE USAO VERSION
IN DISCOVERY DISCLOSURE***

**IN THE BOTTOM CENTER OF THE
RECORD PAGE ABOVE, YOU WILL
SEE 2 OF 20. THE USAO
DISCOVERY DISCLOSURE
RECORDS BEGIN ALTERING
HERE.**

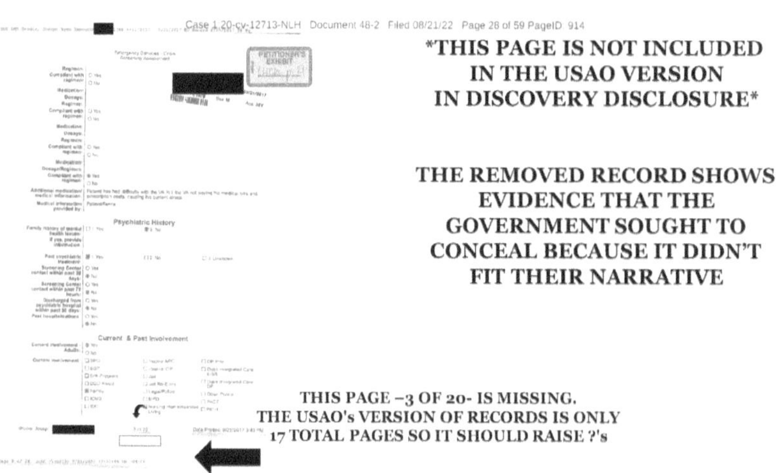

***THIS PAGE IS NOT INCLUDED
IN THE USAO VERSION
IN DISCOVERY DISCLOSURE***

**THE REMOVED RECORD SHOWS
EVIDENCE THAT THE
GOVERNMENT SOUGHT TO
CONCEAL BECAUSE IT DIDN'T
FIT THEIR NARRATIVE**

**THIS PAGE –3 OF 20- IS MISSING.
THE USAO's VERSION OF RECORDS IS ONLY
17 TOTAL PAGES SO IT SHOULD RAISE ?'s**

JOSEPH BRODIE

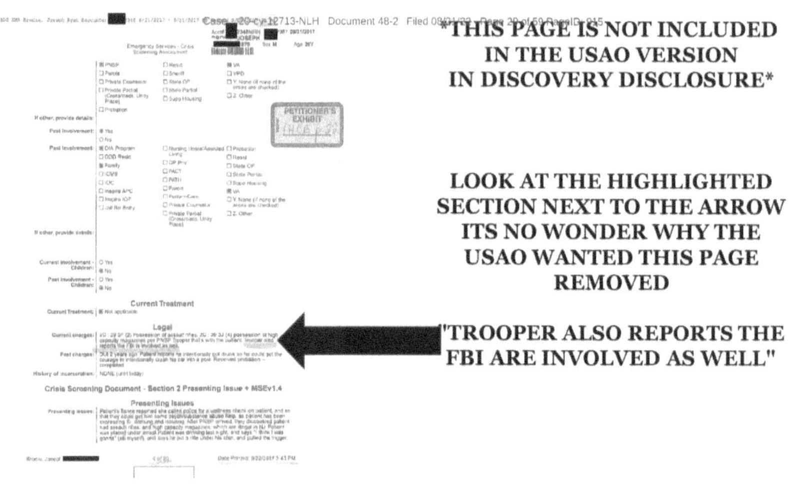

***THIS PAGE IS NOT INCLUDED
IN THE USAO VERSION
IN DISCOVERY DISCLOSURE***

**LOOK AT THE HIGHLIGHTED
SECTION NEXT TO THE ARROW
ITS NO WONDER WHY THE
USAO WANTED THIS PAGE
REMOVED**

**"TROOPER ALSO REPORTS THE
FBI ARE INVOLVED AS WELL"**

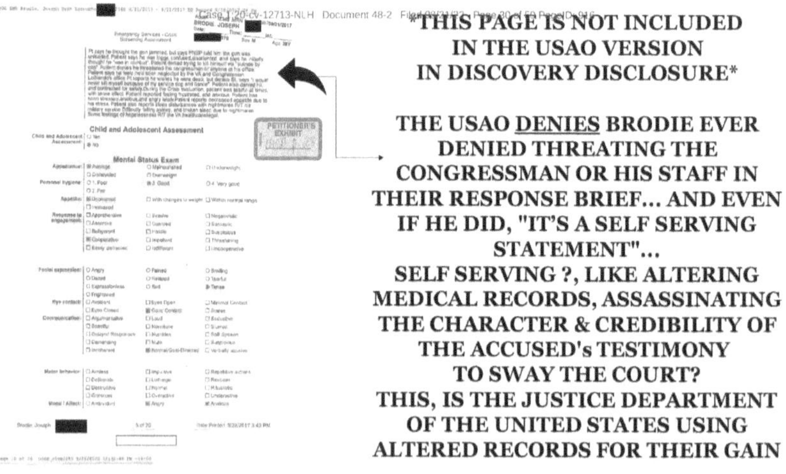

***THIS PAGE IS NOT INCLUDED
IN THE USAO VERSION
IN DISCOVERY DISCLOSURE***

**THE USAO <u>DENIES</u> BRODIE EVER
DENIED THREATING THE
CONGRESSMAN OR HIS STAFF IN
THEIR RESPONSE BRIEF... AND EVEN
IF HE DID, "IT'S A SELF SERVING
STATEMENT"...
SELF SERVING ?, LIKE ALTERING
MEDICAL RECORDS, ASSASSINATING
THE CHARACTER & CREDIBILITY OF
THE ACCUSED's TESTIMONY
TO SWAY THE COURT?
THIS, IS THE JUSTICE DEPARTMENT
OF THE UNITED STATES USING
ALTERED RECORDS FOR THEIR GAIN**

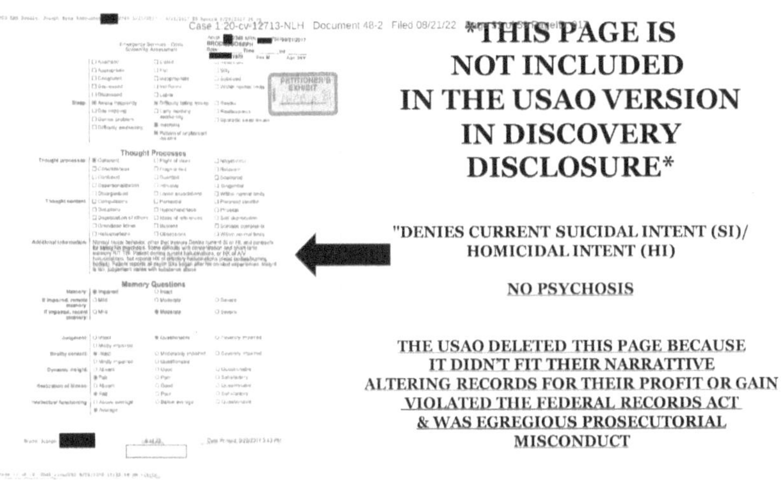

Case 1:20-cv-12713-NLH   Document 48-2   Filed 08/21/22

**THIS PAGE IS
NOT INCLUDED
IN THE USAO VERSION
IN DISCOVERY
DISCLOSURE***

"DENIES CURRENT SUICIDAL INTENT (SI)/
HOMICIDAL INTENT (HI)

<u>NO PSYCHOSIS</u>

<u>THE USAO DELETED THIS PAGE BECAUSE
IT DIDN'T FIT THEIR NARRATTIVE
ALTERING RECORDS FOR THEIR PROFIT OR GAIN
VIOLATED THE FEDERAL RECORDS ACT
& WAS EGREGIOUS PROSECUTORIAL
MISCONDUCT</u>

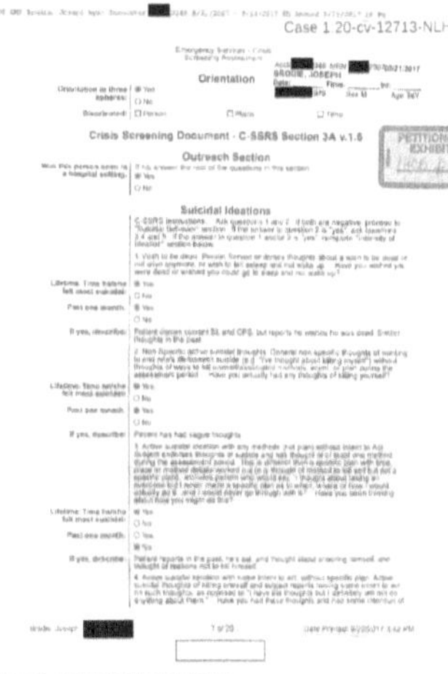

Case 1:20-cv-12713-NLH   Document 48-2   Filed

**THIS PAGE IS NOT INCLUDED
IN THE USAO VERSION
IN DISCOVERY DISCLOSURE***

IT IS DELIBERATELY OMITTED
BECAUSE IT DEMONSTRATES A LOW
RISK OF INJURY OR HARM TO SELF,
OTHERS OR PROPERTY

THIS WOULD BE EVIDENCE IN
DIRECT CONTRADICTION TO THE
ARGUMENT FOR PRE-TRIAL
DETENTION AND PROSECUTION.

IT WAS OMITTED TO HELP
DEMONSTRATE INTENT AND A
PROPENSITY FOR VIOLENCE

JOSEPH BRODIE

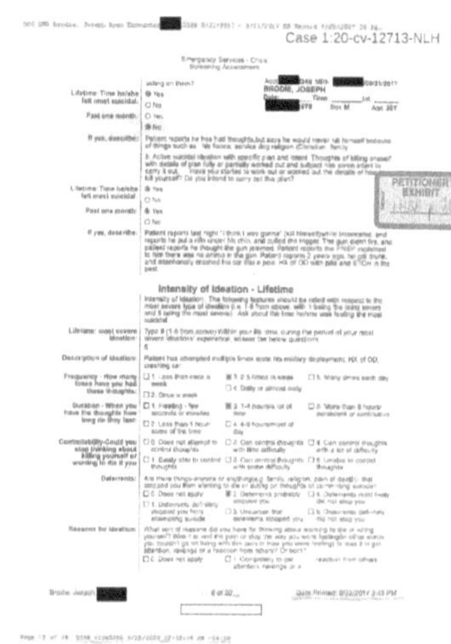

***THIS PAGE IS NOT INCLUDED
IN THE USAO VERSION
IN DISCOVERY DISCLOSURE***

**IT IS DELIBERATELY OMITTED BECAUSE IT
DEMONSTRATES A LOW
RISK OF INJURY OR HARM TO
SELF, OTHERS OR PROPERTY**

**<u>19 of the 20 pages of clinical notes were
deleted & WHAT REMAINED was then
disclosed in discovery
as "true & correct" copies...</u>**

**<u>19 pages omitted JUST in this section
Yet the USAO version contains 17 pages
TOTAL</u>**

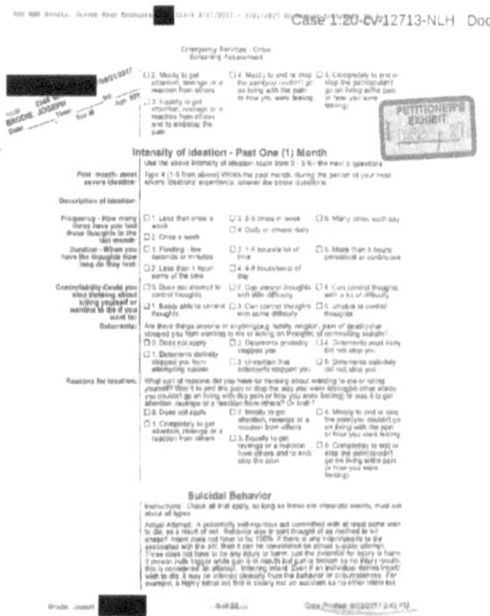

***THIS PAGE IS NOT INCLUDED
IN THE USAO VERSION
IN DISCOVERY DISCLOSURE***

**IT IS DELIBERATELY OMITTED BECAUSE
IT DEMONSTRATES A LOW
RISK OF INJURY OR HARM TO SELF, OTHERS
OR PROPERTY**

**THIS WOULD BE EVIDENCE
IN DIRECT CONTRADICTION TO
THE ARGUMENT FOR PRE-TRIAL DETENTION
AND PROSECUTION, & SENTENCING
ENHANCEMENTS.**

**IT WAS OMITTED TO
HELP DEMONSTRATE INTENT AND
A PROPENSITY FOR VIOLENCE**

THIS PAGE IS MISSING FROM THE
RECORDS DISCLOSED BY THE USAO

IT IS DELIBERATELY
OMITTED BECAUSE IT DEMONSTRATES A
LOW RISK OF INJURY OR HARM
TO SELF, OTHERS OR PROPERTY

THIS WOULD BE
EVIDENCE IN DIRECT CONTRADICTION
TO THE ARGUMENT
FOR PRE TRIAL DETENTION AND
PROSECUTION, &
SENTENCING ENHANCEMENTS.

IT WAS OMITTED
TO HELP DEMONSTRATE INTENT
AND A PROPENSITY FOR VIOLENCE

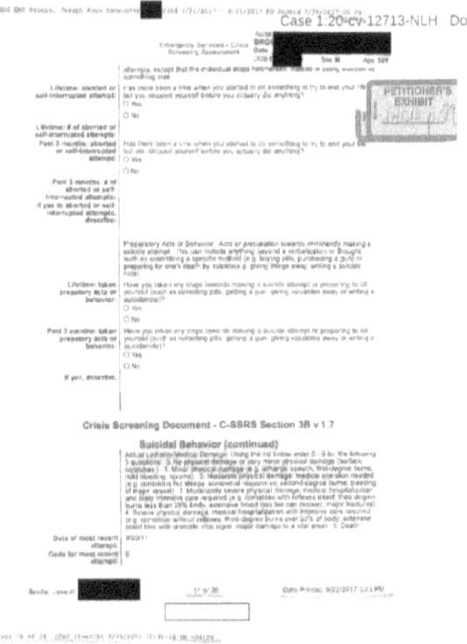

THIS PAGE IS NOT INCLUDED
IN THE USAO VERSION
IN DISCOVERY DISCLOSURE*

IT IS DELIBERATELY OMITTED BECAUSE IT
DEMONSTRATES A LOW RISK OF INJURY OR
HARM TO SELF, OTHERS OR PROPERTY

THIS WOULD
BE EVIDENCE IN DIRECT CONTRADICTION TO
THE ARGUMENT FOR PRE TRIAL DETENTION,
PROSECUTION, &
SENTENCING ENHANCEMENTS.

IT WAS OMITTED TO HELP DEMONSTRATE
INTENT AND A PROPENSITY FOR VIOLENCE

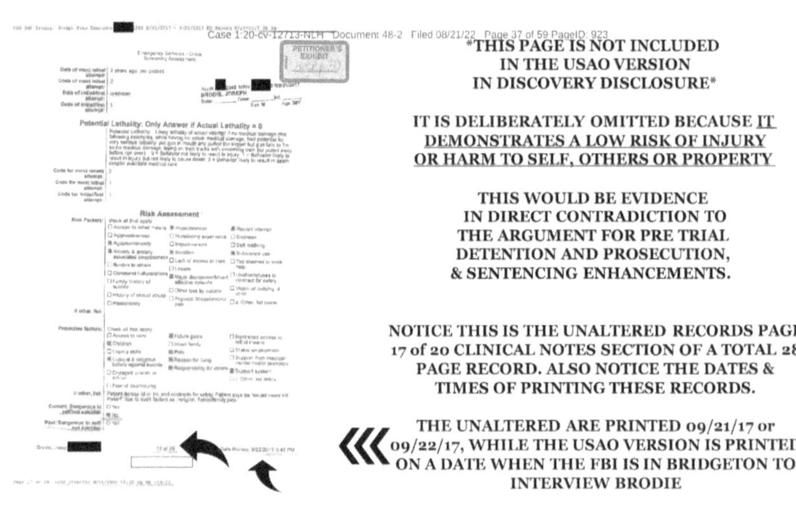

Case 1:20-cv-12713-NLH   Document 48-2   Filed 08/21/22   Page 37 of 59 PageID: 923

***THIS PAGE IS NOT INCLUDED
IN THE USAO VERSION
IN DISCOVERY DISCLOSURE***

**IT IS DELIBERATELY OMITTED BECAUSE IT
DEMONSTRATES A LOW RISK OF INJURY
OR HARM TO SELF, OTHERS OR PROPERTY**

**THIS WOULD BE EVIDENCE
IN DIRECT CONTRADICTION TO
THE ARGUMENT FOR PRE TRIAL
DETENTION AND PROSECUTION,
& SENTENCING ENHANCEMENTS.**

**NOTICE THIS IS THE UNALTERED RECORDS PAGE
17 of 20 CLINICAL NOTES SECTION OF A TOTAL 28
PAGE RECORD. ALSO NOTICE THE DATES &
TIMES OF PRINTING THESE RECORDS.**

**THE UNALTERED ARE PRINTED 09/21/17 or
09/22/17, WHILE THE USAO VERSION IS PRINTED
ON A DATE WHEN THE FBI IS IN BRIDGETON TO
INTERVIEW BRODIE**

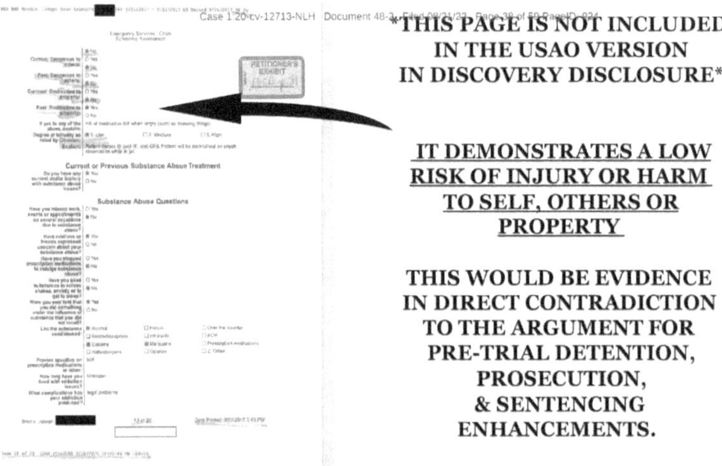

Case 1:20-cv-12713-NLH   Document 48-2   Filed 08/21/22   Page 38 of 59 PageID: 924

***THIS PAGE IS NOT INCLUDED
IN THE USAO VERSION
IN DISCOVERY DISCLOSURE***

**IT DEMONSTRATES A LOW
RISK OF INJURY OR HARM
TO SELF, OTHERS OR
PROPERTY**

**THIS WOULD BE EVIDENCE
IN DIRECT CONTRADICTION
TO THE ARGUMENT FOR
PRE-TRIAL DETENTION,
PROSECUTION,
& SENTENCING
ENHANCEMENTS.**

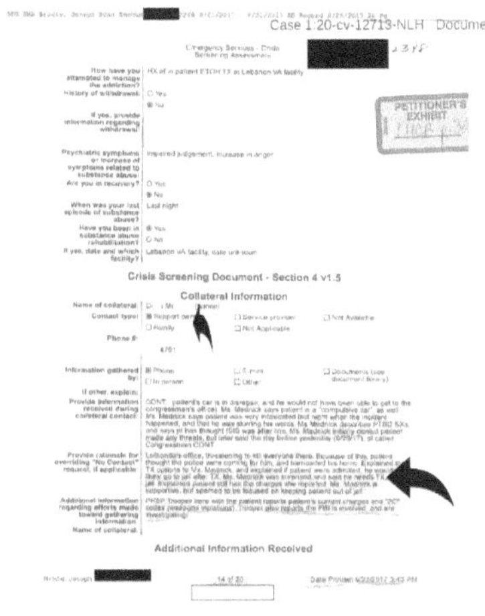

Case 1:20-cv-12713-NLH   Document 48-2   Filed 08/21/24

**THIS PAGE IS NOT INCLUDED
IN THE USAO VERSION
IN DISCOVERY DISCLOSURE***

**THE GOVERNMENT's RESPONSE
NOW CLAIMS IT WAS BRODIE WHO
"CONFESSED" TO THE "NURSE" WHILE
"CALM, ALERT & COOPERATIVE"
IT IS NOTES OF A PHONE CALL WITH "A
SUPPORT PERSON" (MEDNICK)**

**THE GOVERNMENT DELETES PAGES &
DELIBERATELY MISREPRESENTS THE
CONTENT OF RECORDS TO
A UNITED STATES DISTRICT COURT
"DOUBLING DOWN"
ON ITS PREVARICATIONS**

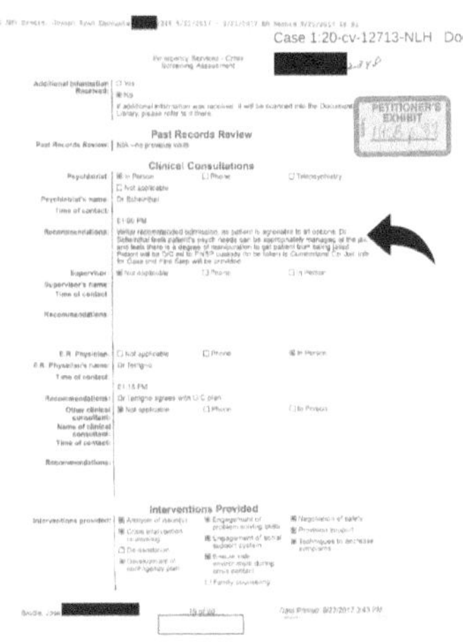

Case 1:20-cv-12713-NLH   Document 48-2   Filed 08/21/24

***THIS PAGE IS NOT INCLUDED
IN THE USAO VERSION
IN DISCOVERY DISCLOSURE***

**THE GOVERNMENT OMIT's THIS PAGE
BECAUSE IT IS EVIDENCE THAT THE
MEDICAL PROFESSIONAL BELIEVES
MANIPULATION TO KEEP BRODIE FROM JAIL**

**THIS WOULD CORROBORATE MS MEDNICK'S
TESTIMONY ON JULY 26TH 2018
THAT SHE SAID "ANYTHING AND
EVERYTHING SHE COULD TO HELP HIM
[BRODIE] GET TREATMENT"**

**EXHIBIT A –MEDNICK's VERIZON CELLULAR
RECORDS-LENGTHY PHONECALL FROM THE
NJSP BEFORE HER INTERVIEW IS
ADDITIONALLY CORROBORATED AS AN
"OFF THE RECORD ATTEMPT" TO COERCE
MEDNICK's RECORDED STATEMENT**

JOSEPH BRODIE

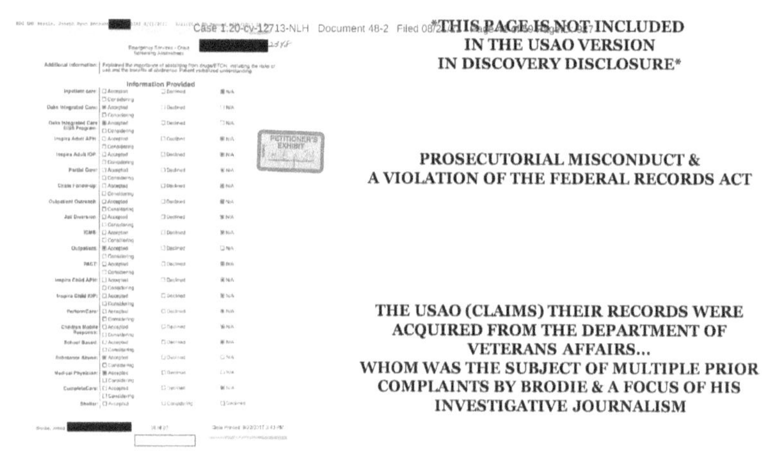

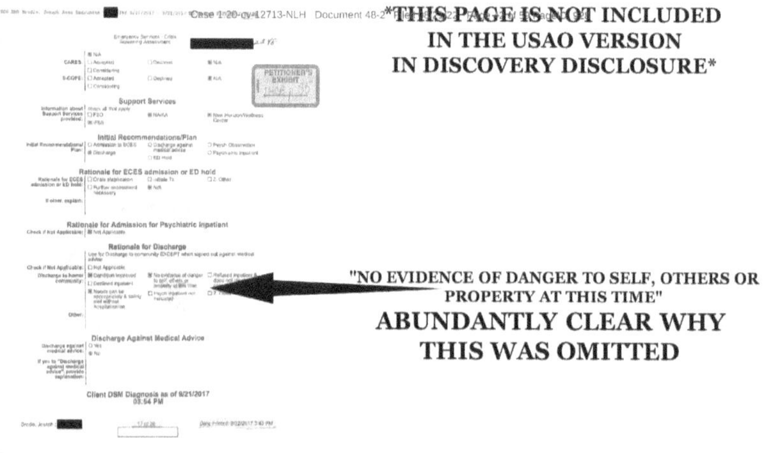

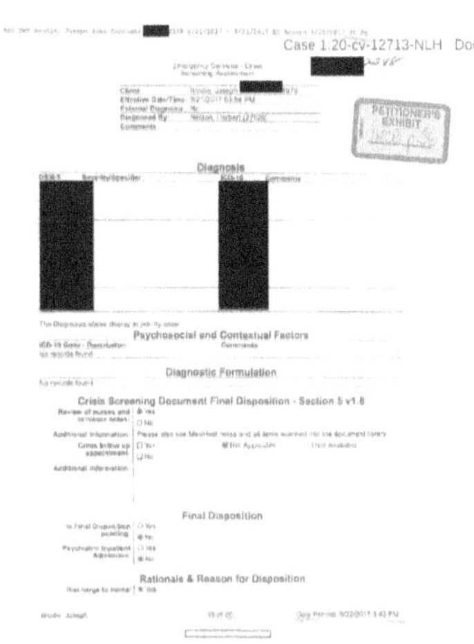

**THIS PAGE IS NOT INCLUDED
IN THE USAO VERSION
IN DISCOVERY DISCLOSURE***

**THIS IS WHY THE CONVICTION OF
MR.BRODIE IS SUBJECT TO
THE STRUCTURAL ERROR DOCTRINE**

**MEANWHILE
THE GOVERNMENT RESPONSE
STILL INSISTS IT PROVIDED
COMPLETE & IDENTICAL RECORDS**

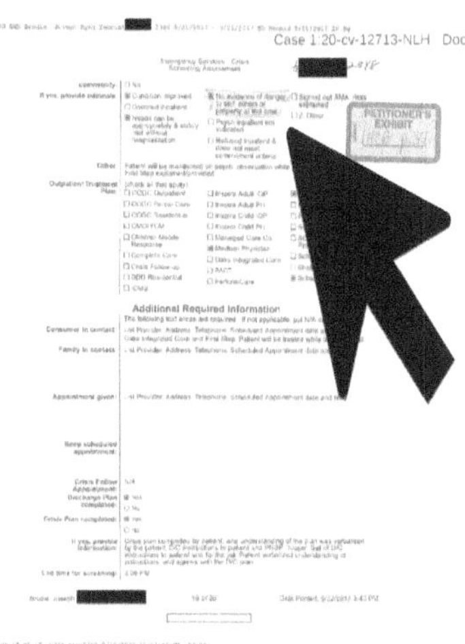

**THIS PAGE IS NOT INCLUDED
IN THE USAO VERSION
IN DISCOVERY DISCLOSURE***

**IF IT SEEMS REPETITIVE, ITS BECAUSE
THE USAO SUBMITTED ONLY 1/3 OF
BRODIE's MEDICAL RECORDS FROM
SEPTEMBER 21, 2017**

**EVERYTHING THE GOVERNMENT SAYS IS FACT,
ANYTHING THE DEFENSE RESPONDED WITH
WAS "OBSTRUCTION OF JUSTICE"**

**BRODIE RECEIVED A 2-PT
SENTENCING ENHANCEMENT FOR
"OBSTRUCTION OF JUSTICE"
DESPITE NO "CONCRETE EVIDENCE OF PERJURY"
(PER THE COURT OF APPEALS)**

**THE MISSING RECORDS ALSO EXIST AS
IMPEACHMENT EVIDENCE
AGAINST THE TESTIMONY OF NJSP
WHO COMMITTED PERJURY AT THE BEHEST OF
LEADING INTERROGATORIES FROM
AUSA SARA A. ALIABADI**

JOSEPH BRODIE

*****MISSING FROM USAO DISCLOSURE*****

THE USAO DELETED 19 OF 20 PAGES IN THIS SECTION ALONE

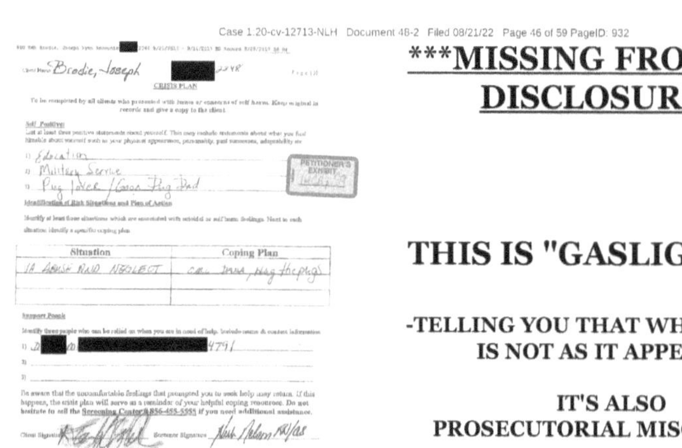

*****MISSING FROM USAO DISCLOSURE*****

THIS IS "GASLIGHTING"

-TELLING YOU THAT WHAT YOU SEE IS NOT AS IT APPEARS...

IT'S ALSO PROSECUTORIAL MISCONDCUT

***THIS PAGE IS
NOT INCLUDED
IN THE USAO VERSION
IN DISCOVERY
DISCLOSURE***

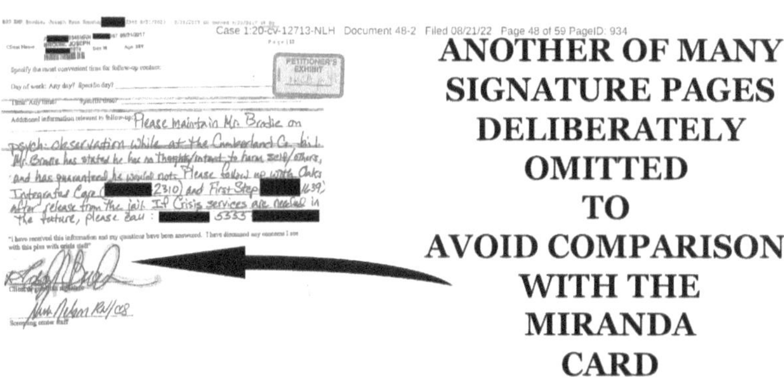

**ANOTHER OF MANY
SIGNATURE PAGES
DELIBERATELY
OMITTED
TO
AVOID COMPARISON
WITH THE
MIRANDA
CARD**

*****NOT DISCLOSED*****

JOSEPH BRODIE

IN THE FOLLOWING SLIDE,
THE USAO's VERSION OF BRODIE's
MEDICAL RECORDS FROM
SEPTEMBER 21, 2017
RESUME...

USAO VERSION - PAGE 10 OF 17

THE USAO HAD THE AUDACITY TO DO THIS IN THE COURTROOM OF THE FORMER CHIEF OFTHE PUBLIC INTEGRITY DIVISION

**SHE BELIEVES THE COURT WONT SEE IT AND
-JUST IN CASE-
CLAIMS IT'S IMMATERIAL**

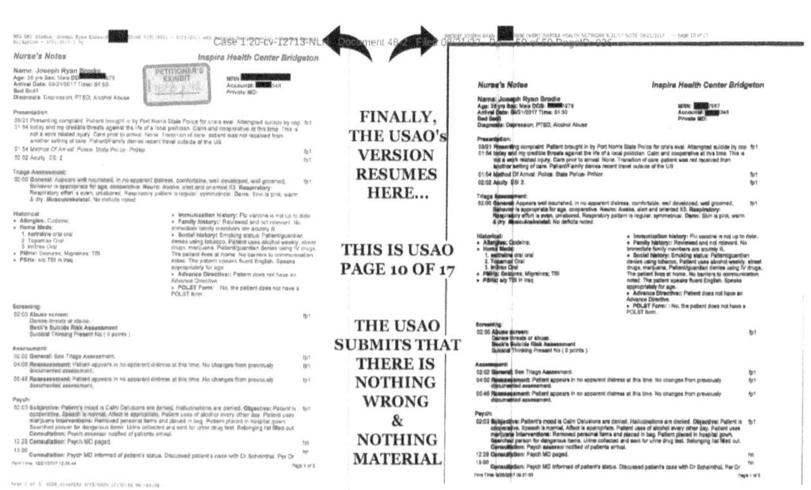

TYRANTS

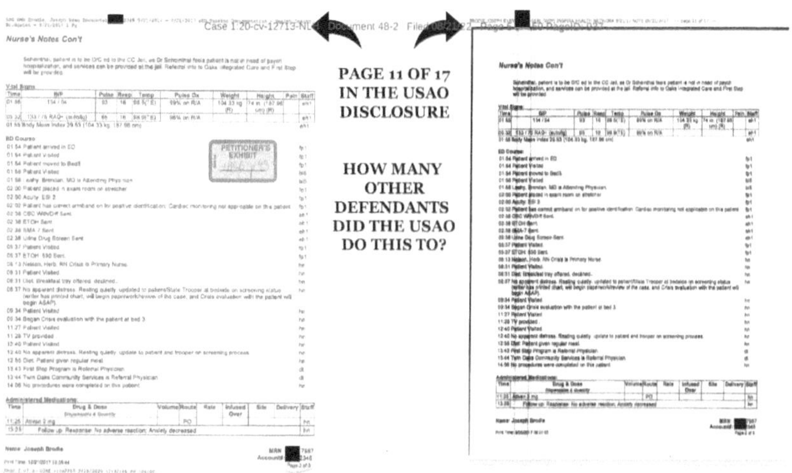

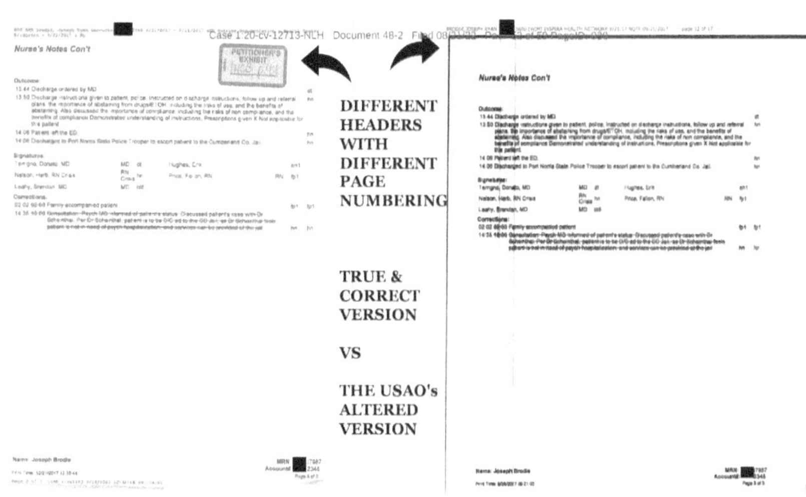

PAGE 11 OF 17 IN THE USAO DISCLOSURE
HOW MANY OTHER DEFENDANTS DID THE USAO DO THIS TO?

DIFFERENT HEADERS WITH DIFFERENT PAGE NUMBERING
TRUE & CORRECT VERSION
VS
THE USAO's ALTERED VERSION

JOSEPH BRODIE

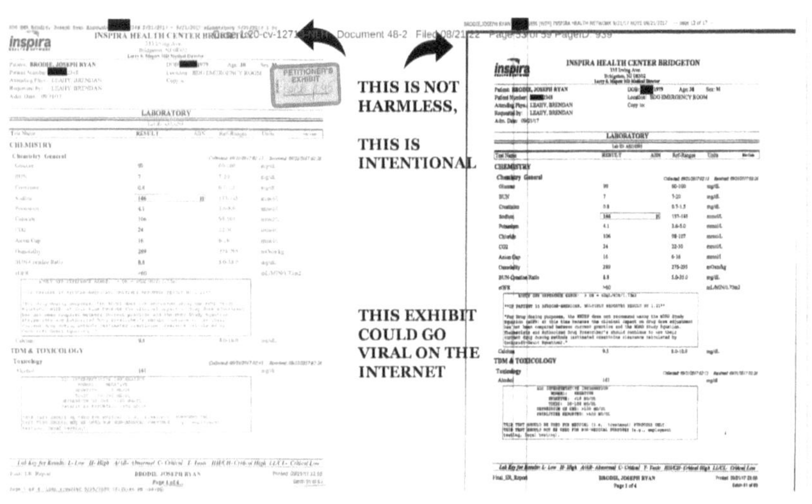

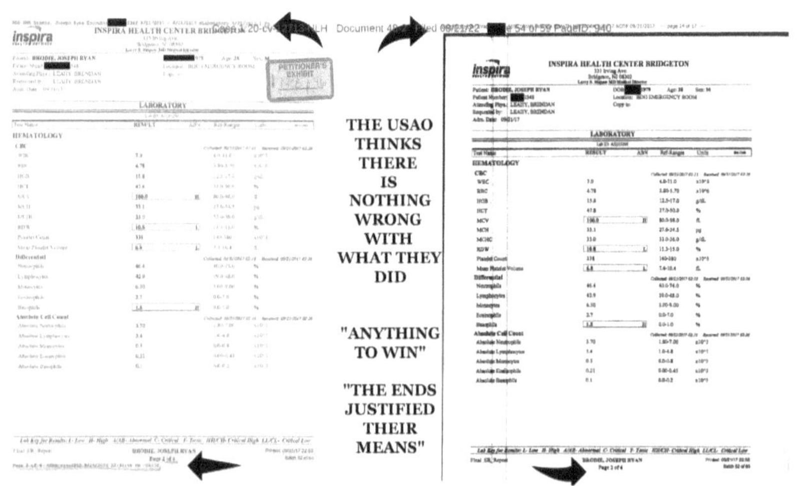

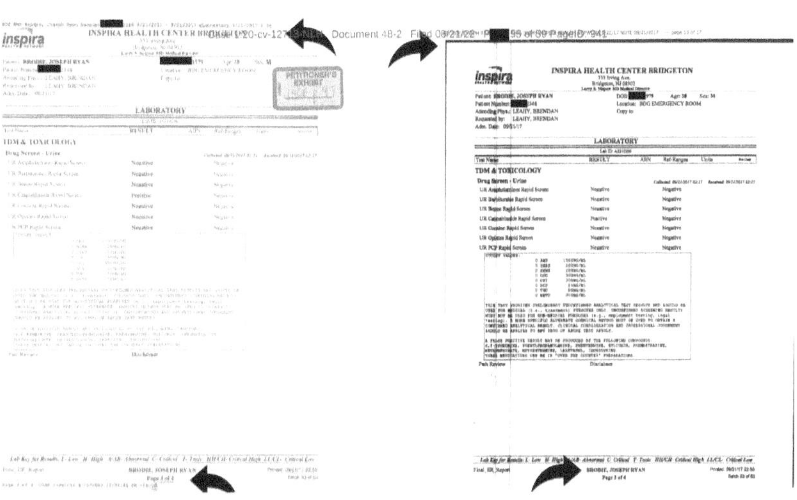

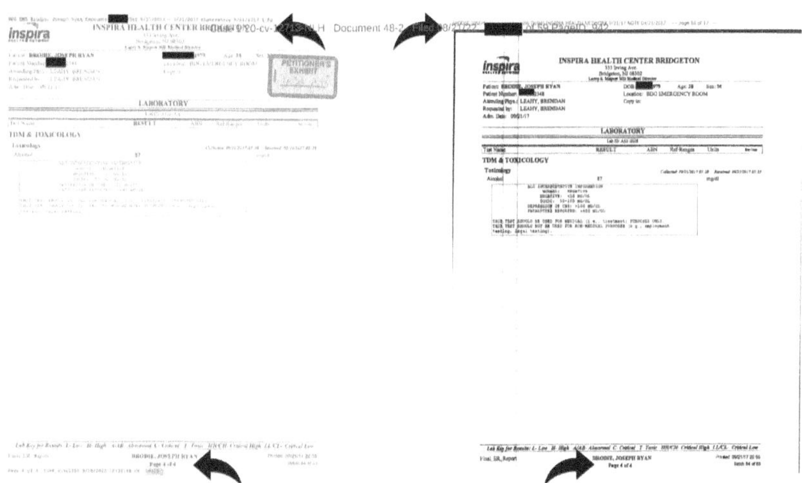

**IF THE GOVERNMENT [TRULY] PURSUED
JUSTICE & NOT POLITICALLY MOTIVATED
PROSECUTIONS,
THEY WOULD BEGIN
BY INVESTIGATING THE PERSON
WHO REQUESTED THESE ALTERED
MEDICAL RECORDS AND WHY?
PERHAPS EVEN QUESTION THE
"COINCIDENCE" THAT THE FBI & USCP
WERE IN BRIDGETON NJ ON THE
DATE THAT THEIR ALTERED RECORDS WERE
PRINTED...SEPTMEBER 26, 2017**

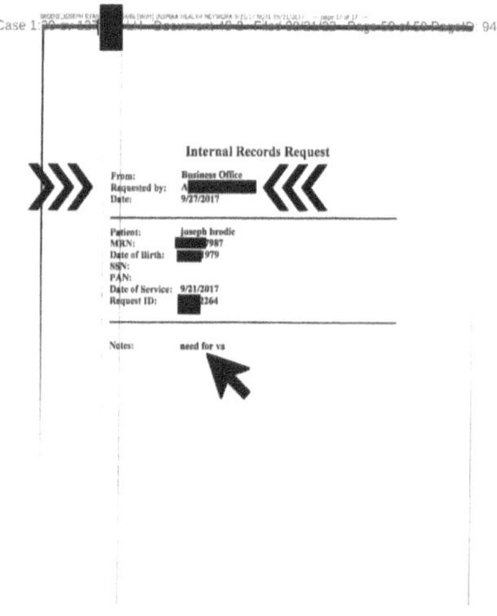

Internal Records Request

From: Business Office
Requested by: A[redacted]
Date: 9/27/2017

Patient: joseph brodie
MRN: [redacted]987
Date of Birth: [redacted]979
SSN:
PAN:
Date of Service: 9/21/2017
Request ID: [redacted]2264

Notes: need for va

THIS IS DISCOVERY DISC 1
IT CONTAINS THE ALTERED RECORDS AS RECEIVED FROM THE USAO

AN EVIDENTIARY HEARING WOULD ALLOW THE COURT TO REVIEW THIS DISC
AND SEE, FIRSTHAND, THAT THE RECORDS HAVE BEEN ALTERED AND THAT THE
MOTION TO VACATE IS WARRANTED
WITH A REFERRAL TO THE PUBLIC INTEGRITY DIVISION

THERE IS AN EPIDEMIC OF PROSECUTORIAL MISCONDUCT
AND ONLY GOOD JUDGES CAN STOP IT!

JOSEPH BRODIE

IN THE UNITED STATES DISTRICT COURT
FOR THE DISTRICT OF NEW JERSEY

UNITED STATES OF AMERICA	:	
	:	
v.	:	Criminal No. 18-162-NLH
	:	
JOSEPH BRODIE	:	

NOTICE OF MOTION

PLEASE TAKE NOTICE that on a date and time to be set by the Court, Defendant Joseph Brodie, by and through undersigned counsel, will move for a new trial pursuant to Rule 33 of the Federal Rules of Criminal Procedure.

In support of said motion, Defendant relies upon the arguments made herein as well as the attached exhibits.

Respectfully submitted,

S/ *Gina A. Amoriello*
____

GINA A. AMORIELLO, ESQUIRE
210 Haddon Avenue
Westmont, NJ 08108
(856) 661-0018
gamorielloesq@gmail.com

DATED: 10/22/19

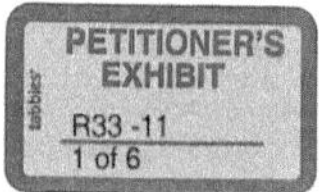

IN THE UNITED STATES DISTRICT COURT
FOR THE DISTRICT OF NEW JERSEY

UNITED STATES OF AMERICA :
:
v. : Criminal No. 18-162-NLH
:
JOSEPH BRODIE :

MOTION FOR NEW TRIAL
PURSUANT TO RULE 33 OF THE
FEDERAL RULES OF CRIMINAL PROCEDURE

Defendant Joseph Brodie, by and through undersigned counsel, hereby moves for a new trial in the interests of justice based on newly discovered evidence, and in support hereof, states the following:

1. Mr. Brodie was convicted on October 10, 2018, after trial by jury, of Counts 1 and 2 of the instant Indictment, Threatening to Murder an Official of the United States in violation of 18 U.S.C. §§ 115(a)(a)(B) and (b)(4).

2. Trial counsel filed timely post-trial motions on October 31, 2018, seeking both a directed verdict of acquittal and a new trial, both of which were denied by the Court.

3. A third attorney was appointed to represent Mr. Brodie for sentencing, but that attorney was relieved when the defendant decided to proceed pro se, with present counsel acting as "stand-by" counsel.

4. In court at the last status listing, Mr. Brodie provided undersigned counsel photographs that he received from his Public Defender representing him in the related pending State Indictment, Kimberly A. Schultz, Esquire, which were

264

taken by the State Police when executing the search warrant in this case, as well as fax records that confirm that Mr. Brodie faxed documentation to the State Police on prior occasions. A portion of these photos are attached hereto as Exhibit A (as well as the fax documentation from Ms. Schultz).

5. In these photos, the following can be observed:

    (a) On page 1, the rifle has the orange hunting tag attached in both top photos (which was how it appeared when recovered) yet this tag is missing in the bottom photo used at Mr. Brodie's trial;

    (b) On page 2, an unassembled gun is also depicted as found, yet it was shown to the jury assembled;

    (c) On pages 3 and 4, the wires from his surveillance cameras are shown hanging in front of the shelf in one photo then removed in the others;

    (d) Page 5 also depicts the wires shown at Mr. Brodie's residence.

6. Exhibit A also shows various photos of the surveillance cameras at the residence which were not shown to the jury after Mr. Brodie was questioned on cross-examination about their existence.

7. During the course of his pro se representation, Mr. Brodie received a hard-drive from present counsel which included any and all evidence provided to her in his federal case, from all prior counsel as well as the Government.

8. Upon review of the hard-drive discovery, Mr. Brodie saw (for the first time) an FBI Extraction Report dated June 4, 2018 (before the Motions hearing); excerpts of same are attached hereto as Exhibit B.

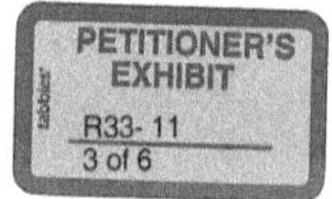

265

(a) Call #s 27, 29, 40, 41 and 42 all pertain to M.F. There are five (5) calls on this report but only two (2) are reflected on trial exhibit D-301, which is also attached hereto to Exhibit B.

(b) None of these calls appear in the official AT&T records used at trial as Exhibit D-300, which is attached hereto as Exhibit C.

(c) Further, the Cornerstone Extraction report for this device (Exhibit D herein) shows that the following calls were also missing from the other records: #18, 19, 21, 22, 47, 48, 49, 139, 282, 292, 293, 387, 388, 447.

9. Mr. Brodie seeks a new trial in the interests of justice, as AUSA Aliabadi stated on the record, on July 6, 2018, at pages 96-97, that the Government had "cracked into two of the devices" and was now handing over entire downloads of those two devices. This was an entire month after the FBI extraction was complete, and it was withheld from the defense prior to beginning motions hearings. The defense contends that the delay in turning over this extraction (which had the evidence of calls being made), whether a mistake, oversight, or intentional, amounts to prosecutorial misconduct by denying him his right to potentially exculpatory impeachment evidence regarding the existence of calls prior to his testimony at the motions hearing.

10. The credibility of Mr. Brodie as a witness was attacked by the Government during his trial, and these records stand to corroborate his testimony regarding the existence of said calls.

11. Had the jury known that Mr. Brodie was telling the truth in that regard, the verdict likely would have been different.

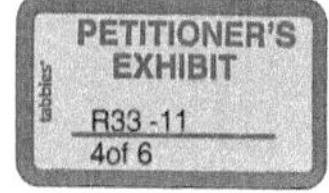

JOSEPH BRODIE

266

WHEREFORE, for the reasons set forth above, it is respectfully requested that this Court grant the requested trial continuance and extend the deadline by which pretrial motions must be filed.

Respectfully submitted,

S/ Gina A. Amoriello

GINA A. AMORIELLO, ESQUIRE
210 Haddon Avenue
Westmont, NJ 08108
(856) 661-0018
gamorielloesq@gmail.com

DATED: 10/22/19

267

CERTIFICATE OF SERVICE

Gina A. Amoriello. Esquire, hereby certifies that, on this day, a true and correct copy of the foregoing was served, via efile and/or hand-delivery, upon all parties of record.

Respectfully Submitted:

S/ Gina A. Amoriello

____
GINA A. AMORIELLO, ESQUIRE

DATED: 10/22/19

ABOUT THE AUTHOR

Joseph Brodie is a graduate of Bloomsburg University in Pennsylvania where he majored in political science.

He earned his masters degree in human services from Liberty University in Virginia. Joseph served honorably in the United States Marine Corps before 9/11 as an infantry soldier in a security, search and rescue element of a Nuclear, Biological, and Chemical weapons anti-terrorism unit stationed at Camp LeJeune, North Carolina. He reenlisted in the United States Army in 2002 as an infantry soldier requesting forward deployment in the War on Terror. Joseph served in the 3rd Infantry Division as a machine-gunner in the armored push into Iraq and participated in the "Thunder Run". He appeared on the cover of the United State's Army's [official] SOLDIERS magazine in April 2003 i.e., The Iraq War Issue. Joseph was medically retired for injuries sustained in combat. He is a patriot member in The Sons of The American Revolution (SAR) with multiple patriot ancestors. In 2009, Joseph taught English & American political thought in Kiev Ukraine. He speaks six languages including: Hebrew, Spanish, Gaelic, Egyptian Arabic, Russian, & German.

He volunteered for the Ron Paul for President campaign in 2008. In 2016, he volunteered for the Donald Trump for President campaign; he was later employed by the campaign while living in the state of Delaware. Joseph is active in charitable work with St. Jude's Children's Research Hospital and numerous charities affecting veterans, first responders, and their families as well as Chabad for their outreach into disaffected communities. He enjoys fitness & exercise and spending time with his Pugs. He is an outspoken critic of the American criminal justice system and has written various op-eds regarding accountability & oversight for all levels of government since 2000.

9 781637 844069